Love That Baby

Love That Baby

Nurture Your Child
With Spiritual Assurance

by

MILDRED E. CAWLFIELD

Peaceful Parenting Press
602 Rue Montand
Ballwin, Missouri 63011-2809

Designed by Sans Serif
Printed in the United States of America
First printing 2000

10 9 8 7 6 5 4 3 2 1

Library of Congress Cataloging-in-Publication Data

Cawlfield, Mildred E., date.
    Love That Baby: Nurture Your Child With Spiritual Assurance.
      p. cm.

Includes index.
1. Infants – Care
2. Infants – Development
3. Parenting – United States.
4. Education – Preschool.
5. Play.
6. Child rearing.
I.   Title

LC 99-98111

ISBN 0-9677944-0-4

The author has made every effort to make the information and suggestions in this book practical and workable, but neither she, nor the publisher, assumes any responsibility for successes, failures or other results by those putting these ideas into practice.

Contents

Contents

Acknowledgments

In giving thanks, I must start with God, the giver of all good. I'm convinced that the Father-Mother of all is cherishing and guiding each parent and child.

I owe to my mother, Emily S. Owen, not only the fine values she has lived and shared, but also her love of children and music. My career with children and parents has followed in the footsteps of her work as a preschool teacher, director, and parent educator.

My husband and partner in parenting, Bill, has been a valuable and continuing support through the years. A testament to that support is the comment from our sons, "We could never pit one of you against the other. You always agreed."

Our sons have been my ultimate teachers on the subject of parenting. Being spaced—two and two—over 15 years, they gave us the opportunity to focus on parenting in two different decades. My deep thanks for who you are, what you have become, and who you are becoming: David, Daniel, Craig, and Christopher (Topher).

I thank my former Acorn Assistant, Christine Telthorst. And heartfelt thanks to Debbie Dutton, who is continuing as Director of the Acorn Program, and to Susan Hosack, her assistant.

I owe a debt of gratitude to those at The Principia who nurtured and supported my work in the Acorn Program: to Arthur Schulz for his vision, to Patricia Piot, Bill Truitt, and Bob Clark for their willing and able backing as administrators.

I thank Laurel Walters whose careful copy editing has been invaluable.

My heart is full of gratitude for all of the wonderful Acorn parents. They have shared their children, their observations, and their schedules. They have been my continuing teachers and source of inspiration in the important subject of parenting.

Introduction

As a child comes into your life, the stage is set for the most rewarding and meaningful experience you've ever had. You discover a love and parenting qualities you didn't know you possessed. You are challenged but also rewarded as you see your little one learn and grow with your guidance. Parents who glimpse the view that their child has a higher source than themselves can be assured that they'll be inspired to do what is best for their child.

As more and more mothers enter the workplace, the role of the parent appears to be diminishing. But parents still make the major decisions for their children and will continue to be the dominant influence in their children's lives. Current research is corroborating previous evidence that the experiences in a child's first years influence his learning throughout life. No one can do more for a child in his early years than a parent who is informed and committed with love for him. I have seen many children excel throughout school after their parents participated in the parent-infant/toddler program I developed and directed. Most of these parents stayed at home with the children for the first three years, but many worked outside the home and were still able to maintain their focus and commitment to their children. Children thrive when they are a top priority for someone who loves them.

This book addresses parents specifically. But anyone who works with babies and young children will benefit from information about the normal agenda for a growing baby and the nurturing that will enhance the first years of a child's life. Today, many grandparents are becoming the primary caregivers of children whose parents both work. This can be a good alternative, because the grandparent is also committed to the baby with love.

The aim of this book is to furnish you with parenting tips that will help you bring forth the best in your child while also encouraging you to listen and trust your own divinely-inspired ideas for your unique child. Each child is different from every other, and each parent is different from every other. It's important for you to listen with an open mind for the ideas that feel right to you. Never accept a parenting idea just because you read it in a book or because someone tells you it's good. Try it on and see how it fits your highest sense of what's right for you and your child. Choices parents make often have far-reaching results. This book attempts to show some of those choices and the likely results so that you can make more informed decisions. In any case, never fear that you will damage your child irreparably by child-rearing decisions you make. Children are marvelously resilient, and the love and care you have already shown by picking up this book indicates that your baby is in good hands.

Most parents have high ideals for their children. They want their children to assume the values they cherish. Children come with the ability to love, to obey, to assume responsibility, to have self-control, and to think intelligently. Children learn language by being spoken to as though they understand. Similarly, they discover good qualities and capabilities in themselves as parents expect these qualities. Certain parenting approaches encourage a child's expression of the best qualities he possesses. The best way to love that baby is to nurture those God-given qualities through loving care and guidance.

There are two opposite poles of advice on parenting infants. One, which was popular some years ago and still has a few adherents, is to put the baby on a predetermined, strict schedule and to adhere to that schedule no matter how much the baby cries. This approach may be comforting to a parent who wants specific guidelines, but it doesn't allow the flexibility to listen to the child and meet his needs—to use inspiration. It can lead to a child's lack of self-confidence and distrust in his ability to communicate and relate to others. Also, the parent often feels concerned if the child doesn't readily adapt to the schedule. Sample schedules for each age are included in this book to illustrate possibilities and give parents a starting point for establishing their own routine.

The other pole of parenting advice that is currently popular supports demand-feeding or "grazing," constant carrying or wearing the baby, and sleeping together in the family bed. Aspects of this approach have worked well in other cultures, but there can be side effects when importing them to a Western culture. This approach can establish a bond that leads to overdependence and lack of freedom. It may be difficult for the child to find his own comfort apart from the parent, and the parent may feel pinned down.

If parents ask, "What is right for us?" a comfortable approach for both parent and child can be found. A good way to avoid autocratic or permissive practices is to see that principle and love are really the same. Love is not wishy-washy, and principle is not harsh or punitive. Most parents and children do best when a comfortable middle ground of loving firmness is found. My aim is to help parents find this position so their children will bloom to full potential with confidence and joy.

Parents should value their role as prime educators of their children. No one will ever teach your children as much as you will. Likewise, you will always be learning from your children. Parenting is a process of transferring responsibility to the child. Parents interfere with a child's progress if they usurp too much of the responsibility that a child should have. Even new infants can take the responsibility (respond to their ability) to settle themselves to sleep and to know how much they need to eat. Problems can arise when parents assume responsibility that should rightfully belong to the child.

On the other hand, parents need to take responsibility in guiding their children to learn the timeless values of humanity. Listening for divine guidance and having some understanding of a child's normal capabilities at any given time helps parents know when and how to transfer responsibility in a way that is comfortable and rewarding for both parent and child.

A toy library is an important part of the parenting program I developed and directed at an independent school in St. Louis for 24 years. The library was set up to provide consultation to individual parents and children for half an hour every two weeks during the child's first three years. I worked with the children using toys to utilize each child's unfolding interests and skills. In addition, I recorded observations and parents' comments about the child's development. The parents would take home three toys for a two-week period and then share comments on the child's response to the toys, as well as observations about the child's development. I thus accumulated a valuable database of information about toys and children in their first years. I'm including some of these comments as "Cameos of Individual Children" to help parents gain the assurance that comes from seeing what other children are doing at a particular time. Parents can be reassured by learning that "my child's not the only one who does that," as well as by seeing the broad range of differences among children.

I use the term "infants" and then "babies" to refer to children in their first year. I call children in their second year "toddlers." In their third year, the term "two-year-olds" is used. Many of the ideas in the second half of the book are useful for children over two.

I use the generic masculine pronoun predominantly throughout the book because I think it reads more smoothly than any alternatives. I hope that having four sons hasn't prejudiced my decision. But I have inserted the feminine pronoun periodically to remind the reader that I don't wish to neglect the precious girls. Be assured that both genders are intended with either reference.

In addition to focusing on parents as educators, this book gives practical tips for parents as caregivers. Thus a busy parent can gain some basic guidelines for parenting from both standpoints. Because children are changing so rapidly in the first year, the first part of the book combines the salient information sequentially in two-month segments. The second part uses a topical format to provide information in the most useful way for the child's second and third years. This is not an exhaustive reference book for parents but includes answers to the most common questions parents have asked.

PART ONE

THE FIRST YEAR

A child's first year is filled with change. Progress is made so quickly that parents seldom remember from one child to the next what babies do at various times or what to do to support their baby's development and learning. Each baby is marvelously unique. The time periods given in this book follow a common sequence, but individual babies will vary in many specifics. Look before and after the age guidelines to find information that will be useful to you and your own precious baby. Trust the inspiration you receive from your own prayers. Then look for information that augments that inspiration.

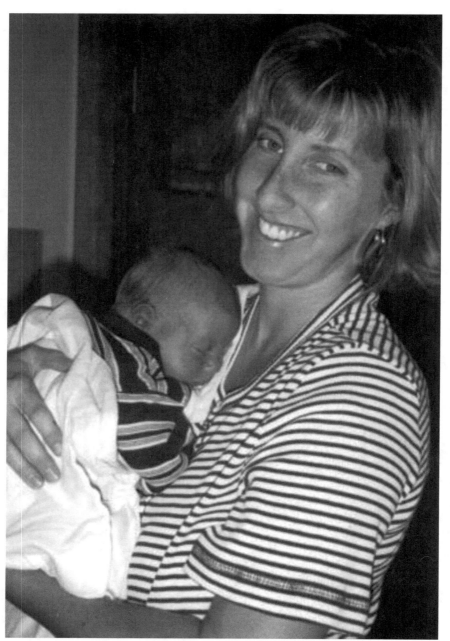

Your child arrives with all he needs.

ॐ

1

Becoming a Parent

He shall feed his flock like a shepherd: he shall gather the lambs with his arm, and carry them in his bosom, and shall gently lead those that are with young.

Isaiah 40:11[1]

Tuning In to Parenting

Opening thought to becoming a parent is true conception. It requires us to make a commitment beyond ourselves to two other individuals—our spouse and our child. It is one of the most enriching and fulfilling experiences one can have. I feel that we each get the very child we need to bless us and be blessed by us. That blessing inevitably includes growth and progress.

It's helpful to think of all the wonderful qualities you are expecting as you await the appearance of your child. You will begin to feel these qualities—the activity of Life, the peacefulness of Soul, the integrity of Truth, and the comfort of Love. Your concept of the birth as the unfolding and appearing of these qualities will contribute to its harmony and safety. Your thoughts form the environment for your child both before and after birth.

In one African culture, the mother makes up a song for her unborn baby and sings it to the baby before birth. She sings it as the child

---

[1] The King James Version of the *Bible* is used unless otherwise noted.

is being born, and it becomes the child's special song after birth[2]. I know parents who have enjoyed talking to the baby, singing, saying prayers and poems, or reading to the baby both before and after birth. Though it may feel strange at first, you can start to communicate with your baby in many ways.

Prayer is the best preparation for childbirth and parenting. Many people today are recognizing the value of praying for the unborn child. Each parent can pray in his or her own way, but the acknowledgment that there is a higher power than oneself loving and caring for this child benefits the child and brings a confidence to parenting that nothing else can. We welcome an individual into our thought before he or she appears in birth, and it's comforting to know that the life and love that appear in our experience have an intelligent source.

Parents' Role as Educator

You, the parent, are the prime educator of your children. You will create their environment. You will care about them more than anyone else, and you will be with them for a long time. Infants learn at a rapid rate from everything they see, hear, and touch. You are responsible for what comes into their experience. This fact is not a burden, but a delight and a focus. You may find it comforting to think of God as the creator and yourself as the caregiver entrusted with His child. You can trust that you will have guidance and inspiration to know what to do to support your child's learning.

A vast amount of learning will take place before your child goes to school. Physically, he will learn to crawl, sit up, climb, walk, run, hop, skip, and more. By communicating with you, he will learn language well enough to communicate with others. He will master an extensive amount of knowledge as well as some problem-solving strategies. By the time your child goes to school, basic building blocks of how to learn will have been established. He will have already learned a majority of the basic elements of your culture and ways to relate to others. You will have already transmitted many of your values.

As you tune in and listen to your child, his needs will become apparent. You will act as a consultant and have many decisions to make.

---

[2] Turnbull, Colin, *The Human Cycle* (Simon and Schuster, 1983).

You may wonder how you will know what is best for your child. A helpful guideline is the question "What will my child learn as a result of my decision and my action?"

You will be a model for your children. They learn from observing you, and if you want them to learn gentleness, you will be gentle with them. If honesty and patience are valued, these qualities will be copied by your children as you work toward expressing them. Your children will learn how to gain self-control by observing how you behave. This may be a challenge, but the growth we make as parents can be satisfying and rewarding. The desire to be and do what is best always confers divine assistance.

A two-year-old looked up at me one day and asked, "What does God look like?" I explained that we don't see God with our eyes, but we feel his love all around us. I could tell that this little one, who was just becoming acquainted with what his eyes saw of the world, wasn't satisfied with this explanation. I asked him what *he* thought God looked like. He said, "Like a father." This reasoning was a credit to his father and a challenge to all parents to examine what they are modeling.

The Working Parent

Staying home with a baby is not always an option for today's parents. But many find it possible to work out of the home or to have flexible hours to enjoy as much parenting time as possible. I know parents who have had fulfilling careers and have planned to go right on working as soon as possible after the baby was born. They didn't know how strongly they would feel about this baby after it came. A number of these parents have changed their plans in order to spend as much time as possible with their children in the first three years. They have gained support from a parenting program and contact with other parents, and then have extended their working hours after the children have started school. These parents have felt that the work with their children was the most important work they could do and have been fulfilled by the results of their decision.

We have seen unique solutions found by parents who need to work and are committed to raising their infants. Some companies allow job-sharing, with two workers covering one job. Some parents find ways to work out of the home with computers or in cottage industries, while others work swing hours with spouses so that one parent can be with the child. Some parents open their homes to care for the children of other working parents.

The best solution for some who are unable to stay at home may be to leave the child with extended family, such as loving grandparents. I have worked with dads and grandparents who are doing a fine job in the primary parenting role.

Efforts have been made in recent years to improve the quality of daycare, and there are many fine, devoted caregivers in daycare settings. If daycare is the best solution for you, do thorough research to make sure the love and care that your baby needs is present. Is there a consistently high standard of caregiving by loving and committed personnel, with a minimum of employee turnover? Visit the location of your choice more than once, and unannounced, to make sure that the high standards you seek are consistent. Are the children all having opportunities to explore materials on their own without too much interference from other children? Do they have frequent contact with a caregiver when they feel the need? A low adult-child ratio is essential for the best experience. Make sure children are not spending a lot of their time waiting for a turn to do something. Most important, do the caregivers have the same basic values that you do? Are they teaching social skills that help the children get along well with each other?

Whether you work outside the home or not, you will find your role as parent to be fascinating and rewarding as you find solutions for problems that arise and take part in the unfolding maturity of your child.

Preparation

*See, I am sending an angel ahead of you to guard you along
the way and to bring you to the place I have prepared.*[3]

Exodus 23:20

Feeding—Breast or Bottle?

Before baby comes, you will want to decide whether or not to breast-feed. Today, the many benefits of breast-feeding for both mother and baby are acknowledged, and most pediatricians recommend it. Despite improvements to baby formula to make it as much like human milk as possible, breast milk is still considered to be the best food for human babies.

It's best to work toward breast-feeding and be prepared for it. Most challenges to successful breast-feeding can be worked out. Breast-feeding is a natural example of supply and demand. As the baby needs more, he feeds more often and takes more. This increases the mother's supply.

If you are planning to return to work soon after the birth of your baby, don't let that stop you from taking advantage of the early benefits of breast-feeding. Some mothers are even able to continue breast-feeding for a time after returning to work. It may be helpful to read further information about breast-feeding. La Leche League (check your local phone book) has information and support for breast-feeding. The League does, however, present a one-sided view, overlooking the fact that many babies have flourished with the bottle.

I bottle-fed my first three children mainly because I didn't have the information or support to make breast-feeding work for me. I was delighted to have the experience of breast-feeding my youngest child. I found the information I needed in books advocating breast-feeding. Since then I have known parents of twins and even an adoptive parent who have succeeded in breast-feeding.

---

[3] New International Bible

The Bottle-Feeding Choice

If breast-feeding doesn't work out for you, don't feel badly about needing to use the bottle. It's important that both baby and mother feel comfortable with the feeding arrangement, and there are some cases in which bottle-feeding is the best answer. Don't allow others' enthusiasm for breast-feeding make you feel a failure if it isn't the best answer for you.

There are many good formulas on the market today that meet the infant's nutritional needs. There are also many types of bottles. In many areas the water is pure enough that you don't need to sterilize water or bottles. You can check locally to see if that is the case in your area.

Space for Baby

You may have a room prepared and decorated for baby. Keep in mind that some colors are restful and others are stimulating. Babies love to look at bright and contrasting colors. I suspect that the decorations are as much for the rest of the family as for the baby. They denote a sense of preparation and expectation. But babies look at their surroundings and learn from what they see.

If you don't have a separate room for baby, you can find another spot in your home that will work out well. A place can be prepared in your bedroom for the early months, in a dining or living area, or in another child's room. The baby's sleep will not be disturbed by other sounds at first. You can decide if the baby's presence would be a problem in a sibling's room. It's best never to leave the baby unsupervised with a toddler.

At first you will want to have the baby in a small bassinet, basket, or cradle. The baby will need to sleep where you can easily hear his cries. When you are getting up in the night to feed the baby, it can be convenient to have him in your room at first. Babies do make noises in their sleep, or even cry briefly, and then go back to sleep. If these noises keep you awake, it's better for the baby to be in a nearby room where small noises won't disturb you but earnest cries will be heard.

If you have the baby sleep in your room in the early weeks, you may want to put him in a room by himself when he outgrows the bassinet, or by three months. The baby will become aware of your presence and may not be willing to sleep alone if kept in your room for more than a few months. You and your baby will have more freedom and independence if you each have your own area for sleeping. An important part of parenting and truly loving your child is learning to let go of a personal sense of parenting and trusting your child to Love's presence. This trust will tune you in to doing what is best for your child and will give him self-confidence.

Preparing Siblings for Baby's Arrival

Older siblings can learn to be gentle with a baby.

Expectation is important in each aspect of parenting. We often get what we expect. It's important to work toward and expect family harmony rather than sibling rivalry and jealousy. Though evidence of jealousy must be met and not ignored if it comes up, you can be assured that enlarging your hearts to include a new baby can bless each member of the family.

Older children can be involved in the preparation for this new family member. They need not get the notion that this baby will replace parents' affection for them, if the parents understand and assure them from the beginning that love is not a limited commodity that must be divided. As a family expands, love expands. It's expressed by parents to each other, to each child, and from one child to another.

Tell your older children that the family will be richer for having another member. The older children will now be brother or sister and will have opportunities to enjoy, to teach, and to love. They can be told what the baby will love about them and what they will love about the baby. Let them know what a new baby is like, so they won't expect an instant playmate.

In preparation for the baby, and after it comes, the older children will enjoy looking at pictures of themselves as babies at different stages. Part of the preparation for the birth can be putting these photos into a book for the older child to look at.

To include an older child, some parents have invited the sibling-to-be to help prepare for a birthday party for the new baby. They have wrapped a few gifts for the baby and for the older child, made and frozen a cake, and had a family party after the baby was born.

To help include the older child when visitors come to see the new baby, you might coach the sibling on information about the baby, such as baby's sex, name, weight, and eye color, then have the big brother or sister tell it to the visitors.

Older children can be made to feel that helping take care of the baby is a privilege, not a burden. Even a toddler can bring a diaper or hand you needed supplies. He'll delight in your appreciation of his helpfulness. You will want to keep the older children informed about the baby's capabilities and interests as the baby grows and give instructions on older brother's or sister's role as a teacher of the baby. They need to know that you are the parent in charge and what they may, and may not, do with the baby.

You will need to keep careful watch whenever a toddler is with the baby so that the baby isn't mistreated. Toddlers don't fully understand the differences between people and objects. Tell the toddler what he *may* do with the baby, not just what not to do. "You may hold the baby when you're sitting on the couch, and when I can help you." "You may kiss the baby gently on his forehead or hand." "You may put on the baby's booties." "See how the baby smiles when you talk to her? She thinks you're a wonderful big sister."

Be sure to show affection for the baby in front of the siblings. Don't withhold it, fearing jealousy. You will be showing the older children what a loved family member this baby is, and you will model for them *how* to love the baby. Setting the stage for a harmonious relationship will lead to continuing peaceful family life.

$\widetilde{\heartsuit}$

2

Getting Acquainted
First Month

And we know that all things work together for good to them that love God, to them who are the called according to his purpose.

Romans 8:28

First Days

The main goal in the first days and weeks is for you and this new family member to get acquainted. You will be listening to your baby's needs, and he in turn will be fitting in to your family and home. You can expect a good adjustment as you let baby know that you are there to lovingly provide for him, and you can trust that he will let you know his needs.

At first your baby will sleep much of the time, but some babies cry frequently. Your baby will be awake increasingly in the coming weeks. Feel free to hold her. Talk to her, even if she doesn't seem to respond right away, and sing to her.

Your baby will get used to sleeping comfortably without being held if you put him down for most of his sleeping hours—a cozy bassinet is good at first. He'll let you know when he's awake and ready to be fed

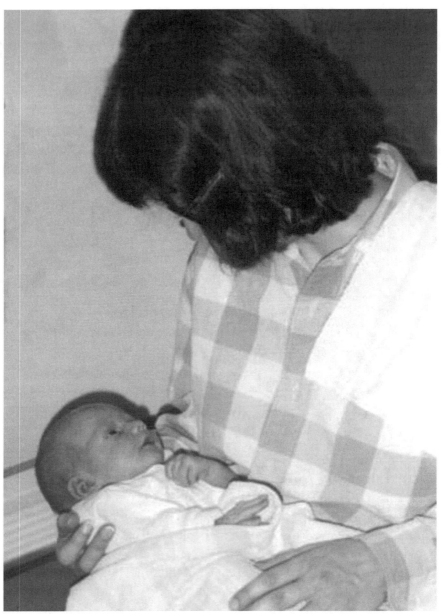

There is nothing an infant would rather see than a parent's face.

and held again. If you carry your baby all the time, he'll get used to it and may cry whenever you put him down. You can move your baby to different locations during the day. He might move himself about more than you expect by pushing with his feet, so be sure to keep him in a safe place. Use crib bumpers if you put him in a crib.

Many babies have fussy times for several weeks. They may fuss as they learn to settle themselves to sleep. It's good to know that if a baby, who has been fed, loved, held, and cared for, cries for 20 minutes or so while settling to sleep, it's not harmful to him. Your sleep will be interrupted for night feedings, and your patience may be tested at times, but know that as you listen for divine guidance, you'll get the answers you need and the strength to do what is right for your baby.

Be good to yourself, and take moments to rest when baby's sleeping. Share joy and humor with your spouse as you both get used to being parents. You're venturing on a challenging and very rewarding experience. If needed, relatives or friends may be able to help you get a little rest in the early weeks.

Baby's Learning

Infants are actively learning from the time they are born—and even before. They learn by what they hear, see, and feel. At first babies seem best able to see objects that are eight to twelve inches from their eyes. They love to look at faces. Your baby's favorite activity, when not eating or sleeping, will be looking at you and hearing you talk. This can be a satisfying experience for both of you. In a few weeks, baby will start cooing and smiling in response to your voice.

When baby starts to be awake for brief periods before or after eating, he will enjoy looking at and listening to a musical mobile hanging over him. From around two weeks to ten or twelve weeks, baby's head will be turned to the side when he's on his back, and he'll be in a kind of fencing position. You can watch and find the best position to place a mobile for your baby to see. Choose a mobile that faces down for baby to see rather than facing out for others to see. There are some that have black and white patterns on one side and bright colors on the other. You can check to see which side your baby prefers. Younger babies usually prefer the black and white patterns.

You can also find pictures and patterns made for babies to look at.

You can hang or prop these in baby's view or make your own patterns and faces of contrasting black and white or bright colors for baby to look at.

In three or four weeks you can help baby start learning to bat with his hands by holding a batting toy (see **Batting Toys**, p. 36) so that it touches his hands.

Sleeping Position

When thou liest down, thou shalt not be afraid: yea, thou shalt lie down, and thy sleep shall be sweet.

(Proverbs 3:24)

At first you may put baby on his side to sleep. Change sides every time you put baby down, so he'll get used to lying on both sides. After several days or a few weeks, he may not stay on his side but may wiggle to his back or stomach.

Today parents are being advised to put babies to sleep on their backs. This comes as a result of some studies of SIDS (Sudden Infant Death Syndrome) which indicated that worldwide, there were more incidents of SIDS for babies who slept on their stomachs than for those who slept on their backs. There are also follow-up studies that show fewer incidents of SIDS since parents have been advised not to sleep babies on their stomachs. In light of these studies, it would be unwise for me to advocate putting babies on their stomachs. But I'll share some considerations that have determined sleeping position in the past.

For years, parents were advised to sleep babies on their stomachs for the following reasons:

- Babies bring up further burps more easily in that position.
- Any spit up flows from the mouth more readily.
- When babies startle in their sleep, feeling the bed beneath comforts them back to sleep, and they can sleep more soundly.
- In the first months, babies can learn to play on their backs and sleep on their stomachs, which gives them signals of when to play or sleep.

- Babies develop the strength to hold their heads up when lying on their stomachs. When they awaken after sleeping on their stomachs, they often practice holding their heads up and also the movements necessary for learning to crawl.
- The back of a baby's head can become flattened by regular sleeping on the back.

Though the vocal pediatricians today are advocating sleeping babies on their backs, there are still some who are telling parents it's all right for babies to sleep on their stomachs if the mattress is firm and there is nothing in the bed that will interfere with a baby's breathing.

I know parents who have started sleeping their babies on the stomach after the first few weeks and reported that their babies are sleeping more soundly and are happier than when they were sleeping on their backs. Likewise, many babies are perfectly happy sleeping on their backs. Parents who sleep babies on their backs can take care to give their babies plenty of tummy time when awake to help them learn to lift their heads to play and crawl in that position.

You will make the best decision as to sleeping position for your baby as you pray and listen for divine guidance. Know that God is caring for this baby, whose life is in His hands, and that He will let you know what is right for your baby. You can then make this decision either way without fear.

In any case, a baby should be able to lift his head enough to move it from side to side before he is left on his stomach. When you put your baby on his stomach for tummy time, be sure that the mattress is firm and that there is nothing in the way that could interfere with breathing, such as blankets, pillows, or large stuffed toys. Babies don't need pillows and should never be left face-down on lamb's wool or soft bedding.

Change your baby's sleeping position from head to foot in the bed regularly, so he will turn his head to both sides when looking out.

Feeding

Your baby will let you know when he's hungry by crying. At first, breast-fed babies need to eat about every two to three hours, and bottle-fed babies every three to four hours. The first days and weeks are a time for both baby and mother to get adjusted. Mother's milk is coming in, and baby gradually adjusts to a pattern of eating and sleeping. Sometimes baby will want to eat more often. Other times he will seem too sleepy to eat (see **Developing a Routine,** p. 20). After the first few weeks, babies can gradually lengthen the time between feedings so that bottle-fed babies eat every four hours. Most breast-fed babies can also lengthen the time to every three, three and a half, and eventually four hours. Babies often cry when not hungry, so look first for other comforts before offering food if baby has eaten less than two hours before. If your baby is small at birth, you may need to awaken him every three hours around the clock to get him to eat enough. Don't be in a hurry to get a small baby to sleep through the night.

When holding your baby, comfortably support her head well above the level of her stomach. Resist the temptation to prop baby's bottle. Feeding is a time of closeness, and your bottle-fed baby should have the same advantage in this way that the breast-fed baby has.

Be sure to burp the baby to bring up bubbles once or twice during a feeding. Do it when baby stops or slows down nursing. Some babies get squirmy when they need a burp. Burp baby again after the feeding. The most frequently-used position for burping the baby is to put baby to your shoulder and firmly pat his back. Other positions for burping are sitting the baby on your lap, leaning him forward on one of your hands while you pat or rub his back with the other hand; or putting baby face down on your lap and patting his back. Place a diaper under baby's mouth to catch any spit up.

Spitting up a little is common for babies after they have eaten. It doesn't mean that the breast milk or formula is not agreeing with them as long as they are gaining well and look healthy. Some babies spit up more than others. The muscle that holds the milk down may need to develop a little more, and that maturity almost always comes during the first year. The milk that baby spits up will appear curdled. This is normal and shows that digestion has started.

Breast-Feeding

Be sure you are drinking plenty of liquids and getting adequate rest. You might like to take a drink of water before you nurse your baby. Sit or lie in a comfortable position and relax when you feed baby. As you feed him, avoid squeezing his cheeks or holding his head so he can't turn it. Make sure the baby takes the areola, or brown part of the breast, into his mouth, not just the nipple. This way he will get more milk and your nipples won't get as sore. If you need to take baby from the breast before he lets go, break the suction by inserting a finger into the corner of his mouth.

As you feed baby, clear your thought of worries or concerns, and relax. Listen for good and peaceful thoughts and talk to your baby about them. See feeding as the natural example of Love's supply of goodness. At first, baby may nurse five minutes or more on each breast and work up to as much as 10–15 minutes on the first breast and 15–20 minutes on the other. Some babies take more time to nurse than others, but most babies get enough milk in half an hour. Alternate the breast you start with at each feeding.

Breast-feeding is a wonderful example of nature's law of supply and demand. Most babies take as much milk as they need and indicate their hunger by crying. The more milk baby takes, the more your breasts produce. When baby has a growth spurt and needs more milk, he will want to eat more often. This will increase your supply so that he can then go back to longer intervals between feedings. One way of telling if baby is getting enough, besides noting his growth, is to see if he usually has six to ten wet diapers a day.

You can eat normally, but be alert to notice if baby might be having trouble with something you've eaten. Strong-flavored foods you eat may make your milk distasteful to baby for awhile or seem to give him extra gas. And it's best to avoid drinks with caffeine, such as coffee and colas.

If you're having difficulty with breast-feeding and want very much to continue, in addition to praying about it, you might read books available on the subject or get in touch with La Leche League before giving up. They can probably answer your specific questions. There are ways to give a baby the nourishment needed, if he's not getting enough from you, that will help you to continue breast-feeding. If you immediately give supplemental feedings, before your supply is established, your supply will be decreased.

Some parents have learned that it's important not to be willful about breast-feeding, however. When it seemed that they were spending all their time breast-feeding and the baby was not gaining properly, they have found peace and the right solution for them by going to bottle-feeding.

Bottle-Feeding

Baby will start by taking two to four ounces of formula every three to four hours. You can start by filling bottles with four ounces. Don't feed baby leftover formula after three hours, but start with a fresh bottle. When baby starts to drain the bottles consistently, fill each bottle with half an ounce more of formula. Be sure the nipple is such that the baby can finish the feeding in about 30 minutes. If baby drains it too fast, try a slower-flowing nipple.

As baby grows, he will take more milk at a time and be able to go longer intervals between feedings. He will start with two to four ounces in eight to six feedings, and progress to six ounces in each of five feedings. Eventually, in a few months, he can work up to 32 ounces a day in four bottles.

Pediatricians disagree on how much milk a baby needs. Penelope Leach, author of *Your Baby and Child from Birth to Age Five*, gives three ounces for every pound of weight as a guide for a daily feeding (24 hours).[4] The Sears, authors of *The Baby Book*, state that babies need between two and two and a half ounces for every pound per day.[5] Fortunately, your baby will let you know how much he needs. He will stop eating when he's full and let you know when he's hungry. You shouldn't urge him to take more, but if he is always draining the bottle, you might add half an ounce more, up to eight ounces.

There's no advantage in trying to move your baby quickly to four feedings a day of eight ounces each. He may be able to assimilate more food in five feedings of six to six and a half ounces. You may note that

---

[4] Leach, Penelope, *Your Baby and Child from Birth to Age Five*, p. 138.
[5] Sears, William, M.D. and Martha Sears, R.N. *The Baby Book*, p. 196.

he regularly wants more at one feeding than another, and divide the formula accordingly.

Though most parents warm the milk slightly, babies can be just as satisfied with milk at room temperature or even out of the refrigerator. It would seem more like breast milk to take the chill off, however. A good way to heat milk is to put the bottle in a pan of hot water before you change baby. Many pediatricians warn against heating baby food or bottles in the microwave, as the milk can be much hotter than the bottle feels.

Delay Solids

There have been varying opinions throughout the ages on when to start solid foods. The general consensus today is to follow the recommendation of the American Academy of Pediatrics' Committee on Nutrition. They say to start solid foods between four and six months because that is when babies are physically capable of handling solids. Bigger babies may need to start solids sooner than smaller babies. Dr. Spock's latest book[6] follows this recommendation, as does *Better Homes and Gardens' New Baby Book*.[7] Lois Smith, in *Baby Eats!*, recommends starting solids when baby has doubled his birth weight. Penelope Leach[8] makes a case for starting around the time baby's weight reaches 12 lbs. The Sears recommend waiting until six months or until the baby starts to show interest in the foods you're eating.

Mother's milk or formula is the best food for babies, and there should be no hurry to replace it with other foods. A persistent belief is that giving solids in the evening will help babies sleep through the night, but there is no clear evidence that this is so, according to studies on the subject. Most pediatricians recommend against trying to stuff babies before bedtime. Many mothers I've worked with have resisted relatives' urging to start feeding baby "real food" in the early weeks. These babies sleep through the night as soon as do those who start

---

[6]Spock, Benjamin, M.D. and Michael B. Rothenberg, M.D., *Dr. Spock's Baby and Child Care*, p. 202.
[7]Kiester, Edwin Jr. and Sally Valente Kiester and the Editors of Better Homes and Gardens Books, *New Baby Book*, p.202.
[8]Leach, Penelope, *Your Baby & Child*, p. 138.

solids early. A better way to get your baby to sleep through the night may be to give more frequent feedings without hurrying him into a four-hour schedule until he is able to take enough milk at each feeding. When babies are able to get enough food during the day, they can go for longer periods without awakening for food in the night. You can help baby lengthen time between feedings at night by awakening him to eat during the day after three or four hours of sleep. If a baby sleeps for periods of five or six hours during the day, he will need to awaken more frequently in the night to get enough food. Another reason babies might continue to awaken in the night for feeding is that they are being fed *too* frequently during the day—less than two or three hours. They are just snacking and are not accustomed to eating enough at one time or to settling into a sound sleep.

Developing a Routine

We all feel most comfortable—free to be ourselves—within defined limits. One of the main roles of a parent is to define the limits for our children. A balance of principle and love helps us do this. It's not principle to be rigidly strict, and it's not love to give in to a child's every tear and whim. A child is happiest when his parents and caregivers seek a balance—when they define boundaries for his behavior and lovingly and consistently teach him these boundaries. Developing a flexible schedule that meets baby's needs and helps him fit into your family's activities in a predictable way gives you and baby a feeling of assurance.

An inflexible schedule tells baby: "My needs don't matter; my cries aren't heard; I can't communicate with others." Demand-feeding after the first weeks, with no regularity, tells baby: "There is no principle here; I don't know what's going to happen from one day to the next;" or "The world revolves around my wants." At first, the baby's needs are changing rapidly, but you can work with baby to establish a comfortable routine. This way, both you and baby will know what to expect.

The early weeks are a time for you to see that the desire for uninterrupted sleep isn't as important for awhile as meeting the needs of this precious child. Most babies simply can't take in enough food during the day to give up night feedings. As baby grows, perhaps as early as five or six weeks, he becomes ready to give up a night feeding.

To develop a routine, make note of the time you begin each feeding. During the day, awaken the baby so that the intervals between feedings are no more than three or four hours. At night, let the baby sleep as long as he will. In fact, let him work into a good cry so you are sure he's hungry. Sometimes infants will fuss a little and then go back to sleep.

Crying is the way baby tells you he's hungry. It's his first form of communication. If you touch the side of baby's mouth, he will open it and root toward the touch as though he's hungry, but don't feed him under three or four hours unless he shows real hunger with a cry. If baby cries after a feeding in less than three hours for a bottle-fed baby, or two hours for a breast-fed baby, look for other means of comfort than feeding (see **Responding to Crying,** p. 25). Try to hold him off until the two- or three-hour period is reached, but if hunger seems to be the real issue, by all means feed him. New infants often act as though they think they should be eating whenever they're awake. Your gentle assurance gets them through this period until they learn that there are ways other than eating to be happy.

Another common infant practice is to fall asleep during a feeding. During the first weeks you can just let your baby sleep until he awakens a short time later from hunger. You might try waiting to change the diaper until the middle of a feeding, or changing breasts to help awaken him to complete the feeding. Sometimes a baby can be awakened to finish a feeding by washing his face with a little cool water on a cotton ball, but it's best not to get into struggles of urging the baby to eat. You want your baby to regulate his own eating.

As you time the feedings, you will see how often baby needs to eat. Each day you can then estimate about when he will want the next feeding, starting with the first feeding of the day. The beginning time will depend on when baby awakens in the morning. To keep the schedule more regular, it's best to awaken the baby for the first feeding at a time that will work out well for you. The baby can fit comfortably into the family's routine. It may take several weeks before a baby's routine becomes predictable, because babies change so much at first. But as you work with baby toward a routine, regularity will evolve.

The three-hour feeding schedule may look something like this: 6 a.m., 9 a.m., 12:00 noon, 3:00 p.m., 6:00 p.m., 9:00 p.m. 12:00 a.m., 3:00 a.m. The beginning time will depend on when baby awakens for the first feeding, and the other feedings will be adjusted accordingly. Let the baby sleep as long as he will between the night feedings. You will see when baby is ready for a four-hour schedule by allowing him to gradually stretch longer between feedings—up to four hours during the day. If he then awakens more frequently in the night, you might go back to three-hour intervals during the day, but he will probably continue to lengthen the nighttime intervals.

A four-hour schedule will look something like this: 6:00 a.m., 10:00 a.m., 2:00 p.m., 6:00 p.m., 10:00 p.m., 2:00 a.m. Continue to awaken the baby during the day to work him into the schedule, but let him sleep as long as he will at night.

Sometimes, instead of skipping the 2:00 a.m. feeding, the baby may prefer to skip the 10:00 p.m. feeding first. If it gets difficult to awaken the baby for that last feeding of the evening, you might go to bed earlier yourself and let the baby awaken you when he will. The time between feedings at night will gradually lengthen until baby sleeps through the night. Most parents feel this is cause for celebration!

(See **Sample Schedules,** p. 39)

Diapering

There are opinions on both sides as to whether disposable diapers are better to use than cloth ones. You can compare local prices of disposable diapers on sale, a diaper service, or buying and laundering your own diapers. The convenience of disposable diapers makes them popular. If you use cloth diapers, a combination of fitted and regular is useful. When the baby sleeps through the night, you can insert a folded regular diaper into the fitted one for extra absorbency. It is easier to clean a dirty diaper if you put a tissue or diaper liner in it before bowel movements (which may be all the time at first). After a bowel movement, rinse a cloth diaper in the toilet. Diaper pail odors are controlled and diapers are kept cleaner if you put used diapers in a pail filled with a solution of one gallon of water to $1/2$ cup of borax. Drain before washing. After you wash the diapers, be sure that they are rinsed well.

For the first three or four days after birth, babies' bowel movements are usually greenish-black. Then babies' stools will vary, depending on whether the baby is breast- or bottle-fed. A breast-fed baby can have six-to-ten loose movements a day. Baby's normal movements can vary in consistency and frequency from no movements for a few days to nine or ten a day. They can be liquid or firm and can be yellow, brown, orange, green, or black. Straining during movements is also common, even when the movements are normal in consistency. Give your baby a little water between feedings if he should both strain and have movements of a hard consistency.

After a movement, change baby as soon as possible, wiping with soft, flushable tissues. (With a girl, wipe feces away from the vaginal area.) Then clean with baby wipes that don't contain alcohol or with a moist cotton ball or washcloth using mild soap and water. Clean in all the creases. Rinse soap off well, pat dry, and dry in creases with a soft, clean cloth or let air dry.

Wet diapers can be changed before and after a feeding, or other times when baby is wet and awake. Even though a wet disposable diaper may not feel as wet as a cloth one, it's best to change it regularly. However, you don't need to change the diaper every time a baby wets a little, and there is no need to awaken baby to change a wet diaper. Powders and lotions are not necessary but may be used. Cornstarch powder is thought to be better than other powders. If you want to use a powder, sprinkle a little in your hand away from the baby so he won't breathe a cloud of it, and then smooth gently on the baby.

You may put baby in a warm place with diaper off for 10 or 15 minutes each day to let him move freely and dry off completely.

Bathing Baby

The baby needs a bath only every two or three days if his mouth is wiped after eating and the diaper area is cleaned during diaper changes. You'll want to keep hands clean as well when they are going into baby's mouth regularly. Daily baths may be welcome in warm weather.

Before the mid-morning feeding was a traditional time to bathe baby, but before any other feeding is fine. You'll probably want to let baby go to sleep after a feeding at first. But if he's too hungry to enjoy the bath, you can look for another time. You can give a portion of a feeding (half or more) before the bath and finish the feeding after the bath. Bathing baby in the evening when he's normally awake can work well.

Have a warm place for the bath. Gather all materials for the bath and have them at hand before undressing baby. Let baby have a little time to kick and stretch with clothes off before the bath. It's common for new babies to get upset and startle at first when they have no covering. You can place a diaper over baby's arms and chest until he gets over the feeling of needing that closeness. During the bath, a warm washcloth on baby's chest may be comforting at first.

Sponge Bath

Sponge baths are usually given to babies until the navel heals, and sometimes after. To give a sponge bath, put a soft towel down on a waterproof surface. Wipe baby's face and head with a soft washcloth dampened in warm water. Baby's scalp may be soaped once or twice a week (but brush it with a soft brush daily). Lightly soap the rest of baby's body with your hand or a washcloth, getting in all creases including behind the ears. Rinse well with clear, warm water. No powder or lotion needs to be put on baby after the bath, but if you wish, put it on lightly.

Tub Bath

For a tub bath, you can use a baby bathtub or the kitchen sink. Pad the tub or sink with a towel or diaper or use a large sponge shaped to hold the baby, and be sure the faucet is turned out of the way before putting baby in. Assemble all needed materials: soap, washcloth, towel, absorbent cotton, diaper, and clothing. Have a towel on a cushioned place to put baby on. Fill the tub or sink (just a couple of inches at first) with lukewarm water, being sure to test it with your wrist or elbow.

Before putting baby in the tub, you may take slightly dampened cotton balls and wipe baby's eyes gently from the inside corner outward. You can also wipe the outer ear and nose with a cotton ball or washcloth. If a swab is used in wiping the ear or nose, take great care to use it in the entrance only. Wash the face and behind the ears with a soft washcloth.

Hold baby in the tub on his back with your arm under his shoulders and your hand grasping the baby's arm that is away from you. Continue holding him this way during the bath. Use the other hand as well to gently and slowly lower him into the water. Wipe his scalp with the damp washcloth (use soap one or two times a week and then rinse). Don't be concerned about washing the soft spot (fontanel) on his head. It is well protected and won't be harmed by normal care. Lightly soap baby all over with your hand or washcloth and then rinse well. Let him kick and enjoy the water. You might add to the joy of the occasion by singing a song. When ready, lift him out of the tub onto an open towel. Wrap him up and dry him well, including the creases. Diaper and dress.

Dressing Baby

Put a cloth diaper or piece of clothing over your baby's bare chest or tummy while you dress him if he startles and cries when his clothes are off.

To put on clothing that fastens in front, put one arm or an arm and leg through the clothing, turn baby to the side with the clothed side up, and tuck the clothes around baby's back. Then turn baby to the other side and bring the clothing around to put in the other arm and leg. Put clothing that goes over baby's head over the back of the head first, then stretch it gently over her face.

Responding to Crying

Babies switch rapidly from contentment to crying and back to contentment again. Their cries are designed to get attention, and it's natural and good to respond to them. Studies have shown that if babies' cries are responded to understandingly in the early weeks, they cry less in later months. Enjoy your baby, love her, and talk to her. Babies often cry frequently in the first weeks, and comforting now will not lead to spoiling, since the cries are usually due to discomfort rather than for attention. Some babies have fussy periods in the late afternoon or evening. If your baby has fussy times, you'll probably try many kinds of comfort. Babies get acclimated and usually cry less often after about three months.

The main need, at first, is regular feeding, and that is the need most cries signal. Sucking seems to be an early need as well, so let baby suck no less than 20 minutes at each feeding. Including time to burp the baby, allow at least 30 minutes per feeding.

If it's been less than two hours since baby has eaten, try other comforts before feeding. Make sure he doesn't have a soiled diaper. Wet diapers seldom bother babies. Baby may seem to be hungry—trying to eat his hands and sucking eagerly—but those signs don't always mean the baby is hungry.

Baby has been used to movement, warmth, and closeness within the womb. Simulating this feeling by swaddling (wrapping securely), by holding, or by carrying can be comforting. A sling is a handy way to carry baby. Babies in many other cultures are carried or worn in this way, and crying is seldom heard.

Other comforts that have been successful are playing music, or the sound between radio stations; putting baby's infant seat on a washer or dryer for the sound and movement; taking baby for a drive in the car; or using a baby swing.

Babies may cry because they are overstimulated and want rest. Then the best thing to do is put them down and let them fuss themselves to sleep. Accustom baby to sleeping by himself in bed for naps between feedings. If a baby is held all the time, he won't learn how to settle himself to sleep. You don't need to pick baby up every time he makes a little noise. Wait for his cries to indicate the need for attention. This doesn't mean you can't hold, talk to, and love your baby when he's awake. Babies thrive on this attention. But there's no reason to constantly hold, hover, and anticipate every need.

The peace you gain from trusting God to shepherd you and your child will assure baby that all is well. Calm your thought if baby's cries are concerning you. Know that if you do what seems to be sensible, your baby will be fine and soon will fit peacefully into the home routine.

Pacifiers

If a baby is inconsolable for periods of time, a pacifier can give extra sucking that may comfort. If you're a nursing mom, you don't need to become the pacifier by nursing far more than is needed for feeding. This can lead to unnecessary dependence. Some babies find thumbs or fingers to suck on and comfort themselves. If you have an aversion to thumb-sucking and your baby seems to need extra sucking for comfort in the early weeks, a pacifier might be an answer. If you try a pacifier, however, be sure not to put it in the baby's mouth every time he cries or before he cries. Look first for other ways to comfort. Also, you might try eliminating the pacifier when baby is about three months old, as other comforts may be sufficient by that time.

When a baby is first introduced to a pacifier, it may fly right out of his mouth, causing the parent to think that he is refusing it. You may need to help him get used to it by holding it in his mouth. Eventually, he will probably get the hang of sucking and holding it in his mouth.

There are many kinds of pacifiers. If you decide to use one, be sure to get one that is well made. Check it regularly by pulling on it to make sure it remains strong and won't pull off or come apart in baby's mouth.

One drawback to using a pacifier is that if the baby gets used to going to sleep sucking it, the parent may need to get up in the night to give it to baby when it falls out of his mouth and he awakens.

Many parents who use pacifiers depend on them too much. They stick the pacifier in the baby's mouth routinely when the baby is perfectly happy, or at the slightest fuss. It appears that the parent is more dependent on the pacifier than the baby is. If parents rely too heavily on the pacifier as a source of happiness for the baby, they can deprive a baby of finding his God-given source of happiness in other ways. A baby who has a pacifier in his mouth all the time isn't as free to use his mouth for exploring sounds he can make, or later, for language. If a pacifier seems to be needed, use it judiciously.

Cameos of Infants from Toy-Library Sessions

These comments are from the records of children who came to toy-library sessions with their parents every two weeks. Parents shared their observations of what the baby was doing at home, and we, the parent educators, added our observations of the child during the sessions. You will see commonality as well as diversity among the children and can get an idea of what your baby might be doing at similar ages.

∞ Chris[9] ∞

24 days. Starting to be happier when awake and not eating. Responds well to sound and music. Likes to be swaddled and held. Moved hand for initial batting with Octopus (dangling, colorful rods). When a rattle with a face moved across his path of vision, he followed with his eyes somewhat jerkily.

∞ Linda ∞

23 days. Alert. Follows well with eyes. Batted well at dangling Ping-Pong balls. Enjoyed sound of Fisher-Price mobile and followed figures with her eyes.

∞ George ∞

24 days. Enjoys looking at faces and contrasting patterns. Eye Catchers (vinyl black and white pictures) a favorite toy to watch. Holds head up well when on tummy.

∞ Sally ∞

26 days. Loves her morning bath—kicks and plays. Evenings most awake times—likes to sit with Mom and Dad. Lots of activity batting dangling balls. With I-Cube that has black and white pictures, focused on face right away. Stared intently when picture changed. Looked from cube to her mirror.

---

[9]Names have been changed

❧ **Nile** ❧

28 days. Stays awake during the morning quite a bit. Nursing every 2¹/₂ to 3 hours during the day. Sleeps on side. Loves watching new Fisher-Price Music Box Mobile. Likes looking at faces of Eye Catchers.

❧ **Lora** ❧

30 days. Looks around at everything. Enjoys being in bouncy infant seat—looks at colors on toy bar. Usually goes to bed at 10:00 p.m. and wakes at 7:00 a.m. Hardest time with crying—around dinner.

Sometimes infants like to be held this way.

ॐ

3

Gazing and Cooing
One to Three Months

And the child grew, and waxed strong in spirit, filled with
wisdom: and the grace of God was upon him.

Luke 2:40

You are probably becoming used to the constant demands of parenting by this time. Listening daily to divine inspiration can help you get through these challenging times when sleep seems elusive and you wonder if you will ever have time of your own again. You have been introduced to a very special love—an unconditional love—that will continue to enrich your life.

During this period your baby will probably recognize you and may stop crying more readily when held. He will be awake more and will look around when you hold him up to your shoulder. Babies often show a preference for being held in this position. You can walk around with baby, letting him look about. Being held on his back in your arms may signal feeding time to baby, and he will turn with mouth open toward you.

Another good way to hold baby is face down across your arm with his head over your elbow so he can look out. You can hold his leg with the hand of the arm he's resting on, leaving your other hand free to pat him or to do other things. Then baby is able to look out while you walk around.

You can talk to baby face to face by holding his head in one hand and supporting his back and neck with your arm and other hand.

Babies love to look at faces, and as you hold and talk to him, you will often be rewarded with a gorgeous smile. Talk to him regularly face to face, and before long he will look at you and make a cooing sound. You can carry on conversations, taking turns with your talking and his cooing. When he turns his head away from smiling or cooing interaction, it means he's had enough for the moment. Later, he'll be happy to engage in the interaction again.

At this age, when on his back, the baby will appear to be in a fencing position with his head turned to the side, with one arm down and the other up. He will reverse the position of his arms when his head turns to the other side. You can place pictures, a mobile, or a mirror to the side for baby to see at this time. Between two and one-half and three months, he will return to a midline position and usually look straight up when lying on his back.

Since your baby is becoming more active, she may kick off a regular blanket during the night. You may want to use a blanket sleeper to keep her covered in a cool house.

Tummy Time

Be sure to give baby time to lie on his stomach when he's awake—especially if he sleeps on his back or side. The stomach is the position from which he'll learn to crawl. When he spends time in that position, he will practice lifting his head. The more he practices, the stronger he will get, and the happier he'll be in that position. Arrange things for him to look at when on his tummy. If he cries immediately when you place him on his stomach, talk to him and encourage him. You can give him some

The more babies work to get the head up, the easier it becomes.

extra tummy practice by lying on your back and placing him face down on your chest. Cheer him on as he struggles to lift his head.

Place baby on his tummy on a firm surface for brief intervals throughout the day to help him get comfortable in that position. Try to have at least one such session during each wakeful period.

Sleeping

As your baby becomes more aware of what's going on around him and enjoys his interactions with you, he may not fall asleep as readily as before. At first he would go to sleep while eating or being held. Now he may find himself awake and feeling sleepy but too stimulated to drop off. The longer he's awake, the more difficult it may be for him to go to sleep. If you put him down, he may cry lustily in protest, not wanting to give up your company.

When you know that all of his other needs are met and he probably needs rest, put him down and let him learn to go to sleep on his own. If he cries, know that crying can't hurt him and that he is safe in his Father's arms. Trust that he can settle himself. He'll probably not cry more than 5 to 15 minutes. If he cries over 15 minutes and gets too worked up, use your intuition as to whether it will be better to pick him up and try to settle him before putting him down again, or whether to leave him and not stimulate him further. Some parents have reported that after the crying got loudest, the baby soon fell asleep.

You might sing a lullaby before putting your baby down to sleep and turn on a special music box or lullaby album to play as she's drifting off. These can be happy cues that it's time to settle down.

While night feedings continue, keep them quiet and peaceful. Resist baby's overtures to get you to play with him at that time, keeping play for daytime hours. Keep the lights low (or off when you can). Parents can overcome the feeling of resentment at having their sleep interrupted by rising to the opportunity to be on watch for the world. Those wonderfully still, peaceful times can be an opportunity for prayer as you feed baby. Prayerful inspiration can come easily in the cozy stillness with your dear one. Your prayerful thoughts can benefit all the children of the world.

Your baby will be happier when he's awake if he's getting enough rest. Eventually, when three naps a day seem too frequent, your baby's naps can be consolidated into two a day—morning and afternoon, with a long sleep at night. This may not occur until baby is four months old or more, but there is considerable variation in how much sleep each baby needs. The two naps usually continue until a baby is around a year old.

Playtime and Baby's Learning

Your baby is learning much by looking and listening. He will like to look at faces, especially yours, and to hear your voice. You will be baby's favorite sight, and the time spent with you will be most valuable. Your baby will love to have you talk and sing to him. When baby is awake in the evening, you can play with him as you undress him in a warm place. You might rub him with a little lotion, and push and stretch his arms and legs while you talk or sing to him. As you talk to him, let him play on both back and tummy, and encourage his efforts to hold his head up.

Your baby will be spending more time awake during the day and will be able to entertain himself for awhile without you. He may discover his hands and be fascinated looking at them.

You can put pictures in baby's crib for him to look at. Baby might like to look at large pictures of family members laminated or hung in clear plastic bags in the crib. Pictures of faces with features in contrasting color or black on white will attract his attention. A mirror may be of interest. Safe crib mirrors are available and may be a source of enjoyment for him. Babies also like to look at black and white patterns and bright colors. You may see baby staring at the intricate pattern of a curtain or clothing fabric.

When babies are just a few weeks old, they begin learning that what they do causes an effect. To their delight they can learn to move mobiles with a ribbon tied to their arm or leg. They can learn to bat at dangling toys to make sound and movement. (See **First Toys,** p. 35.) Given this opportunity, they can then learn to reach out to grasp toys by three months.

Games

Here are some fun games and songs to try:

With baby on his back, hold his feet and move them back and forth away from and toward his body while saying this verse:

Chug, chug, chug go baby's feet.
Walking, walking with the beat.
Chug, chug, chug away we go.
Shall we walk a mile or so?

Hold baby's hands, turning them as you say this verse:

Wind, wind, wind, the bobbin.
Wind, wind, wind the bobbin.
Pull, pull. (Pull baby's hands out to the side.)
Clap, clap, clap. (Touch hands together for claps.)

Here's a comforting version of "Rock-a-Bye Baby":

Rock-a-bye baby on the tree top.
When the wind blows the cradle will rock.
When the bough breaks, the cradle won't fall,
And baby will learn that Love cares for all.

First Toys

A common first toy is the mobile. A musical one is best. Hang it where baby can see and listen. Be sure to get a mobile that faces down at the baby rather than out to the adult. Babies delight in causing an effect. You may tie a ribbon from baby's hand or foot to a mobile so that baby's movement causes the mobile to move. Notice that he will move that hand or foot more than the other and show excitement when he makes the mobile move. He will also love watching a helium-filled mylar balloon tied in the same way. Be sure to keep watch to see that baby doesn't get entangled in the ribbon. Never leave baby alone with ribbons or strings that could wrap around him.

Note that ages given on toy boxes are usually broader than the actual ages of interest in the toys.

Batting Toys

The next interactive toy to give baby is a dangling toy he can bat at. You can make this toy by tying large colored balls onto a dowel with shoelaces. The balls can be wooden, macramé, hollow golf balls, or Ping-Pong balls. Space them one to two inches apart. The length of lace from dowel to ball should be six or seven inches. At first, hold the dangling balls against baby's hand so that his movement puts the balls in motion. Move it so that he can feel it

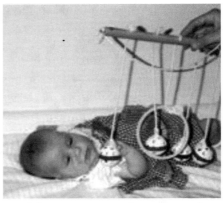

With batting toys, infants learn that they can make something happen.

alternately with each of his hands. He won't reach out for the toy until he has discovered that his movement causes an effect. Then, when he gets the hang of it, you can put screw-eyes in the ends of the dowel and hang it over baby to bat at. You will need to hang it to the side near baby's hand at first. You can string Ping-Pong balls by threading a cord or tip-less shoelace onto a large needle and pushing the needle through the ball. Tie a large knot in the string near the ball. You can string a plastic bracelet or large ring in the center of the dowel between the dangling balls, so that when baby starts to grasp, he will have that to hang onto.

Toys to Make

(These could be made by an older sibling.)

- Draw a bright face with dark eyes and eyebrows on a paper plate. Hang where baby can see it.
- Take a disposable aluminum pie pan and poke a pattern of holes in it with an ice pick, nail, or similar sharp object. Hang it where the light will shine through the holes for baby to look at.

Feeding and Schedule

Your baby should be settling down into a more predictable schedule during this time, if you work toward feeding him at regular intervals during the day and letting him sleep as long as he will at night. He will probably give up one of his night feedings within three months. You can fit your baby's schedule into your family routine. (See **Developing a Routine,** p. 20)

Babies are capable of regulating how much they need to eat. If you are breast-feeding, the baby will be taking all he wants from the breast. Continue to alternate the breast that baby starts with at each feeding. As a bottle-fed baby drains his bottles, increase the amount of formula, half an ounce at a time, up to six or eight ounces. When you feed baby, avoid wiggling the nipple in his mouth to coax him to take more, and don't disturb him by burping him frequently. As long as he is drinking well, just hold the bottle or breast still and let him govern the speed of his drinking. If he stops eating or gets wiggly, take time for a burp.

If you are breast-feeding, your supply should be well established by now. So, if you would like your baby to be able to take a supplementary bottle when you're away, you can express some of your milk before each feeding and store it in the freezer. You can collect enough for a bottle feeding. If you supplement feedings regularly with formula, it will decrease your supply, but an occasional bottle of formula (one or two a week) won't hurt. A breast-fed baby may refuse to take a bottle, but if you start giving a supplementary bottle with your milk no later than a month after birth, the chances of getting the baby to accept the bottle are better than if you wait longer.

Your baby may be taking 20 or more ounces of breast milk or formula by one month, and around 28 to 32 ounces by two months. (Smaller babies will take less, and larger babies more.) Experts don't agree on the amount babies should drink, but they do agree on the fact that babies will take what they need and that a parent should never urge babies to take more than they want. As babies give up the night feedings they need to take more milk during the day. Your baby will work up to four feedings of seven or eight ounces each. If he's not ready for that much at one time, he'll need more feedings.

Gazing and Cooing

Solids should not be needed yet. If your baby is large, 12 pounds or more, and seems to want more food than he can get in five feedings, you may want to start feeding him some solids by around four months. (See **Starting Solids** in the next chapter.)

SAMPLE SCHEDULES

These are schedules in process given by parents, changing as the need changes. The schedules reflect the differing needs of a baby and the family.

Blake is a nursing baby—1¹/₂ months old. His flexible schedule is adjusted to mesh with his Dad's late hours. Diaper changes continue as needed.

Time	Activity
8:30–9:30 a.m.	Awakens, diaper change (clothes if needed), nurses. Awake awhile. Smiley and fun.
11:00 to 11:30	Nurses, then naps 1 to 3 hours.
3:00 p.m.	Awakens, nurses. Mom does errands. Cat naps in afternoon.
6:00 or 7:00	Nurses. Naps 1 to 3 hours. Nurses on awakening.
9:00	Dad gets home. Plays with Dad.
9:30	Parents eat.
11:00 or 11:30	Bathes with Mom and has last feeding.
12:00 midnight	All go to sleep for the night. Awakens every 3 to 6 hours (average 4).

Gazing and Cooing

Nursing baby—2 months 3 weeks. A flexible schedule. Times vary.

Time	Activity
7:30 a.m.	Awakens, nurses.
8:00	Goes back to sleep. Mom naps too.
9:00	Awakens, nurses. Occasionally has bath if not at night.
12:00 noon	Nurses.
Until 2:00 or 3:00 p.m.	Awake, interacts with others and plays independently. Watches family, bouncy chair or swing.
2:30	Nurses, naps.
5:00	Awakens, nurses.
6:00	Interacts with others or plays independently.
7:00	If fussy, swings and has bath. Sometimes naps $1/2$ hour to an hour.
8:00	Nurses.
10:30/11:00	Nurses and sleeps through the night.

A schedule can be flexible and brief, such as this one for a two-month-old.

Time	Activity
5:00 a.m.	Nurses and goes back to sleep.
8:00 to 9:00	Awakens, diaper change, nurses.
Then throughout the day.	Watches family in bouncy chair or swing, plays in crib, playpen or on blanket on floor. Naps, nurses, and is changed every 3 to 4 hours as needed. Mom nurses her before church or outings. Sits in bouncy chair at table where she can see family when they eat.
9:00 p.m.	Bath every night or two.
9:30	Bedtime. Sleeps 7 or 8 hours.

Don't forget the spiritual food

In you're overwhelmed with busyness and possibly feeling sleep-deprived, don't forget to refresh yourself spiritually. Taking the time to pray for yourself and your baby will bring refreshment and peace to your day. It's reassuring to think of your baby, your home, and your community as surrounded by the everlasting arms of Love.

Caring for a baby can be intensive, but remember that the work you are doing as a parent in establishing a good foundation for your little one is the most important work you can do. Make a point of getting out from time to time for a walk or a trip to the store with baby. Plan for an occasional outing with your spouse, leaving baby with a reliable sitter. It's important to keep nourishing your marriage and to get a fresh outlook.

Cameos of Babies

✎ Nile ✎

1 mo. 12 days. Looks all around. Not staying on side in bed any more. Discovered dining room wall paper and stares at it.

2 mos. 2 days Smiles and coos. Batting at toys. Sleeps as long as 6 hours at night.

✎ Elsa ✎

1 mo. 16 days. In fencing position when on back. Prefers batting at dangling toys with right hand. Smiling and cooing. Sleeping longer periods at night.

2 mos. 13 days. Joyous baby. Full of smiles. Plays alone well. Dangling Ping-Pong balls kept her busy for a long time giggling and laughing in crib. Makes vowel sounds and squeals. On tummy, puts fingers in mouth and puts head down to go to sleep.

✎ Jan ✎

1 mo. 18 days. Batting at toys. Still awakens in night for feedings.

2 mos. 15 days. Reaching up and batting overhead. Going into more of a midline position when on back. Smiles. Showed keen interest in hanging Playpath Soft Triplets (soft dangling cloth figures). Batted with both hands reaching overhead. Holds head up well when on tummy.

✎ Alan ✎

1 mo. 20 days. In fencing position. Much happier since nursing Mom discovered a few foods not to eat.

2 mos. 3 days. In more of midline position. Batting at balls. Sleeps 8½ hours at night. Awake most of the evening.

✎ George ✎

1 mo. 22 days. Hands open more and starting to grasp. Getting more efficient with nursing. Does lots of looking and steady staring.

2 mos. 26 days. Lots of smiling. Making vowel sounds. Holds head up well on tummy.

∞ Chris ∞

1 mo. 22 days. Awake a lot during the day, but sleeps well at night. Seems hungry almost all the time. Focusing on close things. Lots of listening. Tuned in to sound. Sucks fist. Learning to comfort himself to sleep. Dangling Ping-Pong balls a favorite toy. Batted and watched.

2 mos. 26 days. Loves looking at hands. Smiles and talks. Looks for what he hears. Happier during day, but still some crying in evening.

∞ Timmy ∞

1 mo. 17 days. Active baby. Has turned over from front to back occasionally since he was one week old. Starting to grasp with hands. Batted and grasped at soft Jingle Balls.

2 mos. 0 days. Mainly in fencing position on back, but easier to turn head. Gaining information visually. Batting and grabbing at toys.

2 mo. 14 days. In more of midline position now. Batting well. Holds head up well on tummy. Smiling and cooing.

∞ Benny ∞

1 mo. 30 days. In fencing position. Evening fussy period. Sleeps 7 hours at night.

2 mos. 13 days. Kicked well at Thumpy Kick Board. Batted well at Dangling Rods, especially with left hand.

∞ Hal ∞

2 mos. 18 days. Discovering hands—watches fingers.

2 mos. 26 days. Surprised Mom by rolling from tummy to back recently. Sleeping 6 hours at night.

∞ Linda ∞

1 mo. 7 days. Follows well with eyes. Parents sing a lot to her. Getting into better schedule. Slept 7 hours last night. Stares at patterned prints on curtains and clothing.

1 mo. 21 days. Found her hand. Squeals when she wants mobile to go. Loved Beautiful Beginnings Mobile.

2 mos. 4 days. Going into midline position. Kicks feet. Keen interest in visual exploration. Starting to grasp and bring objects to mouth.

Gazing and Cooing

Had great fun with Foot Jingles—actively kicking—especially in morning. Loved Dangling Rods. Used with kickboard parents made.

∾ **Cal** ∾

2 mos. 11 days. Sleepy and a little fussy. Enjoyed Mom's comforting. Smiled and watched her as she talked to him. Looked cautiously at me as stranger today. Keenly watched clowns of Beautiful Beginnings Mobile.

∾ **Jody** ∾

1 mo. 29 days. Laughs out loud. Bats at balls.

2 mos. 12 days. Liked Ping-Pong balls. Grins at pictures in book. Going into more of a midline position when on back. With I-Cube black and white pictures, looked at girl for the longest time repeatedly. Liked Musical Mobile Busy Box. Watched animals intently, kicked feet and talked to it.

4

Reaching Out and Smiling
Three to Five Months

Ye shall go out with joy, and be led forth with peace: the mountains and the hills shall break forth before you into singing, and all the trees of the field shall clap their hands.

Isaiah 55:12

It may now be difficult to imagine life without baby. Every time he smiles, you can be grateful for this gift of joy. By this time, your baby has filled out and lost his new infant look. He'll smile readily at you and anyone else who smiles at him. He may look at people and objects across the room and intensely study those that are close. He may turn to look when you call. When on his back, he'll be in a midline position and able to look straight up rather than mainly to the side. During this period, he'll be able to consciously reach out for and grasp objects and bring them to his mouth. He may have discovered his hands (and possibly his feet) and enjoy watching them. He will like to be held in an upright position and may pull his head forward trying to sit up when in a semi-inclined position. He'll like to lock his legs and stand when held in a standing position.

He will probably be sleeping through at least one night feeding by this time and will have settled into a more predictable routine with two naps—morning and afternoon. When you pick him up for a feeding, his cries will quiet in anticipation.

He'll vocalize, cooing in different pitches, gurgling, and squealing. As you talk to baby, he will respond with vowel sounds. You can hold little conversations with him. Take turns with him, talking and listening for his response. At times, echo the sounds he makes back to him. By the end of this time, he may love to buzz his lips with a "raspberries" sound and may squeal loudly.

He will be interested in looking all around and will be gaining much information from what he sees. Take him around the house pointing to and naming items he looks at and touches. Talk to him about what you are doing. "Now I'm going to change your diaper." He'll like to watch your lips if you sing songs or say rhymes as you change diapers and at other times. He may move his lips in imitation as he watches your mouth. Some parents can hear their babies cooing in words, sentences, and paragraphs.

Finding Comfort

Your baby should be crying less than previously. He's probably discovered that he can be awake and happy even when he's not eating. When he's awake, and not hungry, first give him a little tummy time, then give him brief periods to play by himself with his crib gym until he gets fussy. You can also place him in an infant seat and move him around to different locations in the house to give him different views. He may start crying, as well as smiling, to get attention. Enjoy him and play with him, but don't pick him up every time he whimpers.

Now that he doesn't go right to sleep at every feeding, it's a good idea to give him the responsibility of comforting himself to sleep. If you get him in the habit of being fed or rocked, or sucking a pacifier to sleep, you are making yourself part of his going-to-sleep process, and he will then need you to put him to sleep when he awakens in the night. This can interfere with his freedom as well as yours. When you know that all his needs are met, and he's needing sleep, put him down with assurance. Let him cry himself to sleep if he must. Crying is not habit forming, and if you don't give in and pick him up, he'll settle down. Know that he is capable of comforting himself to sleep, and trust him to his Father-Mother God. This is the beginning of the important letting-go process you will go through all of your child's life as you allow him to accept responsibilities. You can still be close to him as you feed him, rock him, talk to him, and play with him at times when he is awake. Of course you will be attuned to special needs for comforting if he's not feeling well, but then return the responsibility to him when he's able to accept it.

Toys and Play

When your baby is awake, you can have her near so that she can watch you while you work around the house, and you can talk to her. She may be in an infant or bouncy seat or on a blanket on the floor.

In the 1970s, playpens came into disfavor because they were overused or incorrectly used. When used properly, they can be an asset. If you have a playpen (play yard, or Pack 'n Play), this is a good time to start using it before your baby can crawl. Dangling toys may be hung from it, and baby can get used to having a special place to play. Then when he's able to move around, he won't object to it as much. You will want to limit the use of the playpen to no more than a couple of half-hour sessions a day, and give baby opportunities to be in other settings. After your baby can crawl, he'll need to have opportunities to explore beyond the limits of the playpen.

Some parents like to use a playpen so they can reserve the crib for sleep alone. It is good to have different places for baby to play. But allowing a baby to have some playtime in his crib with dangling toys will not prevent him from sleeping well in it. Toys should be removed from the crib and the room darkened when the baby is put down to sleep. In addition to the playpen and crib, dangling toys can be tied from chairs while baby plays below on a blanket on the floor.

If you've given baby objects to bat at, he will start grasping them and trying to pull them to his mouth. Cradle gyms and overhead dangling toys will be interesting to grasp and manipulate. Floor gyms work well as an alternate place to hang dangling toys. Get one where the toys face the baby and where you can change the dangling toys and hang rattles or teethers.

If you place a small, circular teether in baby's hand, he will start bringing it to his mouth.

Reaching Out and Smiling

Toys

- Play gyms or floor gyms for baby to reach and grasp when on back
- Rattles and toys that can be easily grasped and mouthed
- Soft, squeezy rubber toys from the pet shop are usually favorites.
- Your baby will probably enjoy looking in a mirror. You can put a mirror made for babies in the crib or by the changing table.

Kicking Fun

Your baby may love to cause an effect by kicking.

- You can position a crib gym toy that has a rotating tumbler center section so that baby can kick it or rotate it with his feet.
- Baby socks or booties with jingle toys on the toes are fun when baby has discovered his feet. He can play with them with his hands or just enjoy the sound as he kicks.
- Fisher-Price has a Kick and Play Piano and Kick 'n Crawl Playhouse which can be used for kicking now and for more advanced play later.
- Another favorite kicking toy is one a parent can make. Paint a piece of plywood and add a picture, such as a face or a rabbit's head. Drill holes in the four corners, and attach one-inch elastic, threaded with large jingle bells, through these holes. Then tie the elastic to the rails near the foot of the crib. Position baby on his back so that his feet can kick the kickboard. Many babies love causing this jingling noise with their feet.
- Tie a mylar helium balloon to baby's ankle. He'll love watching it bounce as he kicks.

Homemade Toys for Batting and Grasping

- Hanging Cans. Most babies love this, but occasionally a baby who is easily disturbed by loud noises doesn't. So you may want to test your baby by clanking a couple of empty cans overhead before making it. 1) Clean out five or six small tin cans (7 to 10 ½ ounce cans), smoothing the inside edges well with a hard object. 2) Cover the can with colorful contact paper. 3) Punch a hole in the top of each can, thread through a thick shoelace, and tie a large knot on the end that will pull up into the can, but not go through the hole. 4) Tie the other end of the laces to a 14-inch length of one-inch dowel so that the cans will be close to touching, or thread them through holes drilled in the dowel and fasten each with a knot. Adjust the laces so the cans are even at the bottom, and the strings are six to eight inches long. 5) Tie additional laces or tape to screw eyes in each end of the dowel, and hang it over baby. He will love touching the cans or making a racket by batting at them. Watch to see if your baby gets disturbed by the commotion, and remove the toy when he has had enough.

- If your baby likes quieter toys, you may make a dangling toy for baby to reach for out of padded cloth-covered jingle bells or with other soft objects, such as a new plastic dish scrubber, a string dish mop or a tied wad of colorful fabric.

Games to Play

- Pull to sit You can hold baby's hands and pull him up to a sitting position. Here are some verses you can repeat for fun as you do this:

  Up, up, up comes baby dear. Reach way up and touch my ear.

  Down, down, down you go cherie. I love you and you love me.

Up you come my little one. Down again you go.
Look and see what I have found—baby's wiggly toe.

- Rock backwards and forwards with your baby singing:

  Rocking, rocking, rocking, rocking.
  Backwards and forwards, to and fro.
  Rocking, rocking, rocking, rocking.
  This is how baby (sing your baby's name) likes to go.

- Listen to sounds with your baby—the tick of the clock, motor of an appliance or car.
- Call him by his name. Does he have any favorite sounds? Shake a rattle to the side of baby, and see if he'll turn to the sound.
- Make a game of holding a tissue high above baby and letting if float down to touch him.
- Make up a song for your baby and sing it as you work around the house or drive in the car.
- Put your baby in an infant seat or swing where he can look out the window. Watching a bird feeder can be good entertainment.

Outings

- Baby will probably love being outdoors. You can walk about your yard holding him and seeing the wonders through his eyes. Let him feel the roughness of the bark of trees and see the beauty of flowers and the movement of squirrels or birds. Have moments of quiet to listen to and name the sounds you hear—the airplane, the bird, or the traffic.
- Baby may enjoy lying on a blanket under a tree and watching the patterns of the leaves. Be sure to keep

watch for his safety. Also make sure that the sun doesn't shine directly on him or in his eyes.

- Baby will be a good traveling companion in a car seat. This may be an easier time to travel with a baby than when he is more mobile and bent upon practicing his physical skills. Babies who ride regularly in the car seat come to accept it as a fact, so it's good to start early with some outings.

Feeding

Whether you breast or bottle feed baby, keep a fairly regular schedule so that both you and baby know what to expect. As the breast-fed baby grows, he may indicate he's needing more food by fussing for feedings earlier than usual. When this happens, feed him more often to stimulate your breasts to produce more milk. In a day or two he'll be getting enough to go back to the regular routine.

If you are bottle feeding, continue to hold baby while he eats even if he can hold the bottle by himself. This is a special time of closeness that can be enjoyed by you and baby, just as it would be if you were breast-feeding. Adjust the amount of formula to suit baby's needs. Baby will take around six ounces of formula at each of five feedings, or maybe by now, seven or eight ounces of formula at each of four feedings.

Starting Solids

Breast milk or formula will remain baby's main nutrition at this time. If your baby seems to want more food, you may want to go back to five feedings a day rather than trying to feed him enough in four. If your baby consistently indicates the need for more food from four to six months, or shows interest in food you're eating, you can start a little solid food.

If your baby is doing well on milk alone, skip this section on starting solids and come back to it when your baby is older and needing more food.

When you feel your baby is ready, start with one teaspoon of

Reaching Out and Smiling

baby instant rice cereal mixed to a thin consistency with formula or breast milk. Don't add solid food to a bottle, since the main object is to get baby used to new tastes and textures and to eating from a spoon. Use a shallow demitasse spoon or baby-feeding spoon with a shallow bowl. Baby might like one with a smooth, plastic bowl.

You may choose the meal that is convenient for you to start the solid feeding. If you are breast-feeding and have less milk at the end of the day, perhaps an evening meal will be best. Otherwise, you might try a morning feeding when baby is fresher. Start offering the solids at the beginning of a feeding when baby is hungry unless your baby is too hungry then to want to bother with learning the new way of eating. If so, offer the solids after the milk feeding. Or, if it works better for your baby, you may give the cereal in the middle of the feeding after offering half of the milk.

Mix infant rice cereal with breast milk or formula in a custard cup and heat to lukewarm in a small pan of hot water. Heating baby's food in a microwave should be done only with great caution as it heats unevenly and can contain scalding hot spots. Always stir and test food on your wrist or lips to be sure it's not too hot before giving it to baby.

Put a bib on your baby and seat him in an infant seat. Take a little cereal on the spoon, put it in baby's mouth and tip the spoon up, holding it there so baby can suck a bit off. Some of it will run out of his mouth, and you can scoop it up and try again. You can talk to baby about how good it is and how nice it is to try a new food. If baby gets upset about it, discontinue feeding, and try again the next day. You may try adding a little more or less milk to change the texture and see what baby likes best. If he shows a distaste for the cereal, try a teaspoon of banana. Take a soft, ripe banana, pull the peel back, and scrape a little with a spoon (pureed, or commercial baby-food banana may be used). Baby might like that smooth texture. If so, after giving banana for a few days, you can add it to the cereal and see if baby likes the combination. Increase the amount if baby is eager for more until he is taking two or three tablespoons.

Watch for baby's signals that he's had enough. Tight lips or turning the face away are baby's ways of letting you know he's through or that he doesn't care to eat a food. Don't force or trick baby into eating. If a food is rejected, make note, and try it again after a few days or weeks. The idea is to have baby enjoy eating new foods. It can take many exposures before baby learns to like some foods, so don't accept a rejection as permanent, but keep each exposure unpressured.

When your baby is doing well with these first foods, you may add other cereals and fruits and give them at another feeding in the day, either morning or evening, depending on which you started with. Smooth baby applesauce is another good first fruit. There is a thought by some that starting with vegetables, rather than fruit, will cause better acceptance of the less-sweet vegetables. However, babies are used to fairly sweet milk, and starting with the sweetness of fruit may make the first solid eating experience a more instant success. You won't have trouble introducing less-sweet foods later if you start with small amounts and convey a positive attitude about eating to baby. The next baby cereals to try after rice are oatmeal and barley. Save the wheat and mixed cereals until later. Introduce one new food no more often than every four days to a week. If a food seems to cause a rash, diarrhea, or extra gas, discontinue it, and try again after a few weeks or months.

Commercially-strained baby foods are fine to use. Or you can use a baby-food grinder or blender to make your own baby food out of any well-cooked food. Food you blend is less expensive and can have fewer undesirable additives such as starches. You shouldn't store leftover food in the container used for a feeding, as saliva on the spoon causes foods to spoil. So keep the serving amounts small, and place the serving of food from the jar into a dish until you are ready for the last feeding from a jar. When the baby wants more, you can increase the amount of food up to half a jar, and then later, a full jar. A jar of food should not be kept more than three days after being opened. You may freeze homemade foods in ice cube trays, store in plastic bags, and take out a cube or two to thaw and heat for a serving.

Other good first foods to offer are cooked pears, peaches, carrots, squash, sweet potatoes and uncooked avocado. All should be strained or blended smooth.

Opinions and beliefs about foods change. One pediatrician will recommend one thing, and another, something else. Since authors of a baby book can't know the individual baby, they always advise parents to check with the baby's pediatrician before following their advice. Before the 1980s, some parents were advised to start babies on orange juice from about three weeks for the vitamin C it contains. Now parents are advised to postpone its use until baby is 9 to 12 months old, because it has bothered more young babies than other fruits such as apple juice. Vitamins are now included in formula and are said to be in mothers' milk, if the mother has a balanced diet including citrus fruits and vegetables. Pediatricians' advice depends on what they have read of research and experienced with individual babies. Since babies are different, it's a good idea to follow the general guidelines of giving your baby small amounts of new foods one at a time, expecting that they will agree with him. Thinking of food as evidence of the supply of God's goodness and care will help you and baby avoid undue suspicion or fear of food.

If you use commercially-prepared baby food, use the separate foods at first, rather than blends, so you know what you're giving baby. Give blended foods only after you have introduced each ingredient separately. If baby prefers, you can thin some foods with formula or mix them for a texture and flavor he likes.

Fruit Juice: It's better not to start giving fruit juice to baby until after six months because a he can prefer its sweetness to the more nutritious milk. (See p. 70)

Sample Guide for Introducing Foods to Baby

There is no hard and fast rule about introducing solids, but some parents might find this guide helpful. Introduce one teaspoon of new food at first, increasing a little each day up to $1/2$ jar (four tablespoons) per meal. Wait about four days before starting each new food. Increase amounts as baby is eager for more.

Give the following foods pureed or mashed. Start lumpier foods after seven months.

Months	Cereal, starches	Fruits	Vegetables	Proteins
4	baby rice baby oatmeal	applesauce banana		
5	barley cereal cream of rice	cooked: pears, peaches	cooked pureed: carrots, winter squash, green beans	
6	zwieback dry wheat toast	cooked: plums, apricots apple juice (diluted at first)	cooked: peas, sweet potatoes	cooked egg yolk
7 introduce lumpier foods	mashed potatoes high protein cereal noodles teething biscuits	cooked prunes	cooked: spinach, yams, beets	chicken turkey yogurt
8	cream of wheat other mixed cereals crushed graham-cracker O-shaped dry cereals	raw pears pineapple	summer squash asparagus artichokes	cottage cheese American cheese crisp bacon veal, beef, pork
9	bagel	orange and orange juice raw apple	celery broccoli cauliflower	lamb liver grated or sliced cheese
10	pasta graham crackers	raw plums nectarines	corn lima beans dry cooked beans	tofu fish (white, non-oily)
11	pancakes muffins	apricots papaya grapefruit	tomatoes okra	peanut butter
12–18 mos.	French toast	grape halves strawberries melon mango kiwi	brussel sprouts cabbage eggplant onions mushrooms cucumber	ham homogenized whole milk whole eggs ice cream salmon or tuna

SAMPLE SCHEDULES FROM PARENTS

Bottle-fed baby—three months on three-hour schedule

Time	Activity
7:00 a.m.	Awakens, 5- to 6-ounce bottle. Watches family from bouncy seat or pumpkin seat.
8:30–9:00	Nap.
10:00	5- to 6-ounce bottle. Bath here or at night. Independent play in crib or playpen.
11:00–11:30	Nap.
1:00 p.m.	5 to 6-ounce bottle.
1:30–2:00	Nap. When he awakens, playtime with Mom and then watches Mom work.
4:00	5- to 6-ounce bottle.
5:00–5:30	Nap.
7:00.	5- to 6-ounce bottle. Then held and talked to by Dad and Mom or near them on blanket, swing, or bouncy seat.
10:00	A few more ounces of formula before bed, but parents stop feeding so he can fall asleep by himself. Sleeps through night.

A nursing baby—four months old

Time	Activity
6:30 to 7:00 a.m.	Awakens and nurses (any earlier, I make him stay in his crib unless he really wails).
7:00–7:30	Bath time (He loves it, and we linger.)
7:30–7:45	Get dressed; tickle/laugh/kiss. (Not crazy about clothes over his head. Doesn't notice when laughing.)
8:00- 8:30	Self-entertained (bouncy chair/swing). Mama showers and has breakfast.
9:00—10:00 or 10:30	Nap—Spiritual study for Mama.
10:30	Nurses.
11:00—1:00 p.m.	Errands, shopping, Laundromat, or walk with stroller.
2:00-3:45	Nurses, then naps. Lunch and serious housework for Mama.
4:00 to 5:00	Playtime with Mama: toy-library toys, singing games, mylar balloon, play "So-big."
5:00-5:30	Nurses.
5:30-6:30	Self entertained—swing, chair, blanket while Mama gets meal.
7:00	Papa's home! Talks with Pop.
7:30	Sits in chair on table and watches while parents eat.
8:00-8:30	Nurses and eats one tablespoon cereal.
8:30-9:00	Rocking, hymn singing, quiet time, bedtime.

Reaching Out and Smiling

Here's another nursing baby at four months. Times are approximate.

Time	Activity
6:30 a.m.	Awakens and nurses, snuggles with Mom.
7:00–7:45	Independent play on quilt or Pack n' Play.
8:00–8:30	Bath, playtime with older brother in bouncy seat.
8:30–10:00	Nap time.
10:00	Nurses.
10:30–11:15	Plays alone in Pack 'n Play or swing.
11:15–12:00 noon	Time outdoors in nice weather on quilt or bouncy seat. Mom and brother sometimes picnic.
12:00–2:00 p.m.	Nap.
2:00	Nurses.
2:30–3:00	Independent play (Busy Gym and tummy time).
3:00–4:00	Outdoors for walk in carrier or stroller or home in bouncy seat.
4:00–4:30	Crib time with toys.
4:30–5:30	Plays alone or with family.
5:30–6:30	Nurses. Naps.
6:30–7:00	Play with family members.
7:00–8:00	Swing time, Busy Gym, maybe some mashed bananas or cereal
8:30–9:00	Nurses, to bed for night.

A bottle-fed baby—four months

Time	Activity
7:30 a.m.	Awakens, diaper change, 6-8 ounce formula. If he awakens earlier, Mom changes diaper. Diaper changed throughout day as needed. Sits in pumpkin seat and watches family while they get ready.
8:30–9:00	Cereal, ripe banana. Playtime in playpen for half an hour.
10:00	Bath (most days).
11:00	With Mom outside or doing errands.
12:00 noon	6 to 8 ounces formula. Playtime. Johnny Jump-Up or tummy time on blanket.
1:00–1:30 p.m.	Goes down on tummy for 2 to $2^1/_2$ hour nap.
4:00 or 4:30	6 to 8 ounces formula. Watches and interacts with Dad and siblings in pumpkin seat, Johnny Jump-Up, or perhaps on blanket near piano while sister practices.
6:00–6:30	Cereal and fruit.
8:00–8:30	6 to 8 ounces formula and to sleep for night

One mom shared her own schedule.

Daily	Weekly
Shower	Monday: Laundry
Spiritual study	Tuesday: Ironing, mending, sewing
Meals	Wednesday: Cleaning, dusting, vacuuming
Bed making	Thursday: Bake a dessert, freeze sauces, cookies, soup stock
Dishes	Friday: Bathroom cleaning
Wash baby's toys	

Cameos of Individual Babies

∞ Jody ∞

2 mos. 26 days. Eyes for Mom now. A bit suspicious of strangers. Almost hums when Mom plays piano. Bringing hands together. Brings objects to mouth. Laughs out loud when Mom swings him around. Loved looking at Eye Catchers (a series of hanging black and white pictures). Had a favorite one—boy with short hair.

3 mos. 10 days. Sound of vacuum cleaner will put to sleep if nothing else does. Smiles at himself in mirror. Loves to be held up in standing position.

3 mos. 24 days. Passes toys from hand to hand. Leans on right side as though getting ready to flip over. Knows people in family well. Gives them big smiles. Predictable about eating and sleeping.

4 mos. 7 days. Plays a lot with activity gym. Laughs out loud.

4 mos. 21 days. Rolls over from front to back. Prefers exploring toys with hands and mouth to overhead toys. Kept going for Cheery Chirper Rattle. Wouldn't look at Octo Teether.

∞ Timmy ∞

2 mos. 29 days. Starting to arch back, trying to turn over from back to tummy. Responds with smiles to "conversation."

3 mos. 12 days. Stares at intricate patterns. Held and shook wooden Cradle Chimes, looking pleased with sound.

3 mos. 26 days. Grasping and pulling items to mouth. Holds head up high when on tummy. Pulled Jolly Jumping Jack to make motion and sound with glee.

∞ Jess ∞

3 mos. 3 days. Loves Mom and Grandma. Acts differently toward them than others. Sleeps 12 hrs. at night and takes two three-hour naps in day. Discovered hand and looks at it. Loved Red, White, and Black Jingle Ball. Would hold it in infant seat.

3 mos. 17 days. Face clouded when Mom left room.

4 mos. 0 days. Squeals with delight. Pulls legs up when on tummy. Liked Crib Activity Arch.

4 mos. 14 days. Turns over from front to back. Kicked at Thumpy Kickboard with glee.

✍ **Hal** ✍

3 mos. 12 days. Brings hands together. Sometimes turns over from front to back. Lots of vocalizing—cooing and squealing.

3 mos. 24 days. Trying to sit up—not liking reclined car seat. Likes tummy time. Rolls over front to back and back to front.

4 mos. 7 days. Works to get things to his mouth. When on tummy, tries to get knees underneath him. "Flirts" with his eyes.

✍ **Elsa** ✍

3 mos. 25 days. Holds head up well when on tummy now, but still prefers back. Grasping well and bringing everything to mouth. Lots of smiles and verbal experimentation with vowel sounds. Loved Hanging Cans. Clanked them together and after several days, tried to get to mouth. Held and mouthed Donut Teether with eagerness.

4 mos. 29 days. Exploring toys with hands and mouth. Makes growling and whispering sounds. Tried to imitate "papa, mama, and baby bear sounds." Now prefers toys she can get to her mouth. Liked Squeezy Lady Bug and Cheery Chirper Rattle.

✍ **Benny** ✍

3 mos. 18 days. Batting well. Seems to prefer left hand. Holds head up well when on tummy. Creeping forward some. Making lots of cooing sounds. Likes to sing when Mom sings to him, even with bottle in mouth.

✍ **Brett** ✍

4 mos. 2 days. Turns from front to back. Still plays on back mostly. Discovered feet. Enjoys vocalizing. Starting to reach out for toy on tummy.

4 mos. 16 days. Grasping and exploring with open hand. Turned from back to front twice.

Reaching Out and Smiling

Diane

3 mos. 26 days. Holds hands together. Grasps and brings objects to mouth. Fingers toys well. When on tummy, reaches out with one hand. Liked hanging cans and Jumping Jack.

4 mos. 9 days. Loves faces and prefers interacting with people to playing with toys. Squeezy Pig gave her great joy—his nose was just right for chewing.

5

Exploring and Rolling
Five to Seven Months

*Thou wilt shew me the path of life: in thy presence is fulness
of joy; at thy right hand there are pleasures for evermore.*
                                        Psalms 16:11

Your charming baby will continue to be full of smiles, probably going readily to parents and strangers alike. (Though some may be more cautious with strangers.) You and baby have probably settled down into a fairly predictable routine, and you may wonder what you ever did without him. His curiosity will become apparent. He'll reach for and grasp whatever he can. He'll continue to learn by gazing at people and objects, but he will also become engaged in the process of exploring objects with his hands and mouth. He learns about texture, color, size, and shape—building blocks for later learning—in this way. Yes, he may love to bite on objects because of teething. But the turning over, examining, and mouthing of objects are part of the learning process, not just a comfort to the gums.

By six months, your baby will reach accurately for objects and explore them with fingers as well as hands and mouth. By the end of this period, he may show interest in small particles, studying them and trying to pick them up. When you put baby on the floor, you'll have to keep it swept and picked up, or small bits of dust (or whatever) will find their way to his mouth.

Babies learn by exploring toys with hands and mouth.

Rolling Over, Crawling, and Sitting

Your baby may learn to roll over during this time, especially if he has become comfortable lying on his stomach as well as his back. If he holds his head up high when on his stomach, he may lean over and suddenly find himself on his back. After this happens a few times, he will do it deliberately. Occasionally a baby will roll from back to front first. When your baby is on his tummy, you are likely to see him extend and lift his arms and legs in an "airplane" maneuver. This position is part of his practice in gaining physical control.

When baby is on her tummy reaching for an object, you can press your hand against her feet and see if she will push with her feet to move forward.

Babies will often get up on their knees and rock back and forth. Then they'll sprawl forward and eventually go into a crawl from this kind of action. Others will develop a commando crawl, pulling themselves forward with their arms, elbows, and legs. Another popular form of locomotion is rolling over and over, but baby then may find himself someplace he had not intended to go.

Many babies learn to balance sitting up at this time. They love to be in this position, and it frees their hands for holding objects. Even if your baby can sit up, you'll want to give him plenty of tummy time to practice crawling skills. Then he'll learn to get himself to a sitting position. Being allowed to gain the natural progression of physical skills gives a child freedom and grace. When you put him down to play, start him on his tummy with plenty of interesting objects to explore. He can be in a playpen or on a blanket near you. If he becomes too fussy in a prone position, you can then move him to a sitting position.

Sitting up frees hands for further exploration.

Use of Bouncer and Walker

When a baby can sit up fairly well, a Johnny Jumper, or similar bouncer that he can sit upright in, will be a joy for him. Adjust it so his feet just touch the floor. A few jumping sessions of about 15 minutes each day are enough. Prone playtime should be the staple.

Since walkers have been associated with some accidents with babies, they have been replaced on the market by the Exersaucer or other seats that rock but don't travel. Use such seats sparingly when your baby needs a change and you are busy, such as before dinner. This activity is also good in places where you want baby to be up off the ground while you are near, such as the basement or outdoors. Baby should have plenty of floor time to practice rolling and crawling. After he's able to crawl, it's better to give him freedom a good bit of the time rather than confining him to a seat.

First Discipline

Discipline is all about learning, and baby is learning much. Parents learn, too, as they provide discipline for their children. As baby becomes more mobile and capable, he needs to find out that what he wants isn't always best for him to have. Parents need to be strong indeed to keep from giving baby everything he asks for when they know he shouldn't have it. We truly love our children when we do what's best for them.

Before mobility comes, baby may seem dissatisfied with his lack of ability to move around. Now, he may cry not only from discomfort but to get you to do what he wants, such as picking him up, carrying him, rocking him, or sitting him up. Instead of running to him to comfort at the first peep, talk to him and try to comfort him from afar. Make sure he has different, interesting objects to explore.

After he can balance in a sitting position, he may fuss at you to sit him up. But, if you sit him up whenever he wishes, he won't practice the skills that will help him get to that position on his own.

You will still want to have plenty of playtime with your baby. She learns much from being with you, but this time needs to be balanced with time on her own to practice the physical skills and explore toys or other safe objects with hands and mouth.

Your baby's new ability to grasp, and her curiosity, may cause her to begin grabbing hair, jewelry, or glasses. Some babies try their new teeth on parents too. You can help baby learn that these are inappropriate activities by simply saying "No!" in a firm voice and holding her away from you. Show her how to pat or give a kiss and express your delight in these appropriate interactions.

Language

Baby may enjoy vocalizing when he's by himself as well as "talking" to you. He'll experiment with squeals, "raspberries" with his lips, and blowing saliva bubbles. He will add consonant sounds to his vowel sounds (ma, ba, pa, da, na) and string them together for babble. You can listen in (unseen) to his experiments with sound when he first awakens.

Have conversations with your baby.

Have conversations with him using his sounds, but also talk a lot to him about what you are doing and what he is doing and seeing. Point to objects and name them repeatedly with single words as well as talking to him in sentences.

Learning, Toys, and Play

If your baby has had plenty of tummy time, he will probably now prefer to play on his tummy rather than on his back. He can reach out for toys that are in front of him and bring them to his mouth. He'll prefer exploring small toys to the overhead ones, because he can turn them around and get different parts to his mouth. When your baby is starting to turn over and move about, all the dangling toys that were used for batting and beginning grasping should be put away, as they will no longer be safe. Now is the time to bring out the rattles and teethers he was given as baby gifts. Kitchen gadgets also make fine toys. Be sure that anything you give baby does not have sharp edges or a finish that will come off in the mouth.

Some babies show preferences for certain textures. At first many babies prefer soft, rubbery toys. Soft, squeaky toys available in pet stores can be real favorites. Later, baby may enjoy exploring wooden or hard plastic toys. Preferences often change over time. After baby has learned all he can about an object, he abandons it for another one. I

Exploring and Rolling

have experimented by showing a five- to seven-month-old two toys—one he has already examined—and a new one. Though I change the position of these toys, the baby always chooses the new one. Rotate your baby's toys, putting some out of sight for awhile. When you bring them out again in a week or so, interest may be renewed.

As baby is able to sit up and play, toys or objects with moving parts become more interesting than simple ones. This is a time when crib activity centers may start to be of interest. Pull toys with springy antenna and turning gadgets may be even more interesting for exploration at this time than they will be later for pulling.

You can make your baby a Button Strip. Get about 6 large buttons (different colors and textures, if possible). Make a strip of doubled fabric with finished edges about $1^1/_2$ inches wide and 8 inches long. Sew the buttons on firmly with strong thread.

Games

Baby will love peek-a-boo games. Cover your face and then uncover it on "boo." When baby's arms are up, you might put a diaper over his arms and face so that he uncovers his face when he brings his arms down to the accompaniment of "peek-a-boo!"

Hide a toy partially with a diaper and let baby uncover it. If you cover the whole toy now, the baby may think it's gone and not continue reaching for it.

Put a toy out of reach on a diaper and let baby learn to get the toy by pulling the diaper to him.

Baby may enjoy airplane games. You can zoom him around through the air holding him face down on your arms. Another way is to bend your knees when you're on your back and place baby on his tummy on your shins. Hold onto his arms and move your legs around, talking, making noises, or singing to him.

Swing baby in your arms as you say this verse, altering tempo:

Mama's arms are a little swing; a-swinging we will go.
We'll swing along, swing along, swing along fast.
We'll swing along, swing along, swing along slow.

Sing the Itsy Bitsy Spider song while walking your fingers up baby's arm or leg.

The Itsy Bitsy Spider went up the water spout.
Down came the rain and washed the spider out. (Slide your hand down his arm.)
Out came the sun and dried up all the rain, (Pat arm.)
Then the Itsy Bitsy Spider went up the spout again. (Walk fingers up again and tickle under chin.)

Feeding

When your baby indicates, by staying awake longer, that two naps are plenty, you can start on a three-meal-a-day schedule with an extra milk feeding morning or evening. As you add more solids, the intake of milk will decrease. If you're breast-feeding, continue to nurse baby about four times a day. If you bottle-feed, baby should still have 20 to 24 ounces of formula each day. (This includes milk added to solid foods.)

If your baby is eating cereal and fruit regularly, you can add vegetables to the solids. Carrots and squash are good ones to start with. Then you can add green beans and peas. With each one, start with a teaspoonful and work up to half a jar. Wait about four days after each new food before introducing another one. You can alternate yellow and green vegetables after baby has been introduced to them. Never force or trick baby into eating a food if he indicates he doesn't want it. Think of the food as good (not just "good for you"), and talk to baby about opening his mouth and eating the "good carrots, beans, or whatever." The vegetables may be given at first with cereal instead of fruit at the evening feeding or you can continue with cereal and fruit morning and evening and add vegetables at a midday feeding.

At six or seven months, you can start adding meats to the noon meal. The meats should be finely ground, strained or scraped, or be commercially prepared, strained baby food. Start with chicken, then beef, then any of the meats. Scrape raw meat with a spoon. This leaves the sinew behind. You can cook it with a little formula in a Pyrex cup. You can scrape liver best if it's cooked first. If baby doesn't take to the meat, you can thin it with a little formula or add a bit of cereal or fruit.

Exploring and Rolling

You may give your baby vegetables and meat at the noon meal or at the evening meal with you.

You can blend the vegetables and meats you're eating for baby. Add a little formula to make it the consistency baby prefers. If your family enjoys casseroles, these may be blended after baby has been introduced to the main ingredients separately.

After six months, potato or pasta may be used instead of cereal at the evening meal.

Starting Juice

You can give baby a little apple or pear juice. Start with just a teaspoon of juice, and work up, over the next couple of months, to no more than two ounces of juice a day. You don't want to give your baby a lot of juice that would replace the more nutritious milk. Leave it unheated. Dilute it at first with half to two-thirds water. You can give it to baby from a spoon at first, then from a cup. This is a good way to introduce your baby to the cup. You may use a bottle if you prefer.

Holding the Bottle and Introducing the Cup

Baby may learn to hold his own bottle, but holding him with his bottle is still a special time of closeness. If you continue to hold baby with his bottle, he can gain his independence with the cup and will be willing to give up the bottle as he seeks independence. Even when baby can hold his own bottle, don't let him take it to bed. Having a bottle to go to sleep with can become a habit that baby may want you to repeat when he awakens in the middle of the night. Also, it's not good for future teeth for baby to go to sleep with milk in his mouth. He should learn to settle himself to sleep without a bottle.

From five-and-a-half months, you can start getting your baby used to drinking milk and juice from a cup. Learning that milk can come from a cup can help with weaning later. Use a cup with a flared rim and put just a little formula or apple juice in it. Hold a diaper or cloth under baby's chin to catch what runs out, and hold the cup to baby's mouth, tipping just enough to go into the mouth. A sippy cup with cover and spout to drink from may be used to give baby independence in holding the cup himself. But give some practice in drinking from a regular cup or glass, as well.

Self Feeding

When baby can sit up well, he may eat in a high chair. At first, it will help to pad the chair a bit. You can give a taste of milk from a cup before feeding solids, and then between bites of food, as baby wants it. Always take the baby's lead and watch for signals that he does or does not want the cup or a food. If baby doesn't take to the cup right away, you can wait and try again in a few days to a week.

At six-and-a-half to seven months, you may give baby a crust of wheat toast, zwieback, or a teething biscuit or pretzel (in baby section of your grocery store) to hold and bite on. It will dissolve as he chews on it and make a mess, so use a good bib and be prepared to clean up after. This will start your baby's self-feeding skills and also help him get used to more lumpy foods. You may give him a little lump of banana or soft, cooked carrot to see if he will gum it and eat it. Allowing a baby to practice self-feeding requires some tolerance to messiness on the parent's part, but baby's neatness improves as the skill progresses.

If baby starts to grab the spoon or put his fingers in his mouth when you're feeding him, give him a spoon to hold. He may bang it on the tray but continue to eat as you feed him. If he puts the spoon in his mouth, you can put a little food on it so that he feeds himself an occasional bite.

Exploring and Rolling

SAMPLE SCHEDULES

Here's the brief routine of a five-month-old girl.

Time	Activity
7:00 a.m.	Bottle, then back to sleep.
9:30	Awakens and plays alone for several minutes. Bath and dressed.
10:00	Cereal and bottle. Plays alone (and with others).
12:00	Nap.
1:00 p.m.	Awake and bottle, fruit. Plays.
2:30	Nap.
4:30	Bottle, cereal, baby veggies. Plays with others—baby games.
7:30	Bottle, bedtime routine including hugs, singing, prayers.
10:00 p.m.	To sleep.

Parents of twins find a schedule essential to keep up with the needs of two growing babies. Twins Abby (A) and Blaire (B)— 5$^1/_2$ months

Time	Activity
7:30 a.m.	(A) Change, 6$^1/_2$ -ounce bottle formula, cereal.
8:30	(B) (May change diaper earlier.) 6$^1/_2$-ounce formula. Both in bouncy seats with toy bar.
9:15	(A) naps.
10:15	(B) naps. (She doesn't sleep as much as her sister.)
11:30 or 12:00	(A) Change, dress, 8-ounce bottle. Play in playpen and blanket on floor.
12:30 or 1:00 p.m.	(B) Change, dress, 8-ounce bottle. Play in playpen and blanket on floor.
2:00 p.m.	(A) Down for nap.
3:00 or 4:00	(B) Down for nap. Swings when fussy.
4:30–5:00	(A) 2 jars baby food—vegetables and fruit, milk from cup.
5:30–6:00	(B) 2 jars baby food—vegetables and fruit, milk from cup. Babies in bouncy seats while family eats, then play with family.
7:00	(A) 8-ounce bottle, then bed.
8:00	(B) 8-ounce bottle, then bed.

Exploring and Rolling

This is a flexible schedule of a nursing six-month-old girl.

Time	Activity
7:00 a.m.	Wake up. Play in bed for a few minutes, then play in Exersaucer while Mum and Dad have breakfast.
7:50	Say goodbye to Dad. Have a little rice cereal, nursing and often quiet play with Mum in bed. Mum does Bible study while nursing.
9:00	Morning nap—varies from 1 to 2 hours.
11:00	Plays with Mum (music, floor play, outside on nice days on blanket with toys). Sometimes a bath.
11:30	In Saucer while Mum prepares and has lunch with Dad.
12:15	Play with Dad for about 15 minutes before he goes back to work.
1:00 p.m.	Adjourn to bedroom. Listen to lullaby tape, nurse.
2:00	Afternoon nap.
4:00	Walk in jogger. On warm days, go to park to swing, slide, see others
5:15	Pick up Dad from work.
6:15	Rice cereal, followed by getting ready for bed, possible bath. Nursing.
8:00	To sleep.

Tracy, six months, has a three-year-old brother.

Time	Activity
6:00 a.m.	Awakens. Has 8-ounce bottle of formula.
7:30	Rice cereal and 1 jar of baby fruit.
8:00–9:30	Bath some days. Plays with toys first on tummy, then on back, then in Exersaucer.
9:30 to 10:30 or 11:30	Naps. When she awakens: 4 ounces milk from cup and 4-ounce bottle. Also finger food such as zwieback or graham cracker.
11:30 to 12:30 p.m.	Lunch: 1/2 jar baby vegetable, yogurt, and fruit. Plays until 2:30 or 3:00.
3:00–4:30 or 5:00	Nap. Has 8-ounce bottle of milk on awakening.
6:00	Cereal and fruit.
7:00	Plays with toys in brother's room.
8:00	8-ounce bottle. Listens as Mom reads books to brother for 20 or 30 minutes.
8:00–9:00	To bed.
12:00–1:00 a.m.	May awaken, and has drink of water in bottle if she doesn't settle down by herself.

Lacy is 6½ months and has a three-year-old sister.

Time	Activity
7:00 a.m.	Awakens, nurses, plays in playpen or bed. Starting to pull up in crib.
9:00	Nurses a little. Naps.
11:00	Awake, nurses.
12:00	Has baby carrots if still hungry. Practices crawling and plays with toys on floor.
1:30 p.m.	Nurses. Naps.
4:00	Dad comes home. Gets excited playing with sister, Dad, and Mom. Loves to sit on lap and hear singing.
5:00	Nurses. Jump seat or playpen while Mom fixes dinner.
5:30 or 6:00	Dinner: rice cereal mixed with formula, fruit (apple sauce, pears, or peaches). Then likes to sit in high chair and play with toys while family eats. After dinner, plays in family room with family.
7:30 When fussy	Bath most nights. Time with Mom while Dad's with sister. Nurses, hymn singing, to bed.

Cameos of Individual Babies

✎ Nancy ✎

4 mos. 25 days. Rolling over both ways. Exploring with hands and mouth. Flaps hands against thighs when she loses a toy. Starting to creep forward.

6 mos. 16 days. Rolling all around on floor and getting to where she wants to go. Rocks on hands and knees. Kicks feet. Likes toys with faces or big eyes. Doesn't like to eat first thing in the morning.

✎ Cal ✎

5 mos. 18 days. Drinking from cup now. Trying to turn over. Airplaning on tummy with hands and feet up. Will play for an hour on tummy. Exploring with hands and mouth. Lots of babbling and making sounds.

✎ Brett ✎

5 mos. 14 days. Turns over both ways. Explores with hands and mouth. Complains when Mom walks away. Expresses disapproval when older brother is rough with him.

6 mos. 25 days. Loves to explore cardboard and paper with hands and mouth. Very vocal about needs and wanting to be with Mom. Creeps backwards. Has four teeth. Squeezy frog is favorite toy.

✎ Jess ✎

4 mos. 28 days. Turns from front to back. Says "Dada." Studied my face for a long time before starting to play with toys. Snuggles head in neck when you hold him. Pushes up high when on tummy and pushes backwards. High-pitched screaming. Liked Play Gym and Squeezy Pig.

6 mos. 2 days. Pulls feet up to play with. Airplaning on tummy with hands and feet up. Making "raspberries" and many sounds with mouth. Prefers hard toys with moving parts to soft, squishy vinyl or fabric toys.

6 mos. 16 days. Rolling over both ways. Gets up on knees and nose dives forward. Full of smiles. Says "Da da da" when around dog. Grunts

Exploring and Rolling

for Mom to turn on fan. Crept around the room following a hollow wooden ball that has holes for his fingers.

∽ Elsa ∽

5 mos. 13 days. Explores toys on tummy for short time, then turns over to back, preferring that position. Pushes with feet and turns in circles on back. Reaches back for toys. Pulls socks off. Put toe in mouth. Looked intently at me.

5 mos. 27 days. Gets toy and turns over to back. Seldom plays on tummy. Plays with her feet.

6 mos. 10 days. Likes to explore soft textures. Squealing and making "buh" sounds. Still likes to make growling sound.

∽ Benny ∽

6 mos. 10 days. Turns over readily. Commando crawl. Moves to where he wants to go. Making a lot more sounds. Carrying on "conversations." Laughing a lot. Talked to self in mirror. Liked Chewy Gummy.

6 mos. 24 days. Goes into airplane position and sometimes trembles with excitement when he sees new toys. Bangs high chair tray and closes eyes to noise. Making "H" sounds.

∽ Nile ∽

5 mos. 30 days. Big smiles. Saying "Oooo" and making lots of other sounds. Saying "B" and "th" and blowing bubbles. Holding head up more and happier on tummy, but still puts hands down at sides instead of using to hold head up. Likes to have Mom sit him and stand him up. Liked Turn and Learn Activity Center. Enjoyed making it rotate.

6 mos. 21 days. Holds head up well when on tummy now and beginning to reach for toys from that position. Not rolling over but loves to sit up and play when Mom sits him up. Great love is getting Mom or Dad to stand him up. Likes Johnny Jumper.

∾ **Mandy** ∾

5 mos. 10 days. Rolls over both ways. Turns toys with wrist action. Loves to interact with people. Vowel sounds and "bababa." Blows "raspberries." Throaty giggle. Likes small vinyl book that opened like accordion and Muppet Teething Rattle. Liked homemade button strip.

5 mos. 24 days. Moves by arching back. Rolls over.

6 mos. 9 days. Crawling commando style. Little toys not as interesting. Likes toys with gadgets to manipulate. Saying "dadada" and lots of "aaaa." Loves to watch people and look at faces. Smiles at everyone. Likes songs, "Allee Galloo" and "Ticka Tacka Tee." Liked Turn & Learn Activity Center and hanging activity center.

6 mos. 21 days. Commando crawling but getting up on knees. Likes to play sitting up. Can go to crawl from sitting position. Copies Mom saying "dadada" and making "raspberries." Sometimes "hams it up."

∾ **Denny** ∾

5 mos. 10 days. Exploring objects with keen interest. Making many different vocalizations. "H" sound.

5 mos. 24 days. Likes vinyl book. Laughs all the time. Turning over both ways. Scooting across floor.

6 mos. 28 days. Crawling on knees and going all over. Goes from crawl to sitting position.

∾ **Karen** ∾

5 mos. 10 days. Likes to sit up for awhile with help. Plays on back and tummy.

5 mos. 24 days. Sits up well. Says "Mama." Just started to eat solids, showing keen interest.

6 mos. 7 days. Enjoys soft, chewy toys. Likes to play with them sitting up and on tummy. Haven't found any solids she doesn't like. Sleeps well through night, but only naps for about half-an-hour during day.

6 mos. 21 days. Working at crawling. Gets up on knees. Can get to sitting position from stomach.

Soon after crawling, babies pull up to stand.

$\mathfrak{F}$

6

Crawling, Sitting, and Standing
Seven to Nine Months

And thine ears shall hear a word behind thee, saying, This is the way, walk ye in it, when ye turn to the right hand, and when ye turn to the left.

Isaiah 30:21

This is a period of unbelievable progress in gaining motor skills. Within a month or two, a baby can learn to crawl, sit up alone, climb, and pull up to stand. Shortly thereafter, he will learn to side step while holding on to furniture. We call it cruising. Children differ in the time they take for this dramatic change in mobility. One baby will be content to sit and observe, or work with objects, perfecting fine-motor skills and gaining concepts. This baby may not walk until fourteen months of age or later. Another will be up and walking alone by nine months. There is no need to be concerned about the baby's development in either case. Time of walking has no relation to later success in school or any other area. Parents of first children are often anxious for them to be up and doing the next thing. With later children they will relax and say, "There's no hurry. It's easier for me if he takes his time."

It's important for parents to refrain from comparisons with other children and cherish the precious individuality of God's child.

Baby may start by pushing backward instead of forward in his crawl. This is common. You can encourage the forward crawl by putting a toy in front and holding your hand behind baby's feet for him to push against. Eventually, he'll start going forward with or without your help. Some babies will get up on hands and knees and lunge forward as they get their crawl together. Others will pull forward for some time on their tummies in a "commando" crawl. As crawling is perfected and the baby picks up speed, you will marvel at how fast he can get from one place to another or get into "mischief."

After learning to crawl, your baby will soon be able to move himself into a sitting position and use both hands for exploration. The mouth will still be used in this exploration, but not as frequently, as the hands and fingers take over in the investigation process. Babies can learn to balance in a sitting position before they can get themselves into that position. If you put your baby into a sitting position, do so only after he has had lots of time to play on his tummy. (See **The Non-Crawler** in the next section.)

Baby will also be able to hold himself in a standing position and will love being placed in this position before he is able to pull himself up to stand. It's fine to give him opportunities to stand this way but don't give in to constant demands to stand him up at the expense of crawling practice.

Climbing and Standing

Climbing is a skill that usually comes before the parent can believe it. Baby always seems to want to get up higher. Soon after he can crawl, before being able to walk alone, he may head for the nearest stairs and start climbing. Going up isn't hard, but baby will probably need help in learning how to come down. Spatial concepts are learned with experience, but at first baby may sit down on thin air and take a tumble. You will want to guard the stairs from baby and be with him when he climbs. Help him learn to turn around and come down feet first on his tummy. If you are able to put a gate on the second step up, baby can practice going up and down on the first step.

Within weeks or even days of perfecting the crawl, baby discovers that he can pull up to stand. He will look for an object that is eight- to twelve-inches high—a cushion, box, stool, stair step, or low table. He'll put his hands on it and pull up first to his knees and then to his feet. You can see the look of triumph on his face as he pulls himself to a standing position. When he gets comfortable on his feet, he will side step (cruise) around furniture and gradually gain his balance. Eventually he will stand, holding on with just one hand, before he takes off to walk. It usually takes from two to four months of cruising before a baby gains the balance to walk by himself.

When a baby first learns to stand, he may not know how to sit down again without falling. If he awakens in the night and stands before he learns to get down on his own, he may cry for you to come and put him down. You can help him learn by bending his knees as you hold his hands and lower them. If you do this a number of times throughout the day, he will soon learn to get down himself, day or night.

When your baby is ready, practicing physical skills will become more compelling than other activities. But curiosity is still keen. Baby will be experimenting with what he can do with toys other than examine them with hands and mouth. He will start shaking, dropping, knocking them together, and tossing them.

Your baby will gain increasing control of his fingers. He'll become able to pick up small objects with thumb and forefinger, and he will use his fingers more in his exploration of objects. He'll like poking his fingers into holes or turning dials and gadgets with them.

The Non-Crawler

Sometimes a parent will say, "I don't think my baby will ever learn to crawl. She just likes to roll from place to place. She likes to sit up and loves to stand when I pull her to her feet, but she doesn't seem interested in crawling."

It's likely that this baby prefers to sleep on her back and has not had the tummy time to practice crawling skills. A parent can hinder a baby's natural process of gaining physical skills by giving in to baby's requests and assisting him too much. Whenever you put baby down to play, put him on his tummy, even if he can sit up well. Give him interesting toys or objects to explore with his hands and mouth. If he has enough time in that position, he'll practice using his hands, arms, and knees to move, to get into a crawling position, and eventually to get *himself* into a sitting position. He'll then learn to pull himself up to stand.

This is a time to realize that you don't have to do everything baby wants you to do when you know it's not best for him. We encourage parents to listen to baby and to tune in to baby's feelings and ideas, but there are times when the parent has reasons to encourage baby to do what's best for him in the long run. Parents play a major role in discipline and training because they have more knowledge about this human experience than the child. A baby who learns, with the encouragement of loving parents, that he can gain skill to do something he didn't think he wanted to do is acquiring strength in more ways than one. When the baby gains the skill to hold his head up and play when on his tummy, he likes these activities, practices them more, and gains the skill of crawling. We've seen parents take a firm stand to resist the beguiling demands of their precious babies to sit them up, to stand them up, and to walk them around. This might also involve resisting the advice of well-wishers to "help your baby along." Though it may take a bit longer for these babies to walk, they gain freedom, independence, and grace. Perhaps they have gained a little patience with themselves and others in the process.

Discipline

Your baby is now able to quiet to your voice. Give him some opportunity to do this. Talk to him rather than going to pick him up every time he fusses if you are busy and there is no obvious need. This will help to prevent overindulgence.

When your baby gets into something he shouldn't, pick him up and tell him firmly, "No, we don't touch the (dog food, plugs, TV, curtains, etc.)." Take him to something he may play with and give him a little praise as he starts to play with it. Remove or cover as many tempting touchables as possible.

If your baby should try to bite you or grab your glasses while you're holding him, you can train him not to do these things. If he is biting, speak to him disapprovingly as you open his mouth by gently squeezing his cheeks. Show him approvingly how to kiss. Hold baby's hand away from your glasses and show him how to gently pat your face.

If the inappropriate behavior is repeated, simply say with a firm voice, "No, don't bite" (or grab glasses). Then put him down and turn away. After he fusses for fifteen or twenty seconds, pick him up again with a hug and talk to him lovingly, demonstrating appropriate behavior. If he repeats the inappropriate behavior, repeat your action. He will soon learn what he may and may not do when he is being held. You might get a set of wooden beads and laces that baby can learn to string in another year and wear them yourself as a necklace for baby to play with at this period.

Some parents wonder if they should refrain from using the word "no" so their baby won't learn to say this word back to them later when exerting his independence. "No" is as good a word as any to stop undesirable behavior. You want your child to learn the signal to stop what he's doing. At first he will respond to your tone of voice, then pick up on the words. You can use other words, too, such as "Stop!" or "Don't touch." My dear Grandmother Grace would say "Tut tut!," and we knew that she meant "Hands Off!" by her tone of voice. It's a good idea not to overuse the word "no" or other negative words when you're not intending to stop undesirable behavior. One admiring observer, who was fascinated by the antics of a toddler, kept saying "No!" in disbelief, and that had a confusing effect on the child. Your toddler will pick up whatever negative word you use and try it out at some point. This is no reason for concern but denotes a step of progress. Your child has learned the meaning of the word, and its power, and is simply testing the rules.

A Safe Place to Play

Baby's mobility and curiosity bring increased interest in exploring. Allowing this exploration with watchfulness provides learning opportunities for baby. There are times, when you are involved with a project or on the phone, that watching becomes difficult, and you'll want baby to be in a safe place.

If you've been using a playpen regularly, baby will probably be willing to play there for brief periods—15 minutes to a half hour in the morning and perhaps again after nap time in the afternoon. Some parents time it by playing one side of a cassette tape. Be sure to save interesting toys for playpen use only. You can save your special activities or phone calls for these times or for nap times.

Crawling, Sitting, and Standing

You will want to close off other safety-proofed areas for baby to explore. Furniture and baby gates may be used. You can put a gate across baby's room and make that into a safe place to play. But most of baby's playtime should be where he has access to you, to watch you, come to you, and hear the language as you talk to him. Therefore, you'll want to safety-proof areas such as the family room and kitchen, where baby will be with you.

Safety Proofing

When your baby starts learning to crawl, it's important to look around your home with safety in mind. This needn't be done fearfully but with confidence that the Love that created this child is keeping him safe and guiding you with wisdom to provide for his safety. Though you'll prepare an area that is safe for baby as he gains more freedom and his boundaries expand, you'll develop a listening ear and tune in to sounds (or silence) that mean it's time to check on baby.

Safety proof any areas where baby can go. Keep small objects (under 1½ inches) out of reach of baby, as they shouldn't be put in his mouth. This will be a time of watching the floor with baby in mind and keeping things picked up. Look at your home from the perspective of a crawling baby to see what he might want to explore.

There are some companies that, for a high price, will come in and safety proof your home. But, with reasonable care, you can do a good job yourself. In any case, safety proofing will not take the place of a parent's watchfulness.

Items that should not be swallowed (including detergents and cleaning products) should be moved out of lower cupboards and drawers—especially check the kitchen and bathrooms. Sharp objects should also be removed from areas a child can reach. In addition, it helps to put safety-proof catches on low cupboard doors and drawers you want baby to stay out of. These catches will prevent bothersome messes but are not fool-proof enough to be a sure protection to baby from hazardous materials.

In stores where baby products are sold, many gadgets are available for safety proofing. Covers of various kinds are available for electrical outlets. You can get plugs to fill empty outlets and also plates to screw on that will cover both outlet and plug. Tying a lamp cord around a table leg can help prevent the baby from pulling the lamp over by the cord. Sharp edges may be covered on furniture baby will be playing near. You can buy corner protectors or devise your own with foam padding and tape.

Stairs and bathrooms are favorite places for crawling babies and toddlers. Find a way to close off the stairs such as putting a gate on the second step. Look for a way to prevent baby from falling through stair railings. Rope wrapped around the rails can work. Some safety-proofing companies use Plexiglas or mesh. Keep doors to bathrooms closed.

As you are watchful, you will see where safety proofing devices are needed. In a few months, you will see different needs, and some of your former devices may be eliminated.

Language

Baby will be adding to his repertoire of vocalizations. Various vowel and consonant sounds will appear and may be strung together. He will make happy sounds and sad sounds and may be able to use these sounds in protest or to engage your attention. It's possible that the sad sounds (mama, nana) and happy sounds, (dada, papa, gaga) may have some historical relation to the terms "mama" (the comforter and feeder) and "daddy" or "papa" (the fun guy).

Baby will be listening to the words around him. Be sure to name with single words the objects your baby is looking at, as well as to talk in sentences. When parents speak only in sentences to their babies, the babies try to imitate the sentences with all the inflections and will start to talk mainly in sentences without understandable words. This is called "jargon." Eventually the words within their sentences will be refined until their language is understandable. It may take longer to understand the language of these babies than of those who hear and copy single words as well. Most babies talk in jargon as well as saying single words.

Social Progress

As babies gain mobility, they also become interested in the people around them. Some delight in engaging people with their smiles. Others are more cautious as they become attached to the primary caregiver and approach strangers with wariness. If baby has regularly been with a few other caring people, this may not be as pronounced. But it's an indication that he is aware of the difference between the people in his life. He's also learning that people and things can go and come back again.

Introduce your baby to others. She will enjoy seeing other babies and will delight in watching older children play. Give her a chance to get acquainted with a friend before handing her over to be held. You can hold her while you talk to the friend. You might have the friend hold one of baby's favorite toys to give to your baby and talk about. That takes the focus off of the baby and allows the friendship to blossom.

When you plan to leave your baby in the care of another, always tell him before you go, even if you don't think he will understand. You can say something like, "Nana will stay with you. I'll be back soon (or later)." Your child will learn to trust you, and this will start to teach him the family rule that we always let each other know where we'll be. Your baby will sense it if you're fearful of causing tears when you leave. Tell him in a matter-of-fact way where you are going and that you will be back. Then leave; don't linger.

Getting to Sleep

Life is so exciting for baby as he discovers the world around him and gains mobility that he may awaken more easily to sounds and be able to keep himself awake. If he awakens in the night, he may want your company. If you have made yourself part of his going-to-sleep routine, he will cry for you and need you to get him back to sleep again. See sample schedules, pp. 95, 112, and 136. So, if you don't want to be awakened in the night, remember to let your baby take responsibility for getting himself to sleep. However, if the issue seems to be discomfort due to illness or teething, you should be discerning to give the comfort needed. Some nursing Moms find that having Dad put the baby to bed helps the baby make the transition from nursing to going to sleep on his own.

You can teach your baby to go to sleep by himself, though it may take some fortitude on your part. If rocking or feeding is part of your bedtime routine, be sure your baby is still awake, though barely so at first, when you put him in his bed. He might have a "lovey" or comfort item such as a small blanket or stuffed animal, but don't let him take a bottle to bed. After you put him down, if he cries, you may come in to pat him and settle him with increasing intervals—5 minutes, 10 minutes, and then every 15 minutes—(a kitchen timer can help you keep track). If your appearance upsets him more, you may just want to let him cry. If you give in and pick him up after he cries for a long time, he will merely learn that if he cries long enough you will pick him up. If you don't give in and pick him up, he'll cry increasingly less and finally be able to settle to sleep without crying. Parents have been amazed at how fast this works. One toddler, whose mom was using this method to teach her to get herself to sleep, cried the first night for over an hour the first time. The second time it was 45 minutes; then 15 minutes. After that, she settled herself to sleep without crying.

You may think your baby will outgrow his need for you to settle him to sleep, but this dependence, if encouraged, deepens rather than lessening over time. The need is for the parent to let go and trust that the child can respond to his natural ability to get to sleep. The sooner he learns this, the more peaceful nights you and he will have. If you have been giving extra comfort because of illness or teething discomfort, you may need to go through the above process again when your baby's feeling himself to give him renewed confidence in his ability to get to sleep by himself.

Night Awakening

If your baby gets to sleep by himself, he is less likely to awaken in the night and need you to get him to sleep again. As you go through the steps of turning over to your baby the responsibility for getting to sleep, you may need to repeat the process when he awakens in the night. Don't get your baby in the habit of eating when he awakens in the night. Though he may enjoy the comfort of nursing or having a bottle, he can now eat enough during the day so that he doesn't need food at night. Settle him down when he awakens in the night with the least amount of attention possible. You may want to check and reassure yourself that everything is all right. Make sure your thought is peaceful, not agitated from being awakened. Just an acknowledgment of Love's ever-presence can turn the tide.

If needed, you may go in and lay baby down with some comforting pats and say, "It's nighttime. We're all going to sleep now. We love you." Don't turn on the lights. If he gets too upset, you may want to hold him for a moment and then put him back to bed, but don't play with

Crawling, Sitting, and Standing

him or feed him. If you feel you must give him a bottle, make it water rather than milk. You may need to let him cry it out as described earlier. This is never easy, but be assured that crying is not harmful to the child or habit forming. You can decide if your coming back every 15 minutes or so helps to reassure you both or if it merely gets him stirred up again. If crying doesn't get attention in the night, it will diminish and stop. Baby will soon learn that it's not playtime or feeding time, and he'll learn to settle himself back to sleep.

Teething

First teeth can appear as early as four months and as late as fourteen or fifteen months. Usually two lower teeth (incisors) will appear. Next, about two months later, the four upper teeth will appear in varying order. Then, the other two lower incisors on either side of the center two will come. The first molars usually come after baby is twelve months old. The canine, or eye teeth, later fill in between the incisors and molars. But babies vary in both the time and order in which teeth appear.

You needn't expect difficulty with this natural process of acquiring teeth. I like to think of it as causing no more trouble than flower bulbs pushing through the ground in the springtime. There may be a little extra drooling, but, contrary to a common old-wives' tale, leading pediatricians say there's no physical reason for illness of any kind to be associated with teething.

Baby may like to chew on a rubbery teether. He may take joy in hearing you tap the spoon on his new teeth. Babies learn to chew with their gums and can handle slightly lumpy food even if they are late in teething.

Learning, Toys, and Play

At this age, baby finds new ways of interacting with objects, and he becomes able to work gadgets. He continues to enjoy simple toys with moving parts—cylinders that spin, dials that turn, and parts that turn to cause interesting effects. This is the best time to use an activity center (such as Little Tikes Early Explorers' Activity Center and Fisher-Price

Activity Center) where the child can manipulate various gadgets. Cause-effect is a compelling interest.

Baby discovers ways to make sounds and will work his tests on each toy. He'll shake, bang on the floor, toss, hit together, and even try to clack his new teeth on the objects he has to explore.

When he can crawl well, he may enjoy a ball to chase. There are a number of balls that make a sound when rolled. A wobbly chime ball about five inches in diameter has been a longtime favorite in the toy library.

Kitchen gadgets and utensils will be favorite play things at this time. If you have room in your kitchen, you may let your crawling baby have access to one cupboard or drawer where some safe objects are placed and rotated. Plastic containers, a pan and lid, spatulas, wooden spoons, measuring cups and spoons, jar openers, etc. may be interesting to your baby. If baby tries to open other drawers or cupboards, you can tell him "No." Take him to his cupboard and say, "This is *your* cupboard (or drawer). You may play with these." You'll need to repeat this a number of times, but he will learn.

If you have take-apart toys such as disks and spindles or containers with balls, the baby may enjoy taking these toys apart but will probably not be able to put them back together until later. One parent made a big circle of take-apart toys. As the baby crawled from one toy to another, taking them apart, the mom followed behind putting them together again. They enjoyed this game, and before long the baby started putting the toys together on her own.

Some Favorite Toys Are:

- Skwish—A ball of wooden rods and beads threaded together with elastic cord.
- Baby Activity Center, Baby Fun Phone, Turn & Learn, Playskool Busy School Bus—Activity centers that rest on the floor with gadgets to spin and turn.
- A mirror to look in.

Babies love to look in mirrors.

- Many babies show keen interest in strings and cords at this time. Pull toys with strings and springy antenna then become favorite toys to explore with hands and mouth.
- Hand-held toys with moving parts such as Fisher-Price Twist-a-Pillar.
- Johnson and Johnson Playpath Clear Rattle. (Makes loud noise when shaken.) Now baby will be big enough to handle it without hitting himself on the head with it.

Games and Play

- Continue to play peek-a-boo games with your face and baby's, and with baby's toys, hiding them partially. When something is hidden, baby will now be more likely to persevere in finding it than when he was younger and it was "out of sight, out of mind."
- Play "So Big" with baby. Ask, "How big is baby?" As you say "so big," start on a higher pitch with "so" and raise baby's hands. With a lower pitch on "big," lower baby's arms. After awhile, when you ask the question, baby will raise his own arms.
- Play lively music for baby to bounce to.
- Hold baby and dance to music.
- Let baby play with water toys in the tub, including a container to pour from.
- When baby shows interest in your face, name face parts—nose, mouth, eyes, etc.
- Before baby can crawl, or holding him on your lap by a table, put toys out of reach on a diaper and get baby to pull it to him. Then when baby has mastered this, give him the string of a pull toy and let him learn to pull it within reach
- Lie down on the bed or floor and let baby crawl on you.
- Stand with your legs apart. Hold baby in your arms and swing him between your legs.
- Bounce baby on your lap to:
  Pony boy (or girl), pony boy, won't you be my pony boy?

Don't say "no;" here we go, out across the plain.
Giddyap, giddyap giddyap, WHOA! (Pull him back.)
My pony boy.

Feeding

Continue to offer different foods to your baby. If he doesn't like something, don't urge him to eat more at the time, but don't accept his likes and dislikes as final. Gaining familiarity by repeated exposure to foods increases likelihood of acceptance, so continue from time to time to offer, with loving encouragement, small tastes of foods he has turned down before. Never force, urge, or cajole him to eat a food, however. The idea is to help him be receptive to eating and trying new foods, not to get the food down him.

Your baby will let you know how much food he needs to eat. If he seems eager for more, give him more food. If he stops eating or merely plays with his food (beyond normal exploration), or throws it, it's indication he has had enough. Just remove the food or take him down from his high chair. Don't try to coax him to eat more. In addition to giving him control over the amount he eats, this will help him learn that food is not for throwing or for play.

Gradually introduce soft lumps to the pureed foods. You can do this both by adding a small amount of lumpier food to smoothly-pureed foods or by giving the baby one lump of food such as a small cube of cooked carrot or a pea with the outer skin removed.

When your baby shows interest in grabbing the spoon, help him learn to use the spoon. Don't worry about the mess. Early attempts will be messy, but let baby learn while he's interested. At first, let him hold the spoon and get some bites in as you feed him. He'll be able to feed himself more as he gains skill.

Baby's ability to use his fingers makes this a good time to give him finger foods. Try giving him bits of table foods or pieces of dry cereal such as Cheerios.

Weaning

This is a time when many mothers have thought of weaning their babies. But, since the value of mother's milk through the first year has been touted, more moms are continuing to nurse into the second year. Do what feels right to you. Your baby is now getting more nourishment from solids and will be able to drink more from a cup. Continue nursing or the bottle if he seems to need the extra sucking. Otherwise, a baby can be weaned directly to the cup. Babies may become more attached to the bottle after nine months. Some babies will wean themselves by refusing to nurse. Others need encouragement. Some mothers enjoy the closeness of nursing and continue through the second year. You can offer your baby milk with a snack either in the afternoon or evening in addition to serving it with three meals. Continue to hold the baby when you give him the bottle, and his desire to move about independently may aid the weaning process.

When you feel the rightness of this step of progress, it can be accomplished easily. You can wean gradually by starting at the noon meal and offering the cup only. Then when you feel ready, another bottle can be replaced by the cup. Finally, when you feel it's time, the last bottle can be eliminated. Weaning can be accomplished the same way from the breast when you are ready for that step. Choose the feeding you feel is best to give up first, then follow with others, taking your cue from your baby's readiness. Don't let other people pressure you into weaning your baby. On the other hand, a willingness to let go of nursing and recognize the maturity of your child might be needed.

One of our sons appeared to need extra sucking and continued with a bottle longer than the others. When he seemed ready to give up the last bottle at about 22 months, he agreed to give it to a baby who lived down the street. I clued in the mom, and Danny walked with me down the street and handed his bottle to the crawling baby. That night he had some second thoughts, but alas, the bottle was gone, and he did feel good about his new maturity. After that, he was fine.

SAMPLE SCHEDULES

Jill is seven months old and has two older brothers.

Time	Activity
7:00–9:00 a.m.	Awakens, is dressed, plays, some cereal, nurses.
9:00–10:00	Nap.
10:00–12:00	Plays, nurses, goes on errands with Mom.
12:00–2:00 p.m.	Nap.
2:00 to 4:30	Plays, walk in stroller, nurses.
4:30–5:00	Goes with Mom to pick up brothers.
5:00–6:00	Plays with brothers; sometimes a short nap, nurses.
6:00–7:00	Dinner. Dad is home.
7:00–9:00	Bath, plays, some cereal and fruit, nurses to sleep.
9:00	To bed. Nurses once or twice in night.

Troy, at 7¹/2 months, has an older brother and a predictable routine.

Time	Activity
5:00 a.m.	Awakens, nurses, is put back in crib. Sleeps or talks until 6:00.
6:00	Nurses, plays, and squeals in big bed.
7:30	Oatmeal and fruit.
8:00	Rides in car to drop off brother at school.
8:30	Asleep.
10:00	Awakens, juice from cup. Loves to play, exploring toys on tummy.
11:30	Lunch—baby vegetable and nursing.
12:00 or 12:30 p.m.	Nap.
Between 2:00 & 3:00	Awakens. Plays and watches big brother.
5:00	Dinner—2 to 3 jars baby food. Likes chicken and vegetables mixed; and fruit. Nurses, but not to sleep.
6:15	To bed for the night.

Alice is eight months old.

Time	Activity
7:30–8:30 a.m.	Wakes up and has 1 jar baby food breakfast.
9:00–9:30	4-ounce bottle.
11:00–12:30	Nap.
12:30 p.m.	Lunch of 1 or 2 jars baby food—vegetable and meat. Milk from cup.
3:00	8-ounce bottle.
3:30–5:00	Nap.
6:00	Dinner: baby-food dinner, vegetable, and fruit. Milk from cup.
8:30	Bath, book, 8-ounce bottle.
9:00	Bedtime. Sleeps through night.

Crawling, Sitting, and Standing

Cameos of Individual Babies

∾ Dena ∾

7 mos. 2 days. Holding head up high when on tummy. Rolls over both ways.

7 mos. 16 days. Sits up with Mom's help. Studies new faces intently. Vocalizing "H" sound.

7 mos. 30 days. Likes chewy objects to explore. Starting to spin around in circles on tummy to reach objects.

8 mos. 28 days. Crawling backwards. Says "Hi" to Grandma. Looks for objects she loses.

9 mos. 18 days. Crawls pulling with left arm and right leg. Sitting when put in that position. First tooth through.

∾ Helen ∾

7 mos. 3 days. Exploring more with hands and less with mouth now. Likes to play sitting up, but plays well on tummy too. Went from sit to crawl to get toy. Says "Mamama" and "Dadada." Explored all gadgets of Baby Activity Center.

7 mos. 17 days. Likes making sounds in different ways—shaking toys, squeaking toys by squeezing with hands and by biting. Likes eating Cheerios. Working on crawling. Lunges forward. Goes into sitting position. Liked Baby Fun Phone.

8 mos. 1 day. Crawls now. Likes stringy things.

8 mos. 15 days. Starting to pull up to stand.

∾ Charity ∾

7 mos. 6 days. Crawls around pulling with arms, fast all over the house. Laughs at older sister. Enjoys social interaction and eye contact with adults. Smiled and cooed at herself in mirror. Favorite toy was Skwish.

8 mos. 18 days. Hits two objects together to make a sound. Trying to pull up to stand.

✎ Chad ✎

7 mos. 7 days. Moves around house pulling with forearms. Explores deliberately, sometimes looking at objects one at a time, sometimes accumulating a whole pile for exploration.

7 mos. 21 days. Pulls knees up under him and scoots forward. Says "Dada."

✎ Vana ✎

7 mos. 9 days. Makes "baba" and "dada" sounds. Gets up on knees. Plays on tummy but prefers sitting. Likes banging objects to make sound.

7 mos. 23 days. Pulled up to stand for first time yesterday. Crawls on knees. Exploring with her fingers. Watches mouth and shows interest in words. Feeds self well eating pieces of table food with fingers.

8 mos. 21 days. More interested in crawling and pulling up than playing with toys. Interest in language. Hearing dog, gets excited and says "Da." Loves looking at pictures in books and hearing language. Watches Mom's lips a lot. Likes to go around house listening to Mom name things. Takes two 45 minute naps and bedtime seems to be pushing later than 7:00 p.m.

✎ Jess ✎

7 mos. Rolls over, carrying toy with him until he gets under furniture or against something, then stops to play. Reaches up to Mom to pick him up. Picking up small objects with thumb and fingers. Says "Ruh ruh" and "buh buh." Likes to make sounds in different ways. Likes vinyl books.

7 mos. 14 days. Rolls and uses commando crawl to move about. Shows object to Mom and "talks" about it. Likes to explore hard objects. Takes them to hard floor to bang them. Liked ringing bell on Activity Center.

8 mos. 12 days. Imitates actions he sees. Waves. Gets to sitting position alone. Sings to music. Says "cuh cuh" for cookie. Crawling all over.

8 mos. 26 days. Pulling up to stand. Bangs on walls with hands. Follows Mom and imitates what she does. Makes a sound, then smiles. Has two teeth. Blows in imitation.

Crawling, Sitting, and Standing

∽ **Hal** ∽

7 mos. 8 days. Crawls and sits to play with toys. Has first tooth. Sits in high chair at dinner time. Likes drinking out of cup and eating table food.

8 mos. 5 days. Looks up with broad smile, engaging a return smile. Turns dial with fingers. Likes to chew on squeezy toys. Pulls up to stand. Says "Mamama." Growls in lower register.

8 mos. 18 days. Cruises all around. Keen interest in people.

∽ **Josh** ∽

7 mos. 7 days. Starting to get up on knees and lunge forward. Has one tooth. Spins all around when on tummy and scoots backwards. Sits alone well. Says "baba, dada, mama, gaga," and makes "raspberries" with mouth. In crib talks to pictures when he wakes up. Likes playing peek-a-boo. Explores with hands and mouth.

7 mos. 21 days. Likes strings. Trying to crawl forwards. When on lap, likes to pull up and hold on to stand. Moves by rolling. Starting to clap hands.

8 mos. 5 days. Sits well and starting to creep forward. Likes to explore hard, wooden textures. Attentive to sounds and wants to know where they come from.

8 mos. 19 days. Goes up onto hands and knees but uses commando crawl to get where he wants. Likes little books. Still prefers wooden-textured toys. Likes dials and things to get his fingers into. Waves bye-bye. Climbs on two-stair landing.

∽ **Kelly** ∽

7 mos. 29 days. Crawling all around. Goes to sitting position. Pulls to stand. Making many vocalizations. Squeak of "Hug-a-Bug" made her cry.

8 mos. 15 days. Likes to manipulate gadgets with her fingers. Lots of babbling. Investigating everything—plants, etc. Loves mirrors.

8 mos. 27 days. Likes making noises with toys and vocally. Very responsive to people. Imitated Mom saying "ba." Claps a lot. Screams with excitement. Smacks lips as she watches in mirror.

7

Cruising to Walk
Nine to Eleven Months

"Now unto him that is able to keep you from falling, and to present you faultless before the presence of his glory with exceeding joy, to the only wise God our Saviour, be glory and majesty, dominion and power, both now and ever."

Jude 1:24,25

As safety becomes a concern for your mobile baby, you can pray to know that he is always in Love's arms. As parents pray in this way, they are frequently alerted to when there is a need to check on baby or take a particular action that protects their baby. This prayer releases parents of needless fear and assures them that there is a higher power in control.

Mobility is still likely to be at the top of the agenda for your curious baby at this time. Mobility and bodily control extends the range of exploration, and exploration remains a key motivator. Crawling will be perfected as the baby practices pulling up to stand and cruising (side stepping around furniture while holding on). Your baby will learn to go from a sitting to a crawling position and back again. When he gets his balance standing, he may let go momentarily and stand alone. A few babies will learn to walk at this time; most will learn to crawl and then cruise; some will be content to sit or move by rolling over. (See **The Non-Crawler,** p. 83)

Walker wagons provide independent practice in walking.

You'll want to give attention to safety proofing when your baby starts moving about. As baby gets more mobile, he'll learn from having room to safely explore about the house. He'll learn about the difference between the hard floor and soft carpet. He'll learn what space he can get in and which spaces are too small. He will learn how to get out of tight spots. He'll discover which objects he can pull up on and which ones give way under his weight. At this time, baby will be interested in exploring and taste-testing small objects, so it's necessary to keep objects picked up that should not go into his mouth. (See **Safety Proofing,** p. 86)

A cruising baby may like to hold your hands to walk around. Others may want the independence of cruising on their own. You may enjoy walking baby around, but don't let him charm you into doing it all the time. If he's unhappy when you're not walking him around, you can encourage him verbally as you work nearby. This is a good time for a walker wagon for baby to push, so he can have the independence of gaining balance on his own.

Climbing will fascinate your baby as soon as he learns that he can pull up to higher levels. Stair steps are an easy height for first climbing and are very appealing to baby at this time. Baby can go up a whole flight of steps before he learns to come down. It takes practice and growing awareness to learn that he can't sit down on the space behind him when he's on the stairs. You'll need to keep him from the stairs except for times that you can accompany his climbing expeditions. Help him learn to come down feet first on his tummy. There might be a way in your home to make a step or two available for your baby to practice on. If not, you can reinforce a cardboard box six or seven inches high and let your baby climb on and off of it.

Baby is also becoming more adept at using his hands and fingers. He can grasp with his thumb and forefinger to pick up tiny objects. This is a handy skill for self-feeding. It also helps with baby's exploration. Index fingers can point, poke into holes, and hook to pull out objects.

Getting to Sleep

Baby may be so excited about his mobility that getting to sleep can be a challenge. He gains the ability to keep himself awake and may prefer to be with you than to settle down to sleep. A cuddly comfort item, such as a blanket, diaper, or stuffed animal, may be helpful for making the transition away from you. A soft, safe, washable item is best.

If baby practices his new skill of standing when he awakens in the night and cries because he can't get down again, you'll need to put him down until he learns to sit down by himself. Help him practice sitting down from a standing position during the day.

It's helpful to keep the time before bed one of quiet activity and routine for winding down, not one of active playfulness. This may take restraint on Dad's part if he wants to play actively with baby. He should choose a time for active play that won't wind baby up before bedtime.

After you have put baby to bed, let him settle himself to sleep. If he cries or awakens in the night, see in previous chapter: **Getting to Sleep** and **Night Awakening.**

Cruising to Walk

Toilet Training?

No, not toilet training until around age two or later. However, a wonderful nurse named Catherine Keith, who gave baby advice to scores of parents for many years, suggested catching a baby's movements after he can sit up well. I did this with all four of my boys, and it turned out to be a good preliminary to potty training. When I expected, from past experience, that there would be a movement after a particular meal, I would sit the baby on a comfortable potty seat on our toilet and look at books with him until he had his movement. If I didn't catch the movement in five minutes or so, I just added a diaper liner to his diaper and changed the diaper later. The baby got used to having his movements on the potty seat and would use the toilet quite regularly. One son seemed to be irregular in his movements until I realized that he was going after every other meal so there would be two movements on one day—after breakfast and dinner—and one on the next—after lunch. Sometimes, if movements were irregular, I would be able to catch the movement when I saw, from the look on the baby's face, that he was about to have it. Importantly, the attitude was always low key—never pressured.

This procedure caused no problem for the baby and was easier for me than changing a dirty diaper. In addition, the babies never formed such a strong habit of having movements in their diapers that they held on to that, as many children do, after learning to urinate in the toilet. They rather enjoyed the attention and time to look at books, and they soon learned to cooperate and go without delay. They also got used to the toilet seat so that regular toilet training, later when they were ready, came quite naturally.

Social Progress

Your baby will know the difference between people he sees often and those who are seldom around. He'll be quite friendly to familiar people but may be suspicious of strangers. If so, this can be disappointing to grandparents and other relatives who can't visit often. Suggest to these visitors that they give your baby time to get acquainted rather than reaching right out to hold him.

You can show your baby pictures of far-away relatives and talk to him about them. You might also play tapes of their voices or show your baby videos of them—particularly before a coming visit.

Baby will love to watch other people—especially children. You may notice him staring intently at them whenever you're out. You can talk to him about what they are doing.

Language

Baby will understand many words that you say. He will show this by looking at a family member or an object you name; by crawling to bring you an item at your request, such as a ball or shoe; or by raising hands for "So Big" or waving "bye-bye." He may shake his head at "No." This is called "receptive language." If a child has a good vocabulary of receptive language at this age, spoken language will come, sooner or later.

Baby may also be making strides in spoken language in other ways. He may imitate a sound such as a cough or a tongue

Sharing books is a special time of learning for baby.

clicking. His gibberish may contain inflections and a wide range of consonants. Some babies will be especially interested in language and will intently watch your mouth as you talk. They may start to say meaningful sounds, such as "Mama" or "Dada," and repeat them. Other babies will not seem interested in language.

Board books (books with hard pages) are popular with many babies this age. They like to open and close books as hinged objects. But they may also become fascinated by hearing the same word each time they see a picture. Your baby may have favorite books to bring you. Name the picture he is looking at, and be ready to stop whenever he has had enough. Most babies this age aren't interested in hearing the story line but like to look at the pictures. Some babies love to hear the rhythm of a rhyme.

Take your baby around the house looking at objects and labeling them for her. She might be interested in seeing all of the lights in the house as you point and say "light." As she sees you pointing to what you name, she will learn to point and ask for words.

Discipline

Discipline is not a synonym for punishment. The word comes from the same root as "disciple" and means *learning*. Baby is learning much about his environment, and he knows nothing about what he should and should not touch or explore except what you teach him. If this teaching is consistent, he will feel happy and secure. Be assured that, since your motive is a good one (to help your baby learn), you will have the strength and the ideas to do what is best for him. Your baby may develop a fondness for a favorite forbidden item. One of our sons loved to crawl to a large, potted plant and eat the dirt. I thought of this as a good time for discipline, and I would take him away, saying, "No no." The minute my back was turned, he headed right back for that plant. We had many struggles over this plant. I later learned that it would have been so much better to have just removed the tempting pot to a closed room until he was old enough to understand.

Babies can be persistent and resistant to distraction. It's best to remove as many temptations as possible during this time of keen exploration. There will still be a few tempting items with which he can learn what "no" means. Consistently take him away from banned items to ones of similar interest that are acceptable. One child learned not to play with the telephone when her family consistently took her away from it and gave her a toy telephone that had buttons that made various electronic sounds.

Don't allow your child to turn on the TV, VCR, or play with a real telephone, even if it seems fun to see his ability and interest in these items. He needs to learn that there are some items for adults only to touch. Keep him away from them (block them off if necessary). Then try to find an acceptable alternative for his play—something that will appeal to his interest in cause-effect. There are a number of simple electronic toys on the market which are appropriate for this age. Baby can have his own controller where the push of buttons causes lights and sounds.

Don't tell your baby not to do something and then allow him to do it. After telling him once, remove him from the area and give him something acceptable to play with. If distraction doesn't work and baby continues to go back to the forbidden item, put him in his playpen or a gated area away from you, telling him that he needs to remember what he may touch. Then walk away. In just about 20 seconds after he starts to fuss, bring him back and give him what he *may* play with. Let him know how pleased you are that he's remembering the right thing to do. If he goes back to the forbidden item, repeat the process. He'll learn what to play with and what to avoid.

Be alert to the temptation to give in to baby's unreasonable demands. He needs to learn that his tears will not get you to give him things you know he shouldn't have. Your persistent teaching will net rewards. One day you'll say "No," and he will look at you and refrain from reaching for a forbidden item. That doesn't yet mean that he won't go to it when you're not around, but it's a big step in the right direction. Babies first learn the effect their actions have on those around them. Later, this can develop into a moral sense of right and wrong.

Independent Playtime

Your baby will probably explore and play independently near you as you work around the house. You can talk to her as you work nearby and periodically take a little time to play with her. You'll have most of the house safety proofed, but there may still be a few tempting places where you can begin to teach baby the meaning of "no no."

If you have been using a playpen or gated room previously, you'll be glad to have a safe place to keep your active, curious baby for moments when you are too busy to keep an eye on him. You can expand the appeal of this place by reserving a few favorite toys exclusively for those times. Use these safe, independent play areas for brief periods only—one or two periods of up to half an hour a day. Your baby will learn most by having access to you and plenty of room to explore.

If you haven't used a playpen or gated room, it may not be welcome now that baby has mobility and a desire to explore a broader area. Your baby may have some enjoyable times to play by himself and experiment with vocalization in his bed before falling asleep or after waking up. You can use nap times for phone calls or work that must be uninterrupted. To get a little more free time and a fresh perspective, you can periodically get a spouse or sitter to watch the baby.

Avoid Diaper-Changing Struggles

Often, when babies get active, they don't want to take the time to lie still for a diaper change. It's best to make this a fun time of interaction instead of a disagreeable task. Your baby will pick up on your mood. If you react to baby's struggle with anger or authority, he may continue to test you. I once tried to change the diaper of a toddler who had been spanked for resisting diaper changing. He wouldn't let me near his diaper but kicked and screamed. There are much better ways that will gain your baby's cooperation and not intensify resistance.

Rather than unexpectedly interrupting baby's activity, give him advanced notice that it will soon be time to change his diaper. Save some interesting items for him to hold while you change his diaper, such as an empty Band-Aid can with a lid that opens and closes. Talk to him and sing songs or say rhymes to interest him. You can say, "Change, change, change. Wipe, wipe, wipe. Pin, pin, pin." Whisper: "Baby (use his name) lies so still while Mommy changes his diaper." My babies liked it when I snapped their gripper snaps with a "SssssssssNAP!" You'll find the interaction that appeals to your baby. Make sure you don't encourage struggles by your tone of voice. A comment such as "Oh no, you little dickens!" can set the stage for a game you don't want to play.

Toys, Play, and Expanding Concepts

Your baby will be gaining lots of information from watching what's going on around him. You may see him steadily staring at people and objects as he satisfies his curiosity. He will continue to learn about small objects by examining with fingers and mouth and also by tossing, shaking, and banging the objects. He'll start to become interested in relating one object to another. He will first take objects out of containers and take apart multipart toys; then, in another month or so, he'll be able to fill containers and put parts together. He'll be able to find a toy that has been hidden or is behind him. He will enjoy looking in a mirror.

Containers, such as pots and pans or plasticware, are interesting to baby. You may let him have a drawer or cupboard in the kitchen for items he may play with. If you can stand it, he may enjoy banging lids together. Let him have some smaller items such as balls, measuring spoons or cups, or blocks to put in and out of the containers. Hinged objects are interesting to most babies this age, so opening and closing the cupboard door can be as fascinating as finding the objects within.

Cause-effect is a continuing interest of babies. Therefore toys that cause a surprise action may hold your baby's attention. Boxes with gadgets that make figures pop up are usually favorites.

Balls for tossing and chasing continue to be popular toys. Baby may love to have balls the size of a golf ball to toss and follow. He'll take one in each hand, clap them together, and may try to pick up a third one. Toward the end of this period, or into the next, baby will learn to consciously let go of an object. Up to this point, he has let go of one object as he reached for another. Now, he will consciously open his hand to let an object drop. When this happens, there will be nothing more appealing than a ball drop. Baby puts the ball into a hole, and it comes out somewhere else. Paper towel rolls covered with contact paper make great ball drops for any ball that will fit.

Stacking rings are a good toy. Ones that have a straight, rather than graduated, spindle are best so that baby can put them on in any order. The skill to put the rings on in graduated order comes much later when interest in this toy has waned.

You can talk to baby about the toys he's playing with and name colors—especially toys with like pieces where color is the distinguishing feature.

Baby will lose interest in toys that are out all the time so you'll want to rotate them. (See **Toy Management** p 221.)

Favorite Toys

- Balls and ball drops
- A drum to beat
- Walker wagon, Fisher-Price Activity Walker, Tomy Multi Gym Walker
- Busy-surprise boxes or boxes with figures that pop up when a gadget is pushed or turned
- Bear-in-the Box, Fun Bus—toys with a figure that pops open when you spin a cylinder
- Happy Pot 'n Spoon (the First Years)—container with plastic fruit, spoon, and lid
- Balls in Bowl
- Toy telephone
- Board books

Fun with baby

Baby is becoming more and more fun to play with as he watches and imitates you. He will continue to like hide and seek, where the hiding of a toy is obvious. But now you will be able to cover the whole toy, rather than leaving part visible. He will remember it and keep looking for it. Peek-a-boo games are still favorites. Songs and rhymes will meet a good response. He may pick up and imitate the rhythm or pitch of your voice.

Here are some games to play:

- Call to baby from another room and let him find you.
- Hold baby and let him turn light switches as you say "off" and "on." Use those words also as he takes lids off and puts them on.
- Say "up" and "down" as you lift and lower baby.
- Roll a ball to baby and try to get him to roll it back. Sing "I roll the ball to baby; he rolls it back to me."
- Play pat-a-cake with baby.

- As with "So Big," ask "Where is God?" or "Where is Love?" Answer "Everywhere," as you hold out your arms.

Feeding

Your baby's ability to pick up small objects with his fingers will make finger foods appealing. It's good to give him plenty of practice eating with fingers. He will be messy at first and then refine his skills as he gets older. He may like to pick up with fingers a cube of vegetable, a bit of shredded, tender meat, or a slice of American cheese. He may enjoy a cracker that dissolves in his mouth. Refrigerate in a square dish some thick, cooked cereal, such as cream of wheat. Give baby small cubes of it to eat with fingers, or slice and fry it and give baby pieces to eat. Cheerios and other dry cereals are often favorite finger foods at this time. When your baby starts grabbing the spoon away from you, you can let him hold his own short-handled spoon. Your baby will be having three meals a day now, with possibly a light snack mid-morning and afternoon, or with a snack in the morning and a drink of milk before bedtime. If he's not weaned yet, this time of physical activity may be a good time to do so. He can help to feed himself milk from a cup. Start with just a small amount of milk in the cup.

He may start to get used to some soft lumps in his food. You can mash the food leaving a few soft lumps, or add a lump or two of soft food to a puree. Baby may accept one or two lumps but not a whole mouthful of them at first.

Egg, softly scrambled, may be added to the menu. Potato, mashed smooth, can be substituted for cereal at one meal. If baby doesn't like it, you can try adding a little vegetable or fruit.

Orange juice may be a good addition now. Start with just a taste diluted with an equal part of water. Work up to two ounces; then gradually decrease the amount of water until baby drinks the juice straight. Juice may be given from a cup.

SAMPLE SCHEDULES

Abe is nine months old and has a teenage brother and sister. His Mom likes to nurse him to sleep and doesn't mind getting up in the night when he awakens to be nursed back to sleep again.

Time	Activity
8:30 a.m.	Awakens. Nurses.
8:30–9:00	Breakfast of baby cereal.
9:00–9:30	Bath time and put into clean diaper and clothes.
9:30–10:00	Mom reads books to him.
10:00–11:00	Playpen time to play with toys, nurses a little.
11:00–11:30	Plays on the floor with toys, diaper change.
11:30–12:00	Lunch of 2 jars of baby food (1 baby dinner and 1 vegetable).
12:00–1:00 p.m.	He plays more, crawling around on the floor. Mom plays with him, hugging and kissing him. Diaper change.
1:00–1:30	Nurses. Often falls asleep for one-hour nap.
2:00–2:30	When he awakens, Mom holds and plays pat-a-cake-type games and songs.
2:30–4:00	Diaper change, plays independently with toys in crib, playpen or on floor. Sometimes nurses a little.
4:00–5:00	Brother comes home and plays with him a little before homework. Abe then plays on floor while Mom starts dinner.
5:00–5:30	Dinner of 2 jars of baby food—a dinner and fruit.
5:30–9:00	Plays: Johnny Jump Up, crawls around and plays with family members, two or more diaper changes, and some nursing.
9:00–9:30	Nurses. Goes to sleep. Nurses once or twice in nght.

Early riser at nine months

Time	Activity
5:30–6:30 a.m.	Awakens, diaper change, nursing or bottle. Breakfast: cereal, toast, fruit.
6:30–8:30	Plays.
8:30–9:00	Juice from cup, diaper change, and down for nap.
10:30–11:00	Awakens, diaper change, and plays.
12:00	Lunch: vegetable, $1/2$ sandwich (grilled cheese, meat or egg salad, peanut butter, etc.), yogurt or cheese. Milk from cup. Diaper change. Plays until 2:00 or when he gets fussy.
2:00 p.m.	Snack of Cheerios, crackers and milk from cup. Diaper change. Rocking, singing, and books, then nap. Cries for few minutes, then plays happily in crib until he falls asleep.
3:30–4:00	Awakens, diaper change, plays with toys or family members.
5:00–5:30	Dinner: baby meat and vegetables, or finger food (shredded meat, parboiled vegetables, pieces of cheese and fruit). Milk from cup.
6:00–6:30	Plays with or near family.
6:30	Bath every other night.
7:30–8:00	Milk from cup or bottle, books, prayers and bed. Sleeps through night.

Alan, 10 months, has a three-year-old sister and two school-age siblings.

Time	Activity
6:00 or 7:00 a.m.	Awakens, diaper change, 7-ounce bottle.
7:00 or 7:30	9–12 tsp. cereal with $1/2$ fresh banana, strip of toast or bagel.
7:30–8:00 or 8:30	Independent play.
8:00–8:30 or 9:00	Nap in crib.
9:00–9:30	Awakens. Out for a walk or shopping, or play in play room with sister.
9:30–11:30	Play period outside or in. Book reading with Mom; listen to music.
11:30–12:00	Lunch: some finger food, some milk-based food (yogurt, custard, etc.) 6–8 ounce milk.
12:00–1:00 p.m.	Plays with sister. Books with Mom.
1:00 or 1:30	In crib for nap.
4:00	Awakens. Interaction with older sister and brother. Outside if nice. Mom works on dinner.
5:00–5:30	Dinner: baby-food vegetable, combo meat dinner, egg yolk, and fruit. He eats first then sits and eats finger food while rest of family eats.
6:00–7:30	Plays with Dad. Bath every other night. Plays around where family is. 6–8-ounce bottle.
7:30–8:00	Hymn, bedtime.

Greg at 10½ months

Time	Activity
7:00–7:30 a.m.	Awakens, smiles, laughs, kisses Papa good-bye.
7:30	Breakfast: bottle, oatmeal, cream of wheat, yogurt, peanut butter on toast, juice.
7:45	Bath (plays there), brush teeth (funny new game), diaper, dress.
8:15–10:45	Plays: sock balls in laundry basket, boxes, kitchen drawers. Likes to be with Mama. Plays in pen while Mama does spiritual study, sometimes reading aloud. Errands with Mama.
10:45–11:30	Snack: banana, graham cracker, cheddar cheese slices. Sometimes a short nap, though outgrowing it.
11:30–1:00	More play or go out for errands.
1:00 p.m.	Lunch: scrambled eggs, omelets, fish sticks, peas, leftovers, burritos, cantaloupe, avocado, formula from cup.
1:30–3:30	Nap. Serious home tasks for Mama.
3:30–3:45	Awakens. Rock in rocking chair, hugs, nuzzles. Mom tells him he's God's child. Snack: bananas, cinnamon grahams, juice or a little formula.
3:45–4:30	Play with Mama: games such as peek-a-boo and pat-a-cake, read stories, walk to park.
4:30–5:00	Start dinner. Plays in his kitchen bin and is usually underfoot.
5:30–6:00	Papa's home, gets excited—rougher play. Likes to chase cat.

Cruising to Walk

6:30–7:00	Dinner: eats what parents eat at the table. Likes shredded cheese, refried beans, pumpkin spice muffins.
7:30–8:30	Plays underfoot, gets into things he shouldn't as parents constantly pull him away and move things higher, parents read him books.
8:30–9:00	Bottle, pajamas, tooth-brushing game, two books, rock a little, put to bed while still awake. He settles himself to sleep.

Cameos of Individual Babies

We can observe a difference in babies' special interests. Some focus on physical skills, some on language, and others on how things work and small-motor skills.

✍ Kelly ✍

9 mos. 10 days Likes making sounds and exploring with hands and mouth. Favorite activity is pulling to stand and taking things off tables. Babbling all the time. Saying "Dada," "Mama," and making "raspberries." Loves books. Mom reads favorite picture board books over and over. Likes animal sounds.

9 mos. 24 days. Keying into language. When grandpa said, "Belt," she said "tt." Crawling all around and exploring.

10 mos. 10 days. Cruises around coffee table. Receptive language: gets book or rattle when Mom asks her to; knows "no,"—turns and looks. Said "Mama" and crawled over to Mom. Says "gogwah" all the time. Loves books. Likes to turn pages and listen when Mom names things. Works to turn one page of book at a time.

10 mos. 22 days. Pointing now. Loved dolphin show in Chicago. Pointed to dolphins. Crawled up stairs at friend's house. Went readily to people she stayed with. Acted to the audience. Loves to play peek-a-boo. Covers eyes (or mouth) with hands. Says "duck" for everything. Repeatedly opened and closed Bear-in-the-Box. Pushed walker wagon all over. Looked, asking for help to turn it, when she got to wall.

✍ Josh ✍

9 mos. 2 days. Pulling to stand. Likes climbing stairs. Does things to get a laugh from Mom and Dad. Looks to parents to get a reaction when he does something new. Talks to toys. "K" sounds and other consonants.

9 mos. 16 days. Beginning to crawl on knees and pulling to stand. Exploring with hands more than mouth. Prefers wooden texture still. Loves to climb on stairs and Mom. Experimenting with sound, blowing and buzzing. Loved opening, closing, and turning Jackpop (clown figure that lifts with lid out of wooden box).

Walked with walker wagon, gaining balance. Took balls out of Balls in Bowl. Turned to make centers spin, tossed them, and started to put back in bowl.

10 mos. 21 days. Cruising. Interest in wooden objects continues. Likes toys with cause-effect. Making more sounds—lots of consonants. Stands, holding two toys. Testing reach as he cruises. "Into everything!" Smiled as he pushed walker wagon. Spun cylinder to make figure of Fun Bus open, then pushed it down.

✎ **Helen** ✎

9 mos. 27 days. Likes making sounds verbally and with toys. Makes buzzing sounds with finger and lips. Plays pat-a-cake. Pulls up to stand. Starting to open drawers. Crawls all around following Mom and sisters. Crawls into bathroom when she hears water running. Loves to drink out of cup. Favorite toy—Discovery Beads. Moved parts with fingers.

10 mos. 10 days. Interest in toys waning. Likes to go all over house exploring and sticking to Mom. Saying "Mama," "Dada." Watching mouths as people talk. Climbs on furniture. Mom has had to put away some plants. Starting to put things in containers. Walked with Fisher-Price Activity Walker and played with gadgets. Put balls in and out of Wobbly Balls and Tray (four balls that fit in tray of indentations).

10 mos. 24 days. Cruising. Practicing physical skills. Empties containers—and drawers. Loves books. When Mom got out a board book, she dove for it with excitement. Studies faces. Waves to everyone in store. Opened and closed Jackpop with keen interest. Started dropping balls into Curiosity Box (ball drop). Also threw balls.

✎ **Denny** ✎

9 mos. 21 days. Pulls up and cruises all around. Likes opening and closing doors. Waves and claps. Bear-in-the-Box a big hit!

10 mos. 5 days. Took three steps. Makes growling sounds and lots of babbling. Cruises all around. Walked all over with walker wagon. Mom needed to turn it around.

10 mos. 19 days. Takes steps alone, but still crawls and cruises for security. Says "kitty" and "ba(ll)" meaningfully.

✍ Seth ✍

9 mos. 4 days All over the house with walker wagon! Lots of "g" sounds. Said "gak" for clock. If he can't get something, screams for help. Also screams at brother to defend himself. Practiced opening and closing Bear-in-the-Box until he got it. All-time favorite toy was Happy Pot 'n Spoon. Took fruit out and put in. Especially liked plastic grapes and orange.

9 mos. 17 days. Stands alone for awhile. Explores all over. Enjoys containers. Starting to fight back if brother does something he doesn't like (has bitten).

10 mos. 2 days. Starting to tune into language—"cu(p)," "ba(by)." Starting to imitate words. Likes books and turning pages. "Speed reads." Put balls in Curiosity Box ball drop again and again. Cruises facing forward resting fingertips on furniture.

10 mos. 15 days. Taking steps now. Loves balls. Throws them. Watches mouth when Mom talks. Says "ba" for book and ball. Keen interest in books. Studies pages and likes to turn them. Less independent play than before. Sometimes hangs on mother's legs.

✍ Diane ✍

9 mos. 11 days. Has crawling coordinated this week. Wants to walk all around holding hands. Said "Hi" to Daddy, imitating his "Hi." Sings and says "da da da." Pushes walker wagon. Stops and backs up.

9 mos. 25 days. Favorite activity is walking holding adult's hands. Gives things to people to hear "Thank you." Takes objects out of containers. Learned to blow toy that whistles.

10 mos. 9 days. Pulls up on wall. Sits down again alone. Has stood up alone and taken a few steps. Making new facial expressions and pouting. Loves to play with clothes. Has started putting them back as well as taking out of drawers. Loves telephone. Holds to her ear and switches hands. Liked Wobbly Balls and Tray. Took balls out and put back.

10 mos. 23 days. Books are always favorites. Turns pages and chatters. Lots of imitating. Points to pictures that are named. Points to eye and nose. Says "boo," "hi," "(l)ight," "Dada," "Mama," "uh" (for pony). Opened and closed Jackpop and said "boo." Taking steps.

Cruising to Walk

❧ Vana ❧

9 mos. 4 days. Continues to watch mouth for words. Pulls up and beginning to cruise. Says "Oh oh" quite a bit. Knocks down blocks when Mom stacks. Sits on legs as well as conventional way. Loves books. Looks at them on her own. Loves Squeezable Kids. Carried around, held, and squeezed. Happy Pot 'n Spoon was popular in playpen. Mom would re-interest her in her play by naming the pieces of fruit and asking her to find them. She would pick up one named.

9 mos. 25 days. Receptive language: at request brushes hair, finds *Pat the Bunny* and other objects. Drinks with a straw. Plays in playpen during one side of a cassette morning and afternoon. Crawls all over and pulls up to stand. Cruises. New vocalization, "twa twa twa" and "ota ota." Liked Curiosity Box. Repeated "ba(ll)" and put in hole.

10 mos. 30 days. Found toys that Mom named. Continuing interest in language. Points with hand and asks "Dat?" to have objects named. Strings sounds together talking jargon. Says "dog" meaningfully. Likes books. Spends time studying catalog after Mom has named objects in it. Climbed in and out of walker wagon and pushed a little.

❧ Linda ❧

9 mos. 6 days. Bangs and shakes toys. Loves her dolly. When eating, offers bite to Mom or dolly. Learned to drop balls into Curiosity Box.

10 mos. 11 days. Has taken seven steps! Plays longest with books. Announces "Uh oh" when she drops things into trash can by high chair. Loves peek-a-boo. Puts things in and out of drawers. Remembers where things are. Pushed Red Walker Cart in different directions, using all sides. Put objects in and out. Followed directions when Mom said, "Give this a ride." "Put this in." "Push it."

10 mos. 27 days. Walking well. Interested in books. Brings objects to Mom. Watching mouths and starting to imitate sounds. Says "Uh oh," "ho(t)." Said, "Bye-bye, Mommy." Putting objects in containers. Tries to say "bottle (baba)" and "up." Put cylinders in holes of Log Boat. Rocked on Wooden Rocking Horse. Said "ah" for on.

✑ **Chad** ✑

9 mos. 2 days. Says "Mama" and "Dada." Wanting to be held frequently now. Discovery Beads a big hit.

10 mos. 2 days. Crawling commando style. Can pull up to stand. Spends lots of time exploring objects. Starting to be less clingy but still has to make sure Mom's in the room. On good sleep schedule—12 or 13 hours a night.

✑ **Charity** ✑

9 mos. 1 day. Uses pointer finger to turn pages, put in Mom's mouth, and touch brother. Bounces by herself. Goes from tummy to sitting position. Crawls. Has one tooth.

10 mos. 1 day. Likes take-apart toys. Doing some crawling on knees, then goes back to commando crawl. Pulls up on everything. Follows older sister around. Busy all the time. Says "Mama" and "Dada." Learned to activate Disney Dancin' Babies with voice.

✑ **Jan** ✑

9 mos. 3 days. Making lots of sounds, some growly and grumbly—others happy: "ma-ma," "ga-ga." Crawls quickly from room to room. Goes up all seven stairs! Has five teeth.

9 mos. 17 days. Giggles and laughs. Moves quickly up stairs, then toward bathroom.

10 mos. 2 days. Stands up alone and has taken one step. Crawling and cruising. Loves to do what she sees older sister do. Has another tooth. Says "Ggg" and "ch."

10 mos. 17 days. Has taken first steps. Stood up in middle of floor by herself. Walked and played with Activity Walker.

11 mos. 0 days. Cruising and taking two or three steps. Eating more foods—table foods. Wants to feed herself. Says "dadadada" and "mamamama" but not meaningfully.

ॐ

8

Becoming a Toddler
Eleven to Thirteen Months

*He shall give his angels charge over thee, to keep thee in all
thy ways. They shall bear thee up in their hands, lest thou
dash thy foot against a stone.*

Psalms 91:11,12

On the Go

The ability to walk graduates your child from the category of baby to toddler. Many children learn to walk during this time. Some have already started walking. Others will wait for another month or more before taking off on their own. Enjoy your child's unique individuality, and resist the temptation to compare him favorably or unfavorably with other children. Rejoice in the wonderful, special qualities of your friends' babies as well, and you will be released from the fruitless feeling of false pride.

Many factors affect the time when a baby will start walking. Some babies are more interested in practicing their physical skills than others. A small, wiry baby may find it easier to learn to walk than a tall or plump one. A key determining factor seems to be the baby's daring and determination. Some seem oblivious to bumps and throw caution to the winds; others appear to think through every step carefully before making the move. In any case, it's surprising what a short time it takes after a child learns to walk before he's running. Crawling can still be a favored form of locomotion for a while after first steps are taken. Baby may quickly crawl across the room, pull up on something, and, with hands up, toddle off for a few steps.

When your baby starts to walk, you'll need to rethink your safety proofing from the standpoint of his greater speed and wider range. (See **Safety Proofing**, p. 86.) Baby will be learning what "no" means as you consistently move him away from plugs, TV controls, telephones, and furniture that he should not climb on. It's still best to limit the number of forbidden, tempting touchables in areas where baby goes. As baby gets more dependable in the next few months, you can gradually give him more access to other areas or objects. This must be a time of careful watchfulness, but throughout the coming year, your child will become increasingly reliable as his communication skills improve and as you establish and teach the rules.

Some parents, who have used a playpen, now put one side down and use it for toy storage rather than for the baby. Others still find it useful for brief periods. It's important for baby to have access to you, the caregiver, during most of his waking hours. As his interest in language intensifies, he'll be bringing items to you and watching your mouth as you talk to him. He'll be watching your feelings and actions and imitating them. He'll learn what you value, what the rules are, and how to behave.

Your toddler will continue to explore everything within reach. The mouth test is still commonly used by many, but fingers take over more of the exploration. Toddlers love carrying an object in each hand and will move objects from one place to another. As their mobility gives them independence, they will range further away, exploring the limits and discovering climbing places. At the same time, your toddler will keep track of you and check on you regularly. Of course you will need to be continually watchful as well.

Bath Time

Now that baby is secure sitting up, bath time can be a fun playtime with toys to float and push around. The tub is a good place to learn to pour. Give your baby cups, containers, and other objects for tub play. Never leave baby unattended in the tub, however.

Becoming a Toddler

Discipline

Remember that your baby is learning as he gets into things he shouldn't. His new mobility gives him access to many more items in the house which he will be intent on finding out about. He needs to learn how to behave in his wider boundaries—what he may and may not do—and it is up to the regular caregivers in his life to teach him. This is an intensive time of teaching on your part. Even if your child is learning what to do in a child-care setting, he will still need to know all of your expectations for him in the home. He loves for you to be pleased with him and will look to you for cues on his behavior. You need to think through what the rules for him in the home should be, teach them to him, and see that he follows them.

Your toddler may be determined to climb and now be able to climb up onto the furniture. If so, look around the house and see what would be all right for him to climb on—a landing, some cushions, or a couch or chair that won't lead to climbing on a table. It's always best, when you take your toddler away from climbing a forbidden object, to take him to where he *may* climb.

The ability to walk extends a child's spatial concepts. Sometimes a few bumps attend this learning. Though you make your home as safe as possible, your toddler, gaining in speed, may take a few little tumbles. He may run into a table or he may stand up under one that is shorter than he. Parents have found it a reassurance to trust that "underneath are the everlasting arms."[10] Your toddler will look to you for a reaction to see if a fall is a comedy or a tragedy. If you're not fearful and can laugh at a little bump, your child will learn to do the same. Of course you'll be ready to give a hug and a kiss and to comfort bigger bumps. Your calmness and trust can have a healing effect, and your toddler will learn what he needs to from the experience as he gets over the hurt.

Let your child know what he may not do by stopping inappropriate behavior and by taking him immediately and consistently to what he may do. If he persists in the wrong behavior, tell him "No," and put him on the other side of a gate from you or in a playpen within view. Tell him firmly what he needs to know, but don't continue to scold him or pay at-

---

[10]*"The eternal God is thy refuge, and underneath are the everlasting arms."* Deuteronomy 33:27

tention to him. When he starts to fuss, let him fuss for about half a minute, then get him, give him a hug, and remind him of what he *may* do. If he goes back to the forbidden behavior, repeat the consequence. No anger should accompany the procedure. You're not punishing; you are teaching.

Language

Receptive language increases perceptibly during this time. Your toddler will probably amaze you by showing that he understands many things you say. He will be able to follow some directions you give, such as "Bring me the ball," or "Go get your shoes." Some toddlers will start saying a few meaningful words also. Those who are keyed in to language may be able to imitate words.

Some toddlers will come into what I call "Velcro™ Time" (see p. 191) during this period. Interest in the primary caregiver will supersede independent play with toys, though practicing physical skills remains a common interest. The toddler will shadow the parent, not from fear of

Books are interesting as hinged objects as well as a means of learning language.

strangers but to hear language. This can be wearing to the parent, but keep in mind that it is temporary and for a good purpose. When the toddler feels well launched on the road to language, he will return to more independent play.

Many toddlers come to prefer books to toys during this time. They will bring board books to parents, turn around, and back into the parent's lap. The parent will point to a few pictures the toddler is looking at and name them. The toddler at some point catches on to the fact that the same word is said for the object or picture each time. The toddler will turn the pages and open and close the book, loving it as a hinged object. Then he will start pointing to the pictures to hear the words. These moments with books may be brief. Let your toddler head off as soon as he wants to, and he'll feel free to come back again when he's ready for more.

Point to and name body parts for your baby. You can also point to parts of his face as you say: " Brow bender, eye peeper, nose smeller, mouth eater, chin chopper, GILLY GOPPER!" and end with a tickle under the chin.

Talk to your child about what you're doing and about what he's doing. Name objects with single words as well as talking in sentences. Your toddler may develop a questioning word as he points, wanting to hear the words. You may also notice that he watches your lips as you say words. He'll bring you an item, hand it to you, then take it away again. He'll watch your lips and listen to what you say. Repeat the words as many times as he likes.

An Expanding Social Scene

Toddlers are often curious about other people. They watch people intently, sometimes trying to engage them with a smile and sometimes expressing shyness. You can introduce your toddler to others in various contexts. Having an object to talk about, such as a toy or a picture on the child's shirt, can help the child to make contact. Toddlers love to be with other children but often spend more time watching than interacting with them.

The toddler may find it difficult to part with Mom, or the primary caregiver, at this time. Be sure to give your child a little time periodically to be away from you with someone he knows that you trust. It's good for babies to learn that they can have happy times with others. Some stay-at-home moms have a high-school sitter come for a couple of hours once or twice a week to give them a breather. Others leave baby with Dad or a grandparent on a regular basis.

Always tell your baby that you are going and will be back soon. Don't try to slip away unnoticed. The substitute caregiver may need to hold your child when you make your exit. After you have said good-bye, leave promptly. Extended good-byes are more difficult.

Time for Yourself—and Dad's Role

In this time of watchfulness, be sure to relax and have fun. If you're not working outside the home, it helps to get a fresh perspective on the home scene if you can get out for a while from time to time. You can take your child out for a walk, a visit with friends, or a trip to the mall or zoo. A stroller or backpack will be useful for these excursions. Look for humor in situations that come up, and enjoy your toddler. Get a good sitter and go out for an evening with

Dads' involvement can bless children.

your spouse or some friends, or take a little time for shopping.

Remember that Dad isn't a sitter, but a parent. Despite some progress in the freeing of gender roles, moms are in charge of the children in most homes. This is natural if she's with the children most of the time, but she can help to strengthen Dad's role as parent by telling him what she observes about their child. She can make notes of daily happenings, on a chalkboard or pad of paper, to share with Dad. Communication is an important factor. Parents should frequently discuss their aims and methods of teaching their children. Moms need to share with the dads, who are more often away, what the children are doing from day-to-day and how incidents have been handled. Moms report that dads get closest to their children, and learn to take the responsibility, when the moms leave the house for a morning of errands, an evening out with other moms, or for work. There should be plenty of family fun together as well.

Some dads are doing a fine job of being the stay-at-home caregiver while their children are young. If Mom is working outside the home full time, Dad will need to communicate the children's progress and daily happenings to her.

Learning, Play, and Favorite Toys

Your baby will continue to be interested in examining and handling toys and objects. He'll spend time steadily staring at objects and people, "taking it all in."

A fascinating concept to the toddler is object permanence. When an item disappears, he now knows it still exists and can come back again. Peek-a-boo is a favorite game, and the baby can find toys that are completely hidden. Baby will like putting a toy in a container, putting a lid on, and taking it off again. A little wooden box called a Jackpop, with a lid that opens and closes revealing a wooden figure, was made by Creative Playthings in the 1970s. The child simply pulls up the lid to reveal the figure (no winding required). This toy has remained a favorite over the years for this age group. Maybe you'll be able to find something similar. Ball drops will become fascinating if the baby wasn't interested earlier. You may see your baby discover the space behind him. He may start dropping objects over his shoulder and then turn around to find them again.

Your toddler will probably love opening and closing cupboard or closet doors. She will likely be enjoying the cupboard or drawer that you have designated as *hers* with objects to take out and put back. She will learn the difference between her allowed cupboard and others as you consistently take her away from the forbidden ones to hers. Change the objects in her cupboard from time to time to maintain her interest.

As mentioned above, books can be favorites at this time, both as hinged objects and for the language. Board books are best. Watch your child with books so they aren't mistreated. If your baby chews on the book or tries to pull it apart, show him how to be gentle with it. If he persists in treating it roughly, remove it for a brief time. Give it back soon, showing him how to be gentle. Repeat the process until he learns, from the tone of your voice and your actions, how to treat books. Name the objects in the books he points to or looks at.

Your child might enjoy pushing and pulling a musical or popping push toy from a crawling or sitting position. If he's just learned to walk, he'll be holding both hands up for balance, so a push toy will tend to get carried rather than pushed. In another month or two, it can be used in the conventional way. A child must learn to walk backwards to enjoy a pull

*When baby can let go consciously, ball drops
become fascinating.*

toy, so these are not usually popular until later. However, pull toys with moving parts and springy antenna can be interesting for exploration.

Balls are usually favorite toys at this time. Your toddler can learn to drop, throw, roll, and eventually kick a ball.

Favorite Toys:

- Objects to explore and take in and out of containers. Plastic or metal bowls with small objects to put in and take out appeal. Hide Inside (Discovery Toys), Happy Pot 'n Spoon (First Toys).
- Objects to climb on and off of—wooden rocking horse, small rocking chair.
- Walker wagons or activity walkers until child is able to walk alone.
- Balls of different sizes to toss or hold.
- Ball drops. You can make one with a cardboard tube covered with contact paper. You can also put a round hole in the plastic lid of a can or the top of a cardboard box. Golf ball-sized balls work well with these.
- Disks and ungraduated spindles.
- Large pegs or rods to put in holes.
- Toys with figures that go down holes (Play-About House— or Discovery Cottage by Fisher-Price).
- Activity centers with cause-effect action and toys that allow child to activate music (Music Activity Center by Fisher-Price, Musical Pop-Up Piano).
- Doors that open and close (Magic Doors).
- Board books.

Games to Play

- Say, while pointing to each toe:

    This little piggy went to market. This little piggy stayed home.
    This little piggy had roast beef. This little piggy had none.
    And this little piggy went wee wee wee all the way home. (Say the wees with a high voice and end with a tickle.)

- When your baby can clap his hands, he'll like clapping with you as you sing:

    Clap your hands, one two three.
    Clap them, clap them, just like me.

- Bounce your toddler on your lap to:

    Alley galloo galloo, alley galloo gallee,
    Al–ley, galloo galloo gallee—wheeee! (Lift him in the air on the "wheeee.")

- Make a hide-away or tunnel by draping blankets over furniture.
- Play hide-and-seek and "Chase me!"
- Make imaginative spaces with large cardboard boxes.

Eating

Growth slows down in the second year and so does a child's appetite. Don't be concerned that your child is eating less than before. If you don't push him to eat, he will be able to regulate the amount of food he needs. Studies have shown that young children are capable of eating just the amount of food they need.[11] If a parent takes over the responsibility by urging the child to eat or playing games to get in "one more bite," the child often resists and doesn't utilize this natural capability.

Continue introducing your toddler to a wide variety of table foods with loving encouragement but without pressure to eat them. Let your child see you eat the new foods, and he may reach for them. Remember that receptivity to eating a variety of food is the goal, not getting the food into the child.

Toddlers can drink regular homogenized milk. Whole milk is said to be better for babies than low-fat milk. Most of the foods you eat are fine for your baby. It's best to limit sugar and avoid chocolate and nuts or foods that could cause choking. Baby will gum foods and take bites but will not be able to do much chewing until the molars come in. Grapes and hot dogs should be cut to sizes that will not cause possible choking.

Continue to let your child eat finger food and practice eating with a spoon. He may enjoy eating bites of pancake or French toast with a small fork. This is not a time to worry about messes. Baby will learn more if you let him do his best and are willing to wipe up the mess. If he throws food, or deliberately drops it, that indicates he's no longer hungry, and the food should be taken away. If he is still hungry, he'll learn the rule that food is for eating, not for throwing. If he indicates he's still hungry, give the food back and let him eat it, but if he throws it again, take him down from his high chair until the next meal. Tell him with a firm, but not angry, voice that food is for eating, not for throwing.

Let him practice drinking from a cup himself by putting small amounts of liquid in the cup.

---

[11]Davis, C.M., 1928; Fomon, S.J. 1974; Birch & Deyshers 1985, and 1986.

SAMPLE SCHEDULES

Ginger, at eleven months, has two school-age siblings.

Time	Activity
7:00–8:00 a.m.	Awakens, talks to herself for awhile, then calls out to let us know she's ready to get up. Diaper change and sponge off. Breakfast: fruit, cereal, sometimes egg, toast, pancakes, milk from cup or bottle.
8:00–11:00	Plays with toys. Periodic interactions with Mom as she works around house. Sometimes in car doing errands with Mom. At 10:00, diaper change, juice from cup, or sippy cup if out with Mom.
11:00–12:00	Lunch from the following foods: vegetables, $1/4$ or $1/2$ sandwich (peanut butter, egg salad, bologna, or other) with whole-grain bread, or graham cracker, thin-sliced meat, yogurt or cottage cheese, cheese, fruit, milk from cup. Diaper change. May have movement on potty after lunch.
12:00 to 3:00 p.m.	Nap time. Diaper change and snack upon awakening—Cheerios and milk from cup.
3:00–5:30	Playtime with toys and with siblings with adult monitoring and supervision.
5:30–6:30	Cleanup. Helps pick up toys. Dinner with family (or before, if Dad is late getting home). Meat, or casserole dish, vegetables, bread, fruit, milk from cup.
6:30–7:00	Bath time, usually with Dad. (Maybe every other day in winter.)
7:00–7:30	Wind down time with cup or bottle of milk and books.
7:30	Bedtime.

Becoming a Toddler

Eleven-month-old twins, Abby and Blaire, have a preschool-age brother.

Time	Activity
6:30 to 7:00 a.m.	Get up and have bottle—eight ounces of formula.
8:00	Instant oatmeal with brown sugar and cinnamon. Finger food or mashed banana. Now using Gerber 3rd foods. (B) takes to bigger pieces. (A) not sure.
8:30–9:00	Go down for nap.
10:30	Juice. Play independently. Mom plays with them for awhile and keeps watch.
11:30 or 12:00	Lunch: 2 jars of baby food each—vegetable and fruit. Or finger foods such as cheese, crackers, Cheerios. Then play.
1:00 p.m.	Nap for about two hours.
2:45	Go in car to get brother from school. Snack in car.
4:30 or 5:00	Dinner. 2 jars of food, including a meat. Also trying new foods from the table. Playtime. Get ready for bed. Play with Dad.
6:30 or 7:00	8-ounce bottle of milk. Play.
8:00	Bedtime for Abby, who needs more sleep.
8:30	Bedtime for Blaire.

Blake, at 11¹/₂ months, is still nursing twice a day.

Time	Activity
7:00 a.m.	Awakens. Dad changes diaper and brings to bed for Mom to nurse.
8:00	Has apple or banana cereal. Gets dressed and plays in dependently. Then explores or plays with Mom and Dad, if Dad is home.
9:00	Four-ounce bottle. Nap.
11:00	Plays until he gets fussy.
11:30 to 12:00	Lunch. Gerber 3rd food, chunky chicken noodle, 1 jar of fruit (pears are favorite), graham crackers or saltines. Likes frozen bagels (¹/4 at a time). Plays.
1:30 p.m.	Nap.
3:00	Nurses, plays.
5:00	Dinner: chunky jar of dinner baby food or food Mom makes—vegetable, meat, pasta, rice. Fruit for dessert. Parents eat later.
6:00	Bath, brush teeth, songs, story, sing hymns.
7:00	To bed for night.

Abe's family, with two teenage siblings, finds it convenient to have him on a later schedule. He is 12$^1/_2$ months old.

Time	Activity
9:30 a.m.	Awakens, nurses.
9:30–10:00	Bath.
10:00–10:15	Breakfast of baby cereal or cream of wheat.
10:15–12:30	Plays independently, periodically bringing Mom a book to read.
12:30–1:00 p.m.	Lunch. Likes Campbell's cream of broccoli or cream of celery soup or one jar of Gerber's 3rd foods.
1:00–3:00	Naps now or from 2:00 to 4:00. Nurses a little before nap.
3:00–5:00	Plays with brother after school.
5:30–6:30	Dinner of chopped fruit, one jar of 3rd foods or mashed food family is eating.
6:30–8:30	Plays with toys. Reads books. Plays with sister, brother, and Dad.
8:30–9:30	Milk from cup, then plays.
9:30–10:00	Nurses and is asleep by 10:00. Nurses a couple of times in the night. [Note: Nursing a baby to sleep usually results in the child awakening in the night to be nursed to sleep again.]

Cameos of Individual Children

∽ Charity ∽

11 mos. 12 days. Stands alone. Says "duck," "quack," "caca" (cracker), "Mama," "Dada." Chases sister, calling her.

11 mos. 26 days. Takes a few steps but prefers to crawl. Cruises all around. Plays pat-a-cake and rolls hands. Says "bye-bye." Climbs on and off of wooden rocking horse.

12 mos. 24 days. Walking alone. Attached to Mom. Points and looks to adult for words. Says "Uh oh." Fusses more, lately, when she can't get what she wants. Put balls in ball drop repeatedly.

∽ Chad ∽

11 mos. 13 days. Watches a lot to see what's going on. Watches twin sister carefully before trying to do something new. Sits and spends more time with small motor exploration than practicing large motor skills. Shows pride in accomplishment by bouncing up and down. Examined and put pieces in and out of Hide Inside (cloth box containing objects of different texture and color).

11 mos. 27 days. Babbles a lot. Gets sad when Mom leaves. Puts objects in and out of containers. Put balls in and out of ball drop.

12 mos. 25 days. Starting to walk pushing activity walkers. Tries to figure out how things work. Watches with awe as twin sister walks. Loves to have Mom walk him next to her. Now, not as concerned when Mom leaves as sister is.

∽ Vana ∽

11 mos. 13 days. Cruises and explores toys. Tosses balls. Says "go(ne)" when she drops something off changing table. Points to things with questioning word "dot?" Sits on legs. Points to objects or pictures her parents name.

11 mos. 27 days. Lots of babbling and keen interest in language. Loves books. Will sit by herself and look for some time at pictures of children in catalogs. Comes forth with soliloquies of jargon. Slides down stairs feet first. Loves playing tag and hide/seek.

12 mos. 11 days. Reaches out with finger on right hand to "work" things. Taking steps holding onto adult's hands. Chatters nonstop. Enthusiastic and dainty eater. Plays peek-a-boo in playpen. Lets Mom know when she has a dirty diaper. Liked pulling string on Activity Cube to make cat sound.

12 mos. 25 days. Walking alone now. Likes carrying things around. Likes books. Still exploring objects. Watches adults' mouths and tries to say words. Uses animated jargon when looking at book. Communicates with gestures. Points to what she wants; pushes away what she doesn't want. Liked Hide Inside. Would find each object Mom named.

∽ **Diane** ∾

11 mos. 6 days. Does a "forced" laugh. Prefers books to toys. Has taken 24 steps. Takes toys to Mom for interaction. Says "bo(ok)," "li(ght)," "puppy," "hi," "bye-bye." Says a word for "up" when Mom picks her up. Whistles for a bird.

12 mos. 11 days. Likes to be on her feet all the time. Kicks balls with feet. Carries object in each hand. Large receptive vocabulary. Works out routine, taking things from one place to another, then adds to routine. Dances with good sense of rhythm and turns in circle. Enjoys books. Not working on new words since walking. Favorite toy was Happy Pot 'n Spoon. Stirred and taste-tested plastic fruit.

12 mos. 25 days. Keying in to language. Watches mouths. Loves books. Little interest in toys now, but carries them around. Enjoys music. Uses word "up" quite a bit. Enjoys watching other little children. Imitates roaring lion. Says "Mama." Has word for Grandma. Played Musical Pop-Up Piano and danced.

∽ **Seth** ∾

11 mos. 13 days. Walking everywhere. Loves balls. Likes to do things his own way rather than the way he's shown. Quickly figures things out, showing he knows what objects are for. Puts brush to hair. Saying many words (getting partial sounds). Throws toys. Shows hurt feeling when told "No." Learned to stack rings on Baby Touch and Stack spindle. Used this in playpen. Liked Pot with Spoon—put wooden blocks in and out and banged large plastic spoon on everything.

11 mos. 27 days. Clinging to Mom, and trying to communicate what he wants by "uh uh." Says "ba ba" for blanket and "gnk" for book. Not falling over as much or tripping on things. Maneuvering around well. Very busy exploring. Loves books. Several times a day brings book to Mom. Paying attention to words instead of just turning pages. Enjoyed dropping balls in ball drop and finding them again.

12 mos. 11 days. In constant motion. Likes pushing toys and containers—also throwing balls. Almost running, now, he walks so fast. Likes to put basketball through hoop. Favorite book: *Dear Zoo* by Rod Campbell. Also likes a homemade book, *Mommy, where are you?*, and a Tana Hoban one.

∾ Helen ∾

11 mos. 7 days. Working on standing and walking. Says "sh" for shoe. Knows meaning of lots of words. Said "bye-bye," lots of times. Not a good napper—too many things to discover! Loves books. Mom can't remember her other children getting so excited about books. Hide Inside favorite toy.

11 mos. 21 days. Likes opening and shutting doors, loading and unloading objects. Acted shy and quietly studied substitute parent-educator in toy-library session instead of playing with toys and showing her usual animation. Crawls and cruises with good balance. Tries to imitate sounds of words. Says "du(ck)." Looks at sisters when Mom names them.

12 mos. 5 days. Stands and squats. Loves containers. Seemed pleased to see familiar face at Toy Library. Played well with toys. Handed them to me, listening for words. Says "bye-bye," "hi," "ba(th)," "ba(ll)." Saw picture of baby in tub and said "ba(th)." Understands and responds to words such as "walk," "stand up," etc. Liked Happy Pot 'n Spoon. Would hold up fruit and say "Ah," wanting to hear Mom name them.

11 mos. 4 days. Cruises, getting steadier on feet. Stands up in playpen and leans against it, not holding on. Making more new sounds verbally. Likes putting objects in containers and flipping through books. Likes *Brown Bear, Brown Bear."

11 mos. 18 days. Cruises all around. Hands objects to people. Looks at and wants to touch eyes and mouths. Learned to shut drawers and keep fingers out. Climbs on drawers and stairs. Turns around to

get down from bed and couch. Pushes Walker Cart. Magic Doors was a favorite. Liked opening and closing doors.

12 mos. 2 days. Good receptive vocabulary. Points and babbles in questioning way. Says "Emma" (cat's name), and "keeca(t)" Looks at piano when it's mentioned. More confident cruising. Sometimes stands alone when holding two small things. Put balls in Curiosity Box repeatedly.

12 mos. 30 days. Likes to shake objects to see if he can make sounds. Taking a few first steps. Likes to move chairs. Into everything. Trying to open things—can twist lid. More vocal about frustrations. Favorite toy was Activity Cube Center.

∽ Kelly ∽

11 mos. 26 days. Loves books! More interested in going to books than playing with toys. Says "Gook?" pointing, to get parents to say words. Throws things. Cruises. Opens and closes cabinet doors. Puts items away in containers. Watches where Mom puts things and gets them. Sits in rocker. When Grandpa said book was upside down, turned it around. Likes Barney and Sesame St. on TV. Likes Activity Walker. Put balls in Curiosity Box repeatedly, and put balls to mouth.

12 mos. 10 days. Takes occasional steps alone going from one object to another. Points to what she wants, such as cup. Drinking from cup rather than bottle. Likes books. Liked Jackpop, Walker Cart, and Play About House. Put men down chimney and opened doors.

12 mos. 24 days. Experimenting with sound of voice. Squeals when she wants to communicate.

∽ Benny ∽

11 mos. 14 days. Curious about everything and fast to investigate, tongue out for concentration. Very vocal. Crawls and pulls up to stand. Likes springs such as antenna on Lady Bug Pull Toy.

11 mos. 28 days. Pushes walker wagon. Walks around holding on to walls. More daring going from table to chair. Loves wheels—likes to turn. Crawls and climbs. Likes animals—friends' dogs. Pushed Fun Bus along on hands and knees. Quickly discovered how to push dog down and make pop up.

12 mos. 12 days. Taking first steps. Likes wheels. Bangs things to make

sound. Loves music. Liked Music Activity Center. Loved pushing walker wagon and getting in to be pushed.

12 mos. 26 days. Very busy—"all over the place." Loves music. Likes to sing and play piano. Has regular time in his room or playpen. Liked Curiosity Box. Put balls in repeatedly.

∽ **George** ∽

11 mos. 12 days. Has more interest in toys than his twin brother has. Walks with walker wagon. Likes balls. Eats a lot—loves Cheerios. Does well with cup. Makes variety of sounds. Good receptive language. Not imitating sounds yet.

11 mos. 26 days. Started to use spoon. Good with finger foods. Likes to feed self. Will put food in mouth if it's put on spoon. Walks well. Loves bath. Likes balls and swing. Put balls in Baby Drum Drop over and over.

12 mos. 10 days. Comfortable walking around outside. Started talking: "dog-gah," "cookie," "ki(tt)y ca(t)," "mama," "uh-oh." Enjoys exploring concepts. Kicks ball around house.

12 mos. 24 days. Loves to take baths. Feeds self with fork and spoon. Likes books. Not talking as much. Follows directions. Put head on brother's lap to comfort him. Shows he understands what is being said. Figured out gadgets on Buttons 'n Bells Cash Register and worked again and again.

ॐ

9

Traveling with Babies and Young Children

The Lord shall preserve thy going out and thy coming in
from this time forth, and even for evermore.

Psalms 121:8

Traveling can be a source of happy togetherness for a family. The expectation of joy and adequate preparation are key to having successful trips with babies or young children. Babies love to be with family members, and they like the quieting movement of a vehicle. Parents are often surprised to find that babies and toddlers can travel happily even though confined to a car seat on long trips. Whether you choose to drive or fly, you can prepare for an enjoyable time. Often babies attract interest from people along the way and make good ice breakers for conversation with friendly strangers. When babies are under seven or eight months, before they can crawl or walk, can be the easiest time to travel with them. When they are more active and love moving about, you'll need to plan more stops or opportunities for their movement.

The baby equipment you need to take will be determined by your destination and mode of transportation. You may be able to rent a crib and high chair where you are going. A call to determine the supply will be worthwhile. If you plan to fly and rent a car, check to see if a safety-approved car seat of the correct size for your baby will be available. You can bring a car seat to use on the plane and in a rental car that will also be useful as an infant seat for feeding and carrying baby. An umbrella stroller is easy to bring on either plane or car and is probably well worth the space it takes.

Bring more than enough baby food for the trip in case there should be a delay, and be sure to bring food you know your baby likes. Count on throwing away any opened jars of baby food. Juice and formula sealed in bottles to which you can attach a nipple are easiest to use. But make sure your baby will drink out of the kind of nipple required. Bring a bottle of water from home.

Car Trips

Of course you will have a comfortable and safe car seat for your child. After eight months of age or so, baby will love looking out the window, so a booster seat that gives good visibility will be a help.

Some couples like to drive when they know the children will be asleep in the car, such as in the evening and into the night. If your children sleep well in the car, there are many options. You may prefer daytime travel so that parents and children can both rest at the same time. If so, plan on frequent stops rather than trying to travel for long stretches. If you have older children, you might consider stopping at a motel along the way for an afternoon rest and swim. Some motels will give you a room for a daytime rate.

You can improvise a diaper-changing area in the back seat of a car with a changing pad and perhaps a pillow. You can also feed baby in a car seat in the back seat. Occasional snacks can help keep babies and toddlers contented along the way. Be sure to bring some wet wipes and paper towels to clean up messes. Bring trash bags as well.

Children seldom take a break from their need to keep busy exploring and learning with their eyes and hands. Before the trip, put aside a few toys that you know will appeal to baby—new ones as well as a few favorite ones. They will be of greater interest if he hasn't seen them for awhile before the trip. Bring them out one at a time throughout the trip. Also bring some books with bright, colorful pictures to look at with your baby.

We camped across the country when our first two boys were ages three and seventeen months. Our toddler, Danny, was contented when he could find a stick at each stop to carry and poke around in the ground. We had to establish the rule, however, that these sticks couldn't go in the car with us. Danny soon became assured that he would find another stick at the next stop.

My mother, a preschool teacher, packed a box full of little wrapped gifts for the boys—things such as magic slates, small books, stickers, little flashlights, small puzzles, and toy animals, vehicles, or figures. We gave the boys three or four a day, making a game of when they could open each one—perhaps after lunch, or when they saw a cow or a gas station. This worked so well that for years I would shop for treasures to wrap before each trip. The party or favor section of toy stores yielded good toys for this. I also put aside and wrapped a few toys we already had that I knew would keep the children entertained. These little gifts led to miles of entertainment.

You can buy or make pockets that hang on the back of the front seats to hold items for the children. These can hold snacks as well as toys to add neatness and convenience. If you have older children, they will like to have their own lap pad and box of art materials, such as colored pencils, crayons, paper, glue stick, stamp pad, and stickers.

Bring some audiotapes or CDs that both you and the children will enjoy. You can intersperse children's' tapes with adult tapes that you like. At other times, you can sing songs together.

Encourage your children to look out the window to discover what they may see. You can name or sing songs about things they see. A song I made up goes like this:

> *When we ride in the car, we sit in the car seat, sit in the car*
> *   seat, sit in the car seat.*
> *When we ride in the car, we sit in the car seat and fasten*
> *   our belts.*
> *Then we ride along and ride along and ride along and ride*
> *   along,*
> *And look out the window.*
> (Spoken) *And what do we see?* (Use child's response or*
> *   your own.)*
> *Tree, trees, trees. We see trees out the window.*
> *(Repeat using cows, trucks, buses, cars, etc.)*
> *(Repeat first two lines of song for chorus.)*

Bringing your child's blanket along may help to make him feel at home. It can be used to play peek-a-boo, to shade him from the sun, or to shield him from the air conditioner.

Take turns with your spouse driving and riding in the back seat with your child. Your spouse may enjoy the change of scene as much as you. We find that changing drivers every hundred miles works well to keep the drivers fresh.

Traveling by Plane

If possible, make a reservation for a flight at a time when the flight is least likely to be full. You will be more apt to have an empty seat next to you and will find the space useful. Ask about children's car-seat regulations when you make your reservation. If an extra seat is available, most airlines will allow you to put a car seat there for your child. If the plane is full, however, you will have to check the car seat at the gate. If you want to guarantee a seat for a child, you must purchase a ticket. You can board the plane first and get settled before other passengers board. If the airline doesn't announce early boarding, you can ask for it. On the other hand, some parents of toddlers prefer letting the child run around by the gate for as long as possible before boarding. Some families like to request the area behind a bulkhead where there is more floor room for the baby. Others like to sit where there is space under the seat in front to store the diaper bag.

Bring along food for your baby. The flight attendant can heat baby food or a bottle for you. Some Cheerios or favorite crackers may help keep baby contented. Be sure to bring wet wipes, too. If you order ahead, some airlines may provide special food for your baby or young child. If you're breast-feeding, have a shawl or loose blouse so you can nurse discretely. Nursing or bottle-feeding a baby on take off or landing can help to relieve ear pressure. A bottle of juice can be used. You may bring on board only items that can be stowed overhead or under the seat. Other items, such as strollers, may be checked through or stored in an area on the plane where it's accessible when you board and deplane.

For entertainment, bring a few favorite toys baby hasn't seen for awhile. Some colorful books will be entertaining, as well. Babies who are standing, or toddlers, may enjoy the freedom of playing on the floor in front of a seat.

A flight attendant will usually be willing to hold your baby while you use the rest room, if you are traveling alone with baby. Many airlines are upgrading their restrooms with built-in changing tables. Otherwise, change baby's diaper on a couple of empty seats or on yours if the plane is full. You can put a dirty diaper in an airsick bag available in the pockets of the seats. These can usually be sealed.

Bring extra diapers for baby and extra clothing both for your child and yourself. After a busy (and maybe messy) flight, it will feel good to have fresh clothing.

Your children will take the lead from you about how they should feel about travel. If you expect a good time rather than an ordeal, this expectation will be picked up by your children, and they will respond accordingly. However you travel, prepare your thought prayerfully for the trip and expect the travel to be harmonious.

PART TWO

THE NEXT YEARS

A Look Back

Reflect on how far you and your baby have come in the past year. He has changed completely from the tiny infant you first met. Now he's able to move about on his own and let you know his interests, desires, and needs. Your baby is a treasured individual, and your home would not seem complete without him. You now know what unconditional love is, and you may appreciate your own parents, and their feeling for you, more than ever.

In the first year, care and feeding have been of primary interest. Your baby has changed perceptibly month by month. As your child continues to gain in capability and develops ideas of his own, discipline, training, and character building will take over as leading parenting topics. You have laid the foundation for a strong relationship that will continue to grow in the years to come.

The next part of the book will drop the month-to-month format and take up general topics vital to your child's second and third year. Sample schedules and cameos of the second and third years are given in Appendix 1 and Appendix 2 so that you can look into the lives of other families and find commonalities and differences among children of the same age.

Overview of the Second and Third Year

The One-Year-Old

The second year brings delightful changes as your toddler explores his expanding capabilities and his world. It's a transition between babyhood and childhood where physical skills blossom, language comes forth, and the toddler gains insights into how to behave.

This is a time where parent vigilance and teaching are vital, since the toddler doesn't know the rules that govern his widening boundaries. Your trust in God's guidance and a sense of humor will help. If a toddler were left to his own devices, he would have a wonderful time opening and closing every door, pulling items off of shelves and out of drawers, streaming toilet paper off the roller, experimenting with toilet water, and climbing over the furniture. All the gadgets and knick-knacks in the house would be fair game. The toddler has no thought of being naughty. He simply has to find out about all of the fascinating things in his environment. Fortunately, you have already been teaching the rules since your baby could crawl, and he probably knows what "no" means. As he picks up speed, however, your alertness must increase. Knowing that God is the true caregiver can reassure you that both you and your child will have the angel thoughts to be in the right place at the right time.

Periodically kneel or sit on the floor to gain your child's perspective of the world. Stoop, kneel, or sit to talk to him eye-to-eye rather than addressing him from above. This shows consideration and gains his attention. Listen to your child, and you will learn much. Every once in a while, observe your toddler for about 10 minutes and take notes—check your watch, jot down the time, and note moment-by-moment what your toddler does and says. This gives a great glimpse and perspective of how busy a toddler is and what is on his agenda.

As the toddler's curiosity causes him to wander off in exploration, he keeps tabs on you, his primary caregiver. He'll come to you frequently for language or for hugs and reassurance. He may also run off, confident that you will follow or hoping you'll play the game of "catch me." This is the time to establish a parenting approach that gives him freedom to flourish in a loving atmosphere with well-defined boundaries.

Conversations with the toddler are still one-sided, though the toddler's ability to communicate nonverbally as well as verbally increases rapidly. There is need for much input from parents in this year, but the rewards are great. By the end of this year you will be in awe of what your baby can tell you about what he's thinking. Two-year-olds often can remember and tell of events that happened, or places they went, before they could talk.

The Two-Year-Old

The two-year-old is wonderful, not "terrible." He has ideas of his own and can communicate them with increasing clarity. He'll better understand the reasons you give him for the limits you establish, but you'll still need to be consistent in teaching the rules and following up with consequences. His ability to remember and follow the rules improves and so does his physical control. He'll be able to climb higher, run faster, pedal a tricycle, and learn such tricks as turning somersaults. Discipline issues related to eating, sleeping, and toilet training must be addressed in this year, and progress in these areas will increase the accord between parent and child in later years.

Drawing and experimenting with different art media will become possible as your child gains reliability in keeping objects away from his mouth. Individual interests will emerge. Topics such as trains, cars and trucks, airplanes, babies, or kitchen play may become the enthralling focus of play.

The length of the two-year-old's sentences will increase. He'll like books with simple stories and start to enjoy pretend play. He'll be more interested in playing with other children. The play will be mostly parallel but will become more cooperative as the year progresses and opportunities to interact with other children are made available. Attention span increases, and the two-year-old can learn to follow directions in a group setting.

Balls provide fun as skills develop.

10

New Ways of Moving

They that wait upon the Lord shall renew their strength;
they shall mount up with wings as eagles; they shall run,
and not be weary; and they shall walk, and not faint.

Isaiah 40:31

As we see fine athletes perform, we can't help but be impressed by the grace, balance, strength, control, and freedom they express. We can help our children express these same qualities as their physical capabilities unfold. The adult's job is to provide opportunity, space, and equipment for them to practice physical skills.

After getting to his feet, the toddler seems intent on continuing to practice large motor skills. He soon moves from a walk to a run, and he'll want to climb to new heights. Some toddlers must be watched more carefully than others as they expand their physical capabilities, but most will find the level at which they can practice safely. It's always better to let (or help) them climb on their own, rather than to lift them on and off climbing equipment and riding toys. This helps them develop the skills needed to play independently. The best way to encourage physical development is to have the appropriate equipment, and let your toddler find his own skill level. But parent encouragement and interaction are also important factors. If your child asks for help climbing on or off a spring horse or climber, you can show him where to put his hands and feet and give a slight assist. It can be hard to resist the temptation to lift a child on and off of equipment. But the reward will be obvious as your child gains confidence and independence.

An important part of teaching is letting your children know where they may practice budding physical skills. They must learn not to climb the furniture, drawers, and kitchen counters. They must learn not to throw toys and where to throw balls. They need to know where they may run and jump. Physical skills can be encouraged by having appropriate equipment available to your toddler—either by taking him to a nearby park or by having the equipment in your home and yard. If your child is in day care, you can check to see that equipment appropriate for his age is available.

If your child is too daring, and wants to climb too high to be safe, you will need to make rules and clearly teach him how high he may climb. Get him to show you he knows how high he may climb and praise him for knowing when to come down. Do this without threatening, which will dare him to climb higher. But be prepared to limit his access to the equipment for a short time if he breaks the rules.

Equipment

Always consider safety when setting up equipment for a child. Make sure there are safe, padded areas around equipment for climbing and jumping. Gym mats, sand, certain kinds of soft mulch, and new, safe materials are possibilities.

Here are some pieces of equipment that allow toddlers to practice physical skills:

For Crawling

A tunnel to crawl through. You can purchase a fun tunnel made of strong spiral wire covered with fabric.

Just as fun, you can make a tunnel out of cardboard boxes or with chairs and tables covered by a sheet, blanket, or bedspread covering.

For Climbing and Sliding

Your toddler will love stairs and will learn on his own how to climb them. You will need to help him learn to come down the stairs safely—

feet first on his tummy. Then when he's ready, he can progress to standing and holding the rail.

Toddler stairs are available with two steps leading up to a platform and down the other side. A railing on each side allows the child to practice going up and down from an upright position.

A climbing frame or jungle gym—either homemade or purchased.

Toddler slide. There are numerous versions of slides for toddlers. Toddlers love to climb the stairs and slide down. Be sure to have a soft landing place at the bottom of the slide. Toddlers can learn how to catch themselves and can experiment with various ways to go down the slide. If your outdoor slide loses its slipperiness, rub it with waxed paper.

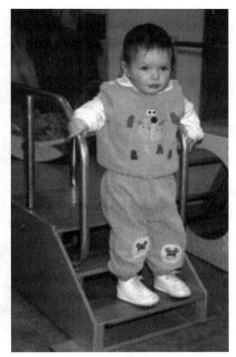

Toddlers love practicing on these toddler stairs.

A bar to hang or swing from can help develop arm strength.

For Jumping

An inclined board is one of my favorite pieces of equipment for young children. You must make it yourself, but it's not difficult. Purchase a 1"× 8" board 8 feet long. Screw a 2"× 2" cleat across the underside at each end of the board and finish the board with a polyurethane varnish or a good paint so there will be no splinters. Place one end of the board over a block or box 6" or 8" high. The child can first crawl up and down the board. Then let him hold your hand or finger as he walks up. You can say "Jump!" as he jumps off the end of the board. Later he will walk up and down by himself, and still later, jump the length of the board. A child learns about gravity as he uses the board to roll balls and small cars

New Ways of Moving

153

down. You can raise the end of the board higher as the child gets older to increase the incline. You can also raise both ends of the board so the child can jump on a horizontal "jumping board." If your child jumps on a bed or other furniture, you can tell him to jump on his "jumping board" instead.

A small trampoline. Some beginner models include handles. Make sure the surrounding area is soft or padded in some way.

An old mattress on the floor, covered with a fitted sheet, is great fun for jumping.

Your child will also enjoy jumping into a large beanbag chair or a pile of cushions.

A jumping board is a favorite piece of equipment.

For Riding

A sturdy spring horse or rocking horse.

A four-wheel riding toy. Be sure it doesn't tip over easily and that the wheel base gives the child's feet room to move without running into the wheels. The child may start pushing backwards with his feet before learning how to push forward.

When a child is close to three years old, he can learn to pedal a small tricycle or three-wheel pedal toy. A good way to help a child learn to pedal is to get behind him and push the tricycle just until a pedal is up. Then gently touch or push the top of the child's leg to help him push that pedal down. Next, touch or push the other leg as that leg's pedal comes up. This will help the child feel how to push with alternate legs.

A low vehicle such as the Big Wheel is good too. It doesn't tip over as easily as a tricycle.

For Ball Handling

Have balls of various types and sizes available for your toddler, and play ball with her. Balls that are soft—made of yarn, foam, or soft, rubbery material—are best at first for learning to catch.

Beanbags are also useful for learning to throw and catch.

A basketball hoop, box, or wastebasket may be used for throwing at a target.

Children enjoy swinging at a ball with a plastic bat.

For Swinging

Swings are always popular. A toddler swing with strap will hold the child as you push him. Later when he can hold on reliably, he can use a regular swing.

As children get older, they can make a glider swing before they learn to pump a regular swing. A toddler must be watched carefully around a swing in use so that he doesn't move into its path. Hold him back a safe distance, and let him watch how the swing moves.

Play With Your Child to Encourage Skills

A child learns some physical skills best by having someone play with him. Some children are more inclined to practice physical skills than others. But, with encouragement, all can learn. Practice should be fun and unpressured. A parent can help by keeping the practice at a level commensurate with the child's ability, so that the child is not discouraged by failure.

For games to play with your child, see **Active Games** (p. 227)

Ball Handling

Your child's ball handling starts when he throws and chases a ball. You can teach him how to sit with legs apart to roll and catch the ball. Then when he's steady on his feet, you can start throwing a large, soft ball to him to catch. Start at a close distance, and show him how to hold his arms; then move further away. Seeing other children, or you, playing ball will help him see some of the possibilities of ball handling. Two- and three-year-olds, whose parents or friends play ball with them, can learn to throw, kick, dribble, and catch a ball and to bat a T-ball.

Swimming

Babies and young children who are exposed to the water come to love it and can become good swimmers. There are swimming classes for parents and babies that will acquaint your baby with the water in a fun way. As your baby sees you put your face in the water, blow bubbles, float, and go under water, he will want to do the same. Before playing with your baby in the water, you will need to release yourself from any fear of the water so he won't feel your fear. Never push your baby beyond his comfort level in the water. It takes longer for a child to regain confidence after a scare than to progress at his own rate with trust.

Children love to play with water. Give your child a small amount of water and let him pour and play with toys that sink and float. The bathtub can be a fun place to play with constant supervision.

Safety around water is essential. You can't assume that swimming lessons will safety-proof your toddler around water. You must maintain watchfulness to keep your toddler away from water unless he is carefully supervised. Life vests are a must if your toddler is in a boat or playing around a pool. To maintain safety without fear, pray to know that God is always protecting your child and alerting you to any danger.

11

Growing Independence and Discipline

*Train up a child in the way he should go: and when he is
old, he will not depart from it.*

Proverbs 22:6

It's a thrill when your child shows that he has ideas of his own and can communicate them to you. At some point in the second year, he will let you know he wants to do things by himself and may start to struggle with you when you try to help him. You can find ways to empower him by giving him some choices that are acceptable to you. You will also learn how to gain his cooperation—sometimes by turning the chore into a game or by accompanying it with a song.

You will need to continue to teach your toddler the rules of behavior which allow him to get along well with you and others. You can establish a discipline style in this year that brings joy to your relationship with your child. Discipline is teaching, not blaming and punishing. When disciplining your child, you always want to be on his side against the error of thought and action that would cause difficulty. Your approach should assure the child that you love him but not the inappropriate behavior. Love for the child should not allow him to do anything he wants but should help you take the time and thought to teach suitable behavior. Think of each discipline problem that comes up, not as trouble, but as a learning opportunity. Your toddler has much to learn, and you are the primary teacher.

*Children can early learn rules that help
them get along with others.*

The teaching in the second year is demanding for the parent, but it reaps great rewards. You're not likely to have a "terrible two" or disagreeable child if you establish and consistently enforce good behavior from the beginning. You will still have discipline issues to work through, but you maximize accord with your child by building a strong basis for working through problems.

Spanking is not necessary and can teach some lessons you don't want your child to learn. It teaches the child, by example, to use physical aggression to get what he wants, and it causes more resentment than repentance. You should be ready to take action in terms of logical consequences when your child tests the rules. For example you might say, "Will you come right now? (pause) Or shall I carry you?" Or: "You forgot to stay on the sidewalk. We'll have to go into the house. Next time you will remember that we stay on the sidewalk. Cars go in the street."

You have the knowledge and experience to know what's best for your children. You can continue to listen to their needs but must resist the temptation to give in to their unreasonable desires no matter how much they fuss. You'll need to take the responsibility of defining the rules for your children, understanding that many of these rules will change as the children grow and as circumstances change. You will also want to consider what choices you can give your children to help them develop responsibility.

Your toddler's tempo is slower than yours. Give her time to respond, cooperate, and obey. If she says "no" and then obeys, ignore the "no."

You don't want to interrupt a child's play unnecessarily. Think through requests before you make them. Give directions simply and clearly with a positive tone of voice, expecting obedience. Don't give a choice if none is intended. For instance, say "It's time to come to lunch," not "Do you want to come to lunch now?" Say "You may come and get your coat on now. It's time to go," or "After one more turn, you may come."

If a choice is involved, you can make that clear. "Do you want to bring your Teddy bear? (long pause) Or will you leave him here?" If you give more than one question, pause before asking another. "Do you want to do it by yourself?. . . Or shall I help you?"

Define Rules

Great peace have they which love thy law; and nothing shall offend them."

(Psalms 119:165)

Parents need to define the limits or boundaries for toddlers. This gives the children a sense of security. They then have freedom to move within those limits. Toddlers respond better to rules stated in positive terms than to "don't" statements. Well-defined rules help children respond to government by principle, not by person. Everyone will not agree on just where the limits should be, but parents have found these to be good rules to teach toddlers, stated as you would tell them to a toddler:

- "Tables (certain furniture and kitchen counters) are not for climbing. You may climb on the climbing frame (jungle gym or special pile of cushions)."

- "We eat sitting down." This eliminates crumbs and sticky fingers throughout the house. Give the child food only when he's sitting down. If he wants to walk around with some food, state the rule, "Food stays at the table." If he persists in getting up, take the food away. There's no need to allow a child to carry a bottle or sippy cup around. It's better for him to get the idea that we sit in one place to eat. A bottle can become a comfort item if the child is allowed to carry it around. It's best not to let food become a comforter.

- "No! (Sandi) doesn't touch that." Take her hand away from the item and lead her to something she *may* touch. Certain items in the house, such as parents' drawers and desktops, electronic dials and buttons, are to be touched only by an adult. Children need to learn what they may touch and to ask before touching other items. This training will help your children be more-welcome guests when you visit the homes of others.

- "Toys and food are not for throwing; balls are for throwing." A soft ball, such as a yarn or Nerf ball, is good for throwing in the house.

- "You may have *your* telephone. *This* is for Mommy and Daddy." A real telephone may be used only by an adult or when an adult holds it to the child's ear. This will be modified when the child gets old enough to learn how to answer the telephone properly.

- "When we ride in a car, we must be in a car seat with the seat belt on." Some parents have found that children respond well when they state strongly, "It's the law."

- "We use gentle hands with our friends and animals." You'll need to demonstrate gentleness.

- "We walk on the sidewalk. Cars go in the street."

- "We hold hands crossing the street and in a parking lot." A child may have the choice of holding our hand, having us hold his hand, or being carried.

- "We stay in our own yard (unless we are with a parent or have permission to go elsewhere)."

- "We don't scream and hit to get our way. Use your words and people will listen to you."

Teach Rules and Redirect the Toddler

Children learn more by action than by word. Showing them how to follow the rules and praising right behavior teaches them better than telling them what *not* to do.

A parent was having trouble getting garden work done because her fourteen-month-old daughter, Teri, kept running out of the yard and needed to be brought back. The mom was advised to teach the child the boundaries of her yard. So every time they went outside together, she took her around the boundaries of the yard saying, "This is Teri's yard. This is where you can play." She stayed close to Teri and praised her for knowing and playing in her yard. If Teri started to head across the boundary, she led her back saying, "No, Teri doesn't go in the neighbor's yard. She stays in Teri's yard." If Teri was determined to cross the line again, her mom brought her into the house. Since Teri loved to be outside, this was a disappointment, and tears sometimes resulted. Her mom comforted her and said, "Next time you will stay in your yard." The next time they went out, the boundaries were taught in the same way. Within days, Teri stayed in the yard while mom did her gardening. However, adult presence, if not direct supervision, was still needed whenever her young toddler was outside.

This parent's experience is an example of how it pays, in the long run, to take the time to teach the rules. Also, parents report that they get more work done when they take time periodically to play with or read to the child, and to comment on how well the child is playing, than if they wait until the child demands attention.

Most rules can be taught as Teri's boundaries were. Always tell and show your child what he *may* do, not just what he shouldn't do. Give him some coaching and provide the opportunity to practice appropriate behavior. Praise him for doing the right thing. If he persists in disobeying the rule, you may need to either remove the temptation by limiting his access to the forbidden item or find a consequence that will teach him it's better to follow the rules. Praising appropriate behavior will lessen the need to correct misbehavior.

Give Appropriate Choices

Children seek independence, and they should be given appropriate choices in order to feel some control over their lives. The choices of a toddler should be well-defined and limited. At first, two acceptable choices may be given. For instance:

> "Do you want to ride in a stroller or walk holding my hand?"
>
> "Would you like peanut butter and jelly or an egg-salad sandwich for lunch?"
>
> "Would you like carrots or celery to munch?"
>
> "These two shirts go with those pants. Which shirt would you like to wear?"

Global choices—such as "What do you want to wear?" or "What do you want for lunch?"—can be overwhelming and lead to argument. A child shouldn't have to make choices at every turn but should have charge of certain areas of his life such as, "Which of your toys are you going to play with?" or "How much do you want to eat?"

If your child asks for an unacceptable alternative, say, "I know you would like to . . . , but that's not a choice."

Watch Your Tone of Voice

When disciplining your child, work to use a no-nonsense tone of voice—not shouting or angry—but firm. Listen to your voice as you talk to your child. It may help to record it. Toddlers can always sense if you are indecisive about your request or if you are not convinced that they will obey. Your expectancy that they can and will do the right thing will carry over in your demeanor and tone of voice. Your tone of voice when you playfully say, "I'm going to get you!" should be very different than when you say, "Chris! Come now!"

Your tone of voice should reflect your confidence that you are making a right request. If a parent inwardly sympathizes with a child's desires, the child often continues to whine and cry to get his way. When an older sister wanted to play with her toddler brother's new toy, the parent half-heartedly told her it was her brother's and that he wanted to play with it. The sister continued to try to have her way, as the parent struggled with indecision, until a big scene with tears emerged. The parent should have said, "Your brother is playing with his new toy. You may not touch it until he is all through with it and brings it to you for a turn. You have the same right to play with your new toys. You may find another toy to play with here, or you may go to your room to play by yourself until your brother is ready to give you a turn." If the whining and fussing were to continue, the parent then should enforce the room option.

Be Consistent

If a child is corrected consistently, he will learn the rules much faster than if he's allowed to get by with misbehavior one time and not another. Discuss your expectations with others who are caring for your child and, insofar as possible, come to agreement on those expectations and how to enforce them.

Some of your child's new, mischievous discoveries and capabilities may seem amazing or cute at first, and you may fail to stop them until you see that they are inappropriate. But it helps to establish the rules as soon as possible. Your child may love the effect of turning on the TV or turning the dials of the VCR. Tell him, "No, that's not for (Jamie)" and take him to a toy that has dials he may turn, such as a busy surprise box. Tell him that he may turn his dials, and give him affirmation when he does it.

Take Action

Telling your child what *not* to do or what *to* do is of little value unless you see that he does the right thing. Vigilance and action are needed on the part of the parent. Your child will learn what your words mean by the action you take.

If redirecting doesn't do the trick, changing the location of a toddler is a good way to let him know that it's better to obey rules than to break them. If he throws his food from the high chair, he can be taken down from the high chair and the meal ended. If he pulls the dog's tail after being shown how the dog likes his "gentle hands," he can be put into a play yard, or behind a gate away from the dog, for a brief time. At first, just 30 seconds to a minute after he starts to show his unhappiness should be enough. Then show him again how to pet the dog gently. These should be consequences, not punishment. Speak in a matter-of-fact way. Don't get angry or give long explanations. When you go to your child, give him a hug and remind him of what he will do next time.

If your daughter opens a forbidden drawer (or does any other inappropriate activity), you'll have to take her away from that drawer as you say, "Not for Sally. Here is *your* drawer to open," and take her to *her* drawer. Be sure to show your approval when she does the right thing. "Good. You're opening *your* drawer and finding your toys to play with." Sometimes you'll feel like ignoring misbehavior because it seems easier than helping a child obey, but in the long run, consistency is easier because the child learns faster. Repetition is needed for learning to take place, and some persistent children seem to require more repetition than others.

If Sally goes back to the drawer for the fourth or fifth time after consistent redirection, she may be enjoying your attention. If you think this is the case, you may need to put her for a short time in a location where she will not be able to get to the drawer. Put up a gate (or playpen) to keep her away from the drawer *and you*. Tell her "No!" when she opens the forbidden drawer, and put her behind the gate, turning away from her until she starts to fuss. Then after a few minutes, let her come back. Take her again to the drawer she may open, telling her, "This is Sally's drawer. You may open this one."

After you have taught your toddler the rules consistently, there comes a time when you need to expect that he will obey. As a mother saw her son going back to a forbidden drawer after much teaching, she was about to correct him again, but intuition held her back. She waited and didn't let him know she was watching. He opened the drawer a little way, told himself "no," and closed it again. We can trust that our children can listen to the "still, small voice," as well as *we* can.

Replace Crying and Whining

"Weeping may endure for a night, but joy cometh in the morning."

Psalms 30:5

Don't allow your toddler's crying to sway you from doing what you know is best for him. Remember that a year ago, cries were your baby's major form of communication. It's not unusual for him still to cry to convey his wants. If he wants something he shouldn't have, simply stick to your decision, and don't allow him to have it. Help him learn to use words for legitimate requests. Stay calm when he cries, whines, or screams for something. In a quiet voice, try to verbalize what he wants with a question. "Drink of water?" "Read a book?" Then, when he quiets and makes an attempt to say a word, or nods affirmatively, respond to his request. A good word to teach him to say is "please." He can learn that an attempt to say "please" brings him what he needs faster than a cry or whine. When he brings objects to you, if you say "thank you," he will pick up on those words as well. When he sees that crying doesn't get him what he wants, and words do, he'll soon replace the disagreeable sounds with words.

If the child continues to cry with anger over not getting what he wants, you can put him in his room or crib "to gain his control." Assure him that when he has found his control, he can come back to be with you. As soon as he quiets, ask him if he's ready and let him rejoin the family.

I smiled when I heard a "toddler" cardinal bird in our yard. It was just out of its nest and flying from place to place with a raucous "chi, chi, chi." I could imagine its parents sighing and asking, "Why is my baby so noisy? All the cats in the neighborhood will hear it!" But the parent birds were following and feeding it, teaching it to find food for itself and to flee danger. How like the toddler cardinal is a noisy human toddler. Human parents also need to patiently meet the needs until the toddler learns the language and more mature ways of behaving.

Security and Comfort Items

Children often latch onto an object of some sort to give them a sense of security or comfort. Whether this is a thumb, pacifier, blanket, diaper, stuffed animal, or other toy, it is a symbol of comfort to the child. The child may want to use these comforts as transitional objects when going from a familiar person or place to an unfamiliar one. When a toddler must leave the primary caregiver, he may find it a help to have his familiar comfort item at hand. As the child matures, learns that his parent *does* come back, and gains social skills, he becomes ready to give up the security item.

It's possible, if you feel your child is ready, to teach him that the blanket or pacifier stays in the bed or car. Whether you do this or not will depend on the apparent need your child has for the item in other settings. One family kept their child's pacifier in a basket on the dresser for use at bedtime only. The child gained motivation for going to bed and enjoyed that nighttime comfort as long as it was needed.

Some parents get overly concerned by these objects and wonder when the child will ever give them up. It's best not to add your worries to your child's by periodically taking away, nagging, or teasing him about his comfort item. You can trust your child's maturity to come forth at the appropriate time.

Sometimes a parent will hold on to the need for a comfort item after the child is ready to give it up. When we were on a long trip, one of our sons left his beloved snuggly in a motel. We had traveled half a day before we discovered its absence. I didn't know how he could get along without it. We called to ask the motel to send it to our home. Our son shed a few tears over it that night and the next, but soon forgot about it. When the snuggly came in the mail several days later, the need for it was gone.

Discipline Problem Solving

Parents are usually full of questions about how to handle current discipline problems: "My son has started biting when he plays with his friends." "My daughter is squeezing her baby brother too tightly when she plays with him." "Our toddler takes forever to eat (or dress)." "Our daughter always seems to get into mischief when I'm on the phone." "We can't get our son to go to bed." "What should we do?"

I developed a problem-solving method that has helped parents resolve such problems. When an inappropriate behavior has been repeated, you can ask these four questions and talk over answers with other caregivers involved.

1. **What needs to be learned?**

   Since discipline is learning, there is always something to be learned when a problem develops.

2. **What are the spiritual facts?**

   Taking the time to think through these facts prayerfully can lead more directly to a solution of the problem.

3. **What rules should be established?**

   Seeing what rules should govern the situation helps both parent and child realize that principle, rather than human will, is in control.

4. **What action should we take to teach the needed lesson?**

   Now we're ready to look for the action that will bring forth the solution.

Of course, the problem-solving method can't be used in the heat of a difficulty.

But if a misbehavior is becoming a repeated problem, take the time, when you have a few minutes, to think through answers to the questions. Do it either by yourself, with your spouse, or with any other involved caregiver. You'll find that, as the learning takes place, the misbehavior disappears.

Let's look at some of the answers that can be found to these questions with two of the discipline problems mentioned above. You can think of other answers.

For the child who is biting:

1. What needs to be learned?
- He needs to know what he *may* bite.
- He needs to know that biting hurts and that we don't hurt others.
- He needs to learn how to communicate and play with friends.
- He needs to learn what to do instead of biting when he feels frustrated.
- *We* may need to learn to watch the play more carefully and teach social skills.

2. What are the spiritual facts?
- Our son is governed by Love.
- It's natural for him to love his friends and not want to hurt them.
- He has the God-given strength to control his actions.
- He has the intelligence to learn beneficial interactions.
- We have the ability and patience to monitor and correct his behavior.

3. What rules should be established?

- Teeth are for biting food only.
- We love our friends and never hurt them.
- We use words to let others know how we feel.

4. What action should we take?

- Watch our son closely when he's with other children, and try to prevent him from biting. Show him ways of communicating if he is becoming frustrated.
- If he bites, hold him away with one hand while comforting the bitten child with the other. Then include him in the comforting process.
- Tell him that we wouldn't let anyone hurt him, and we won't let him hurt another.
- Take him to the refrigerator and give him a large, peeled carrot to bite. Tell him that he may bite food, not people.

For the daughter who gets into mischief when parents are on the telephone:

1. What needs to be learned?

- That parents need to talk on the phone without disturbance.
- That certain times are better than others for getting a parent's attention; when they are talking on the phone is not one of them.
- That children can entertain themselves when their parents are busy.
- Parents may need to learn not to make long phone calls when their children need supervision.

2. What are the spiritual facts?

- God's children are not in conflict but work together.

Growing Independence and Discipline

- Our daughter has the capability of entertaining herself.
- She can feel love without constant attention.
- She is being governed by Love.

3. What rules should be established?
- We listen to God and do the right thing all the time—even when our parents are on the telephone.
- We find something to play with when parents are on the phone.
- If we have an important need and parents are on the phone, we can go to them and hold their hand until they can talk to us.
- Parents should save long phone calls for times when children are not needing supervision.

4. What action should we take?
- Have a toy telephone and/or basket of special toys put away that can be brought out when parents are on the phone.
- Talk to our child to let her know what to do when we're on the phone. Practice by pretending that the phone is ringing and letting our daughter show what she'll do. Praise her for remembering how to cooperate while parents are on the phone.
- Keep phone conversations short when children are around.
- At a time when the child will enjoy it, sing this song to the tune of "The bear went over the mountain."

When Mommy's on the telephone,

When Mommy's on the telephone,

When Mommy's on the telephone, I play by myself.

And what do you think I do? And what do you think I do?

I play with my kitchen things. I play with my kitchen things.

I play with my kitchen things, . . . when Mommy's on the phone.

(*Can be sung replacing "Daddy" for "Mommy" and using child's ideas for the play.)

You might plan a time to go out to dinner with your spouse, or have a special time at home after the children are in bed, to work through current discipline problems using the above questions. Remember to never discuss children's behavior with another in their presence. You could also work through the questions yourself when children are napping. If the misbehavior arises again, you'll be prepared to act purposefully, rather than react to the situation. The needed learning will take place and behavior will change.

"I Can Do It By Myself"

Some children push for independence before we think they're ready for the next step. Others are laid back and wait for us to encourage them and to give them the responsibility. Likewise, children can resist some steps of progress and relish others.

After one of our sons was potty-trained, he wanted me to continue to pull up his pants. For awhile, I pulled up the back and asked him to pull up the front. But finally, when I knew he could easily accomplish the task, I would busy myself with other duties and leave him to do the job by himself. He protested at first but soon discovered his own capability. This same son wanted a two-wheel bike with training wheels when he was three-and-a-half. He wanted it badly enough to show his maturity by stopping his thumb sucking. After he was given the bike, he wasted no time in learning to ride it.

It's not always easy to know what responsibilities to pass on to our children as they mature. We all know parents who give children too much freedom too soon and others who hold the reins tighter than necessary. Prayer for guidance usually gives the right answer at the right time. Some parents have found that a self-help checklist is useful in knowing when children might be ready for a new task. Children are so individual that they can differ greatly in readiness. But here is a list that might give some ideas of when to try certain activities.

Babies under one-year-old may:
- ❑ Reach for toys and bottle
- ❑ Direct the bottle by pulling it toward the mouth or pushing it away
- ❑ Hold out arms to be picked up and for dressing
- ❑ Go to sleep without assistance
- ❑ Drink from cup held by you
- ❑ Feed self with fingers
- ❑ Hold sippy cup with two hands and drink
- ❑ Put spoon to mouth with help

From one to two years a toddler may:
- ❑ Eat table food with a spoon and small fork by self
- ❑ Hold and drink from a regular cup with two hands
- ❑ Retrieve specific items when asked
- ❑ Put on a hat and take it off
- ❑ Pull socks and shoes off
- ❑ Push arms through sleeves and legs through pants
- ❑ Take off coat when unfastened
- ❑ Take off pants
- ❑ Zip and unzip large zipper once started
- ❑ Climb on and off of a spring horse or riding toy

A two-year-old may:
- ❑ Wipe hands and face with towel
- ❑ Brush teeth in imitation
- ❑ Use a straw to suck liquid

- ❑ Scoop with a fork
- ❑ Put on shoes
- ❑ Use potty when taken
- ❑ Use stool to get drink from the faucet
- ❑ Wash hands and face when adult regulates water
- ❑ Place coat on hook within reach
- ❑ Use napkin when reminded
- ❑ Wash own arms and legs in bath
- ❑ Put on socks
- ❑ Put on coat, sweater, shirt
- ❑ Carry a plate of food or drink without spilling (small amounts)

Sometimes a child will balk at a task he has been doing for awhile, and a parent may wonder why. He may want to be carried when he is capable of walking or be undressed when he can do it himself. Sometimes children fear that independence will bring them less attention, especially if there is a younger sibling. When baby sister needs to be nursed and have diapers changed, an older sibling may want to revert to diapers. The attention that only an older child can enjoy usually makes such trials short-lived.

Instead of chiding an older daughter for acting like a baby and telling her she's a big girl, you can look for opportunities to rejoice in her maturity. Here are some examples: "I'm so glad I have a big girl to share this book with." "I'm glad I have a big girl to help me with our baby." "See how our baby loves his big sister! He watches everything you do." "I bet our baby wishes she could swing and climb like you do. She'll be able to play with you when she gets bigger."

Prevent Problems

A little foresight and the expectation of good behavior can prevent many problems. Here are some ideas to help maintain your family's peace:

- Match your expectations of your child with his capabilities. Can he be involved with an activity or outing for as long as you are expecting without eating, sleeping, or playing? You may need to cut an activity short to keep it within his limits. A walk outside or around the lobby of a restaurant while food is being prepared might help your toddler to sit for a longer time after the food arrives. Be sure your child will have some food he enjoys, and don't linger too long over the dinner.

- Remember your toddler is curious and needs to be active. Take along interesting toys or provide activities when you are going to be where none are available. (See **Traveling with Babies and Young Children,** Chapter Nine.)

- Let your child know ahead of time what to expect—where she will be going and what she will do. Think through what rules will be needed and teach them to her. For instance: "You're going to be sitting in the cart in the grocery store and can watch to see what I buy. You may put some of the packages in the cart (or click a counter, or eat a box of raisins)." Here's another instance: "We're going to Aunt Hettie's house. She has lots of precious things that are to look at, but not to touch. When you look at her precious things, you'll remember not to touch. We'll take a bag of toys for you to play with."

- Remember to state rules and requests in a positive form. Children seem to hear only the words that follow "don't" and ignore the word itself. For instance: "You're being careful the way you hold your glass" works better than "Don't spill your milk." "Use your gentle hands" is better than "Don't hurt your friends." "Crayons stay at your table" works better than "Don't draw on the furniture."

- Each day, prayerfully acknowledge the goodness of your child as God's child. It will help you to treat him accordingly, and he will act the part.

꽃

12

Eating, Sleeping, and Toilet Training

Most questions about a toddler's discipline center around the topics of eating, sleeping, or toilet training. These areas needn't become battlegrounds. Some common questions are: How do I get my toddler to eat? to finish a meal? to try new foods? to stop playing with the food? How do I get my toddler to go to bed? to go to sleep? to stay in bed? When and how do I toilet train my child? These three areas of discipline are most challenging because they are the areas in which the child has the last word—the ultimate control. We can't make him eat, sleep, or eliminate. The need is to gain the child's cooperation and lead him to achieve socially acceptable habits.

Avoid Eating Problems

The meek shall eat and be satisfied.

Psalms 22:26

Food is evidence of Love's supply. It stands for goodness, and we want our children to be receptive to good. Food is not the source of life, and we're not responsible for keeping our children alive by making them eat. They have been given life, hunger to eat, and the ability to know when they're full. We have the ability to provide good food at appropriate times and to respond to our children's needs.

Children's growth slows down after their first year and so do their appetites. They don't need as much food as they did during their previous rapid growth. This is the time that parents often make the mistake of worrying about the amount of food a child eats, with the possible result of initiating meal-time battles. Trust your toddler's ability to know how much food he needs to eat. If a parent urges a child to eat or goes back to feeding him to get in "one more bite," the child may further resist eating and allow the parent to usurp his normal responsibility for eating.

Meal times should remain happy and stress-free. The goal is for the child to be receptive to eating. The parent should be responsible for providing a balanced variety of good foods for the child and establishing a regular time and place for eating. The child should have the responsibility of deciding how much and which of the foods offered to eat. Most toddlers are ready and willing to feed themselves. Give them finger foods. They soon learn that some foods, such as hot cereal, soup, or pudding, can't be picked up with fingers and that a spoon works better. Present the food as good, rather than "good for you," and offer it in an appealing form. Try to have something you are sure your child will eat at each meal, though children's tastes may be fickle. They may love a food one day and turn it down the next. They may eat a lot of food at one meal and little at another. Serve small amounts of food, and allow children to request further helpings. Give your toddler a small amount of milk in a cup so he can learn to drink it by himself without spilling. Then give refills as needed.

If your child rejects a food, encourage him to take a bite, but never force the issue. You might ask, "Can you take two bites or one?" If he continues to reject the food, don't push. Let him see you enjoy it, and tell him that he'll like it when he gets bigger. Don't take his dislikes as final, but keep presenting foods in different, appealing ways. You don't have to become a short-order cook. Present some foods you think your child will like along with ones he doesn't care for, and let him eat what he wants; then have him wait until the next scheduled meal. A little hunger does wonders for picky eaters. You can schedule a small snack of wholesome food between main meals if you feel it's necessary. Limit the availability of non-nutritious sweets so the child doesn't substitute them for nutritious foods.

Desserts should not be offered as rewards for eating other foods.

That will cause the dessert to become the preferred food and will promote resistance to the required food. You can give an amount of dessert proportionate to the amount of other food eaten without threatening it as a reward. This can help a child regulate his appetite and learn about what makes a balanced meal.

The consequence for not eating or for bad behavior at the table, such as throwing or dropping food, is a simple one. Remove the food and ask, "Are you all through?" If you get a negative response, you can give the food back. But if the misbehavior is repeated, simply say, "I see you're all through," and take your child down from the high chair or table, giving no more chances and offering no more food until the next meal. This can be done without anger and in a matter-of-fact way.

If your child is given his responsibility for eating and is offered a variety of good foods in a nonpressured atmosphere, meal times will be harmonious, and your child will eat what he needs.

There is an exception to the usual eating guidelines given here. If a child's appetite should take a precarious dip, as when recovering from an illness, it may be necessary to give small amounts of food the child will eat about every three hours until the appetite is built up again. This procedure was needed with one of our sons and also with my niece. In each case, they were given Instant Breakfast mixed with milk about four times a day until they were feeling stronger and their appetites for regular foods returned. There are some canned, balanced-food supplements on the market that could work as well.

Food for Toddlers

Here is a list of foods to try:

Finger Foods

Toddlers enjoy the independence of eating by themselves. Before a child has the skill to use utensils, eating with fingers is a good way to gain this independence. As your toddler sees you eating with utensils, he'll want to develop that skill, and you can give him opportunities to use utensils successfully. Here are some finger foods you might like to try:

Fruits—cut into appropriate sizes

Apples, peeled and raw or cooked
Banana
Blueberries
Canned fruit and fruit cocktail
Canned Mandarin oranges
Cantaloupe
Dried fruits softened by soaking in a little hot water or chopped
Figs
Grapefruit sections
Grapes, halved or quartered
Kiwi, peeled
Oranges, sectioned
Peaches, peeled
Pears
Plums
Strawberries, halved
Sweet cherries, halved and pitted
Watermelon

Vegetables

Cooked asparagus tips
Ripe avocado
Steamed broccoli (plain or with mayonnaise dressing dip)
Carrots, steamed or grated
Cooked cauliflower (plain or with cheese dip)
Celery, with strings removed
Cooked green beans
Shredded lettuce
Cooked mushrooms
Slightly cooked green peas (Many two-year-olds like frozen peas.)
Potatoes, mashed, French fries, or oven baked
Cooked squash, zucchini and yellow
Tomatoes, peeled

Meats

Beef roast, sliced thin or ground
Crisp bacon
Chicken or beef liver
Chicken or turkey, diced or sliced very thin
Frankfurters cut in small pieces that could not cause choking
Ham, cut into bite-sized pieces

Hamburger, meatballs, or meatloaf pieces
Lamb
Luncheon meats
Tuna
Cooked turkey, sliced thin or ground
Veal

Dairy

Cottage cheese (add fruit, or blend and make into dip, or serve on
   crackers)
Cream cheese on cracker or bagel
Eggs, scrambled, hard-boiled and deviled, omelets
Mild cheese—small pieces or grated

Breads

Arrowroot cookies
Bagels
Biscuits
Bread pudding
Breads—white or dark
Cereals, hot or cold, unsweetened varieties (with or without milk)
Cooked pasta, different shapes and colors (noodles, macaroni,
   spaghetti, ravioli, and many others)
Cookies
Corn bread
Crackers
French toast fingers
Graham crackers—plain or with peanut butter
Milk toast
Pretzels—without excess salt
Sandwiches—egg salad, lunch meat, tuna or chicken salad, peanut
   butter and jelly, and many more
Toast strips, with a little butter
Zwieback

Other Toddler Foods

Drinks

A 15-month-old can drink from a cup, rotating it with wrists,
but will have spills. By 21 months, most children can handle

drinks without spills. Help your toddler put the cup down away from the edge of the table to prevent it from being knocked over.

Milk
Fruit juice
Milk and fruit juice blends
Eggnog
Smoothies—blend varying combinations of milk, juice, banana, and yogurt with frozen fruit

Spoon foods

Start with a child's spoon. It's common for children under 24 months to spill food from a spoon. Practice will bring neater eating skills.

Casseroles of meat or fish, vegetables, and pasta
Cereal with fruit
Cooked, chopped spinach
Custards or puddings
Eggs (soft-cooked, baked with milk, creamed hard boiled)
Gelatins
Ice cream
Junket
Soups
Puddings, including tapioca or rice pudding
Yogurt (plain or vanilla, or mixed with baby fruits)

Maintain a Bedtime Routine

"I will lie down and sleep in peace, for you alone, O LORD, make me dwell in safety."

Psalms 4:8[12]

Sleep is an activity that is allowed, not mandated. You can mentally place your children in their Father-Mother God's arms as you put them to bed. They will feel the sense of peace you establish in thought. If you've given your child the responsibility of comforting himself to sleep,

---

[12] New International Version

as described earlier in this book (p. 88), he will probably continue having peaceful bedtimes. Most children test the bedtime rules at some point, however.

If Mom and Dad early start taking turns putting a child to bed, the child is less likely to become prejudiced about who puts him to bed. Children can show preferences from time-to-time, but if both parents remain good-natured about it, they can each come into favor and enjoy that special time of sharing with their children.

It's good to have a short, regular routine before bed, which can include potty, brushing teeth, and a hug and kiss. But it may also include a bath, a game or story, and a prayer. A routine shows your child that bedtime is on its way and helps him settle into readiness for rest and quiet. Let your child have some choices within the routine, such as which book to read or which way to go to bed (tip toe, gallop, creep like a cat, or be carried). You can tell him that he may decide *when* he wants to go to sleep, since that is his choice anyway. But the rule is to stay in bed when it's bedtime. You should determine the time for bed and the length of the routine.

Many bedtime problems are solved simply by realizing that the child needs less rest and should go to bed later or have a shorter afternoon nap. In other cases, perhaps the child is too stimulated by an exciting evening or extended bedtime.

If fear of being separated from you or fear of the dark seems to be an issue, providing a tape with your voice or a night light might make a helpful transition. You can also talk to your child about how to pray for himself to feel God's love and presence.

When your child learns to climb out of bed, simply take him back and tell him to stay in his bed and to call you when he awakens and is ready to get up. As you establish this rule, choose a time to let him practice calling you and having you come in. You can let him call you once at bedtime to show you how he will call in the morning and how you will come in, but tell him that you won't need to come in again at bedtime. Don't give in to the common requests for another drink of water, more potty, or another story. Those needs have already been met, and the appeals for more, no matter how they tug at your heartstrings, are just for more attention. If you respond to "just one more," you will perpetuate the tactics.

Tell your child, if you wish, that because he stays in bed so well he may choose whether to have the night light on, the door open, or to listen to a tape. If he gets out of bed, you can remove one of those privileges. Tell him that you will listen, and if he's staying in bed, you will soon return and restore the privilege. If he gets out of bed again, tell him that he may not have the privilege back again this night, but he may show you how he will stay in bed so that he can have it again tomorrow night.

Some toddlers go from a crib to a junior bed or a mattress on the floor. Others go directly to a single bed. When you think your child is ready for the change, appeal to his maturity. Tell him that he is ready to sleep in a big bed and that means he knows how to stay in bed. Some parents like to keep the crib up until their children have demonstrated that they can stay in the big bed.

Bedtime can be a special time to review the day with gratitude. It can include prayer and an opportunity to talk of God's love and presence. Our children liked to tell the "happiest thing that happened today." Your child can learn to look forward to bedtime and settle into a peaceful sleep.

Toilet Training

"Thou hast possessed my reins: thou hast covered me in my mother's womb. I will praise thee; for I am fearfully and wonderfully made:"

Psalms 139:13,14 [to :]

Toilet training is not a difficult process. Some authors on the subject call it "toilet learning" rather than "toilet training," but it is truly a training process. The parent knows what the outcome will be and trains the child to eliminate in the socially acceptable way—by using the toilet. The discovery method of learning doesn't work well when training is needed. Waiting for the child to discover the toilet and decide to use it can postpone the process needlessly.

Your attitude and readiness for toilet training is as important as your child's. Be ready to focus your thought on helping your child. Choose a time when you can be home with your child for consecutive days. Look for his readiness for this step and be ready to respond to it with support. There's no need to rush the process before readiness is there, nor to postpone it unnecessarily. Address your own thought prayerfully to remove any fears or concerns about toilet training.

See cooperation as natural and expect it. Your manner should be matter-of-fact. Rejoice in your child's success, but avoid *excessive* praise for accomplishment or disappointment with failure. Excessive praise or reprimand can put pressure on the child and cause resistance.

There's no significant difference between boys and girls in toilet training. There are many different methods of toilet training that work, and you can determine what will work best for you and your child. The goal is to gain your child's interest and cooperation in the process. Expect harmony and success. Here are some ideas. You can choose or modify the ones that best fit your own and your child's needs.

Readiness

You can prepare a child for toilet training in a number of ways:

- Let him see other members of the family using the toilet.
- Tell him that he will use the toilet when he gets bigger and that he will wear big-boy (or she will wear big-girl) pants instead of a diaper.
- Talk to him matter-of-factly when you change a diaper about how his diaper is wet or dirty and how you are putting on a dry or clean one.
- If you see him straining to have a movement, tell him what he's doing. Use the words you want him to use (BM, poop, etc.)

If you have been catching your baby's movements on the toilet (see p. 104), he is probably already also urinating in the toilet at those times. He has gotten used to the toilet, but you still need to focus on toilet training when he is ready to keep his diapers dry. If you haven't caught his movements, you can do so whenever he's cooperative. If you can't catch his movements, just wait until you see readiness for urine training and proceed with that first.

The following signs of readiness may appear around the age of two or later:

- Your child is able to keep his diaper dry for two hours or more, unless he drinks a lot of liquids.
- He shows that he is aware of when he is urinating or having a movement in his diaper.
- He becomes interested in watching when other family members use the toilet.
- It's best to choose a time for toilet training when he's generally cooperative and not frequently acting contrary to assert his independence.

Using cloth diapers or training pants helps the child feel when he is wet. If you've been using disposable diapers, you might switch to cloth diapers, if you have them, when you start thinking of toilet training. Keep your child in cloth diapers until he has had some success at using the toilet. Then put him in heavy training pants so he will feel it even more when he wets and so the pants can be taken down easily. If you don't have cloth diapers, you can go directly to heavy training pants.

Wearing "big-girl (or -boy) pants" can be an encouragement, and they're easy to get on and off. You may want to put plastic pants over training pants, unless the child is outside or play is confined to a floor that can be mopped. If a child feels the dampness or makes a puddle, he may readily make the connection between his action and the result. Disposable diapers or pull-ups don't help with diaper training because they are designed so that the child won't feel the dampness.

For ease of training, dress your child in outer pants that will be easy to get on and off. Pants with elastic waistbands are better than overalls or pants with belts and zippers.

Method Using Child's Seat That Fits On Regular Toilet

Many parents prefer a seat that fits on a regular toilet because you don't have to empty and clean a small pot, the child uses the same toilet he sees you using, and flushing is often an incentive.

Get a small, comfortable toilet seat that fits securely on the regular toilet seat. A boy's seat will have a guard in front. Show the seat to your child and tell him what it's for. There's not much point in having your child sit on it with his clothes on to get used to it unless he shows fear of it, which is unusual. The first goal is to get your child to sit on it when he can succeed at urinating there. When your child wakes up dry in the morning or after a nap, sit him on his toilet seat and tell him what a big boy he is to sit on the potty. Tell him he's going to tinkle (trickle, pee, urinate) in the potty, and listen with him. You can run a little water in the sink or tub, as the sound sometimes helps to release the urine. Giving him a drink of water might help. You may sit with him and look at a book. The extra attention at this time may add to his willingness to cooperate.

On the other hand, if you think your child might be purposely holding back when you are there, you can tell him that you have to do something or get something in another room. Tell him you'll be right back. Then give him a few minutes alone, staying within listening range to see if he uses the potty successfully.

Have him sit about five minutes or until he is successful (no more than ten minutes). If he gets restless or fussy, take him off. If he uses the toilet, say something like, "Good! You're tinkling (or doing B.M.) in the potty. What a big boy (or girl)!" Then wipe. (Show a girl how to wipe from front to back.) Say, "Now you can flush the toilet!" Most young children love this example of cause-effect. Generally, if you don't wait too long, there won't be fears connected with the toilet. If the child doesn't use the toilet, say something like, "I guess you don't need to go, now? We can try again another time."

Tell him he will keep his pants dry by using the potty. Keep track of the time, and have your toddler try to use the toilet again just before snack time or before or after lunch—about every one-and-a-half or two hours. While the tub fills before a bath is a good time to try too. If your child has just wet, there's no point in putting him on the toilet, since success at eliminating on the toilet is what you're looking for. From time to time, comment about your child's dry pants. "You're keeping your pants dry. Don't they feel good."

If he wets, don't scold or make a big deal about it. Just say, "Uh oh! You wet your pants. We'll get dry ones. Next time you can do it on the potty."

At first, don't ask if he needs to use the potty. You are likely to get a "No!" Instead, say, "It's time to use the potty again." Or make up a song to sing as you take him to the toilet. Be consistent until the toilet habit is established.

If you meet strong resistance that doesn't dissolve with loving encouragement, maintain your cool, back off, and wait for another time.

Method Using a Small Toilet Seat Chair

This method is outlined in many books on the market. It can work best if your child is older (around three) and/or very independent.

Get a small toilet seat chair that your son or daughter can sit on comfortably. Introduce it to the bathroom a couple of weeks before you plan to start toilet training, when you are seeing signs of readiness. Tell your child that this is his potty seat, and he can use it as you use the big toilet. Let him sit on it, if he wants to, while you are in the bathroom. Let him pretend his doll or stuffed animal is going potty, if he wishes.

Proceed much as in the former method, taking him to use the potty to keep his big-boy pants dry. Show him how to pull down his pants and sit on the potty. Then show him how to empty the potty into the big toilet.

After he gets the idea of using his potty, you can talk to him about using it when he feels he needs to. Go with him, if he prefers, but you can encourage his independence.

Extra Tips

After your child is successful at using the toilet, you will still need to take the initiative, in most cases, by telling or reminding your child to use the toilet. The habit needs to become well established before the child is reliable about knowing when to go on his own. He may get absorbed in his play and not want the break. Also, it's good for you to ask him to use the toilet before you go out or start an activity that you don't want to have interrupted. If the child says he doesn't need to go, you can say, "You don't *have* to go, but you need to *try* before we go out."

Children are better prepared for preschool if they are able to use the toilet at a time scheduled, or suggested, by an adult.

Teach your children the good habit of washing their hands after going to the toilet. A song you can sing, making up your own melody, is: "First we go to the toilet. And then we wash our hands."

Children can soon learn to sit on the regular toilet seat after becoming toilet trained. Show your child how to balance, holding on to the seat. Boys may feel secure sitting on the regular seat facing backwards. They have fewer accidents this way, bending over and holding on to the back of the seat. The disadvantage of this position is the need to take his pants all the way off to spread the legs far enough apart. Other positions to teach boys are to sit facing forward by leaning forward and holding down the penis or to sit at the very back of the seat leaning forward. When boys get tall enough, they can stand (on a sturdy block at first) to urinate.

Nighttime Reliability

When children are toilet trained during the day, some will also stop wetting at night. It's best to keep a diaper on them at night until you are certain of their reliability. When they can stay dry at night, they can go to training pants, and then to just their night clothes.

Some children sleep so soundly that they continue to wet at night. Put them in diapers and let them know that when they keep the diapers dry at night, they will be ready to wear "big-child pants." Put no shame on them for wetting at night. Let them know they have control, are doing well during the day, and will soon be able to stay dry at night as well.

If your child is still wetting at night when he is around four, you may want to take such measures as limiting the number of drinks before bedtime or getting the child up to use the toilet before you go to bed. A night light or flashlight may encourage him to get up to use the toilet by himself in the night. If you think a little extra incentive will help, you can make a chart entitled "Harry's (name of child) Dry Bed Chart." Let him put a sticker on the chart every time he wakes up dry. Don't chide him if he doesn't get a sticker, and retire the chart without comment if he's having more failure than success.

Resistance

If you meet great resistance to toilet training, you may need to back off for a time and give the child the choice of wearing diapers or underpants. If he or she chooses to wear diapers, say, "All right. Maybe you will feel like a big boy (or girl) tomorrow." Then don't nag about it. Give the choice again the next day.

Sometimes it helps to give extra motivation if the child knows how to use the toilet but doesn't want to. Often children don't want to be bothered with the interruption to their play. It helps to make toilet time part of the routine before or after snacks or meals. If extra motivation is needed, some children respond favorably to putting a sticker on a chart every time they go, or getting a raisin, marshmallow, or other treat. One of my sons, and later, a grandson, strongly resisted using the toilet until a plastic honey bear filled with tiny pastel candies appeared in the bathroom. I told them, as I shook the bear, that Honey Bear gives candies to children who use the toilet. One was given to older brother when he went, too, as an example. In less than a week in each case, the younger boys were trained, and the bear was retired. The satisfaction of accomplishment was then reward enough.

Learning is often a spiral affair, so don't be concerned if there are successful days and less-successful ones. Be consistent. Don't let toilet training become a battle of wills. If there is too much continuing resistance, it's better to back off, drop your own sense of will about it, and wait for the child's willingness. You can be sure he'll be trained when he starts to school. Know that control is a divinely given attribute of your child. Support his maturity with your prayers, and you will find him eager to cooperate.

ॐ

13

Blossoming Language

"I will be with thy mouth, and teach thee what thou shalt say."

Exodus 4:12

Language development is nothing short of miraculous. In less than three years, a child learns to communicate effectively with language without prior experience of decoding or producing sound. Though linguists can describe the acquisition of language, there are still unanswered questions about how a child is able to acquire it in such a short time. Major milestones in the development of language generally take place during the second year.

Adults bring meaning to the sounds a baby makes. He says "dada," and his parents get excited and say, "Yes! This is Daddy." He will later say the word more meaningfully, looking at Daddy. "Mama" comes in the same way. Spoken language generally starts with these single words being given meaning. Baby aptly chooses first words according to his interest and the sounds he is able to make. If parents name objects, people, and pictures in the baby's environment he'll pick up more words. "Ball," "dog," "bottle" may enter his vocabulary, though they may sound like "bah," "dah," and "bahbah." Parents generally do just the right thing naturally to help children learn language. They respond to the meaning of the communication rather than getting hung up on the correctness of the sound. Baby says "bah" while looking at a ball, and the parents say, "Yes that's a ball. Do you want the ball?" (They don't say, "no, it's not a bah. Say ba*ll*.") By hearing the word correctly, the child

Toddlers give toys to you to cause interaction and hear language.

eventually corrects himself and refines his speech. Constant correction by the adult can interfere with fluency of speech.

Many babies speak jargon—sounds strung together like a sentence, complete with inflections. The words are usually unintelligible, but because of the familiar-sounding inflections, you think you should be able to understand. If you speak mainly in sentences to your child, rather than labeling with single words, he may speak more jargon than words at first. He may seem to be language-delayed, but gradually he will clarify the words within the jargon, and his speech will become understandable.

Receptive Language

A child usually understands many words by the end of the first year. This is called *receptive* language and is a more significant milestone than spoken language, which can begin anywhere from eight months to two years and still be considered normal. If a child is not understanding many words you speak after twelve months, his hearing should be checked.

Your child will show you that he understands what you say by following directions. He may respond correctly to your requests: "Go get the ball," or "Take the ball to Daddy." He may get his shoes, or point to them, when you ask, "Where are your shoes?" You can ask him, "Where's Daddy?" or name other family members and see if he will look at them.

Your toddler may show you that she understands the meaning of words by pointing in books to pictures you name. She may also point to pictures, wanting you to name them. She may be an expert at mime, showing you just what she wants by her actions. She may point, take you by the hand, or gesture, to let you know what she wants. Many children whose spoken language is delayed develop such good non-verbal communication that they may think they don't need to talk. Then parents can help them see that verbal communication gets better results by responding more readily to verbal attempts than to body language. On the other hand, some parents have discovered that using sign language with a baby can facilitate earlier communication. Whatever form of communication you use, your baby will pick it up in order to communicate with you.

You can expect of your child spiritual receptivity as well as receptivity to language. Repeat some of your favorite Bible verses and prayers, and sing hymns to him at special times of closeness, such as bedtime. He will become quiet and thoughtful as he responds to your inspired thought.

Velcro Time

At some time in their second year, children frequently lose interest in playing independently with toys in favor of following the primary caregiver around. When Mom goes to another room, the toddler follows. He wants to be involved with whatever Mom is doing. He will bring objects to her and then take them back again. Whoever is the primary caregiver will receive that attention. If picture books are available, the toddler may prefer these to toys. He'll bring them to Mom or Dad and indicate that he wants to settle into a lap and hear the words in the book. After looking and listening briefly, he may toddle off again.

We have noted a dramatic change in the way children play with toys in the toy library during this time. The child's attention span appears to be much shorter than before, and we may show many toys be-fore finding ones that will engage the child. A toy that responds to a child's action with a surprising effect is now often the best choice. Single-piece puzzles may interest the toddler when the adult names the pieces as the child removes them. A child will play longer with toys at this time if the adult is involved and talking with the child.

During this time, your child may have a questioning word or sound that is repeated over and over, asking for you to name objects she points to or looks at. She may look at your mouth as you talk, and even-tually she will try to repeat the words she hears.

This phenomenon appears to be language related, and I have dubbed it "Velcro Time." It comes at a time of intense interest and growth in language development. It's natural that a child should seek closeness to the adult at this time, since language must be heard to be learned. Parents, who have been concerned that this velcro behavior might lead to overindulgence, are relieved to learn of its language con-nection. The results of my study of this behavior were reported in the article "Velcro Time: The Language Connection," *Young Children* (The Journal of the National Association for the Education of Young Children) May 1992. (See **Appendix 3**.)

Parents find that if they freely give the language that is sought dur-ing this time their child is soon saying many words. We have observed that once the child has a vocabulary that is satisfying to him interest in independent play returns.

During this demanding time, the parent or primary caregiver should talk a lot to the child. Talk about what you are doing and about what your child is doing. Continue to consistently enforce the rules and to keep your joy. If you are constantly with your child, periodically take some time for yourself away from the child. Some parents have a high school student come in for a couple of hours once or twice a week. Others leave the child with a relative or friend. Explain your child's cur-rent interest in language to the substitute caregivers.

First Sentences

Your child's first words may not sound close to the word he's trying to say, but you will notice that he makes the same sounds whenever he looks at or points to certain people or objects. You will want to stop imitating your child's sounds now and give him a correct model of language to copy. He will correct and refine his words until they are intelligible to others as well as to you.

At first, a child may put only one consonant at either the beginning or end of a word. "Dog" may be "(d)og" or "do(g)." The first two-syllable words will probably have repeated consonants such as "mama," "dada," or "bahbah" (bottle). As you let your child know you understand his words, and then say the words correctly to him, he will clarify his speech.

One word can stand for a whole sentence at first. "Cookie" might mean "I want a cookie." "Up" may mean "Pick me up." "Side" may mean "I want to go outside." The child chooses the most salient word of a sentence to convey his meaning. "Uh oh" and "No" may be early words he hears and picks up.

After using one-word sentences for awhile, your child will start putting two words together. Again, he will choose the best words to bring out the meaning. He might use a noun with a verb such as "Car go." A two-word sentence may denote possession, such as "Daddy car," or "my b(l)ankee." The child will continue to expand and clarify his sentences.

Consonant blends in words don't usually come until later so words like "p(l)ease," "b(l)ankee," and "(s)chool" will commonly be heard.

Generalization and Expanding Vocabulary

Don't be surprised if your child looks at a picture of a cow and says his word for "dog," or points to a man and says "Dada." That's called *generalization* or *extension*. It doesn't mean the child can't differentiate between animals or people, but he chooses the word in his vocabulary that most nearly fits. As he learns more words, the generalizations will disappear. You can affirm his attempt and give the correct word. "Yes, that's a *cow*." "Yes, that's a *man* like Daddy."

You can use many specific words with your child. Children are adept at differentiating between things they see and can pick up an extensive vocabulary. You don't need to be conservative with the words you use. Feel free to name specific flowers, animals, birds, and so forth. A two-year-old who lived in the country said "Guernsey," or "Holstein" rather than just "cow." To another child, flowers were "rose," "marigold," or "dandelion."

Bilingualism

If you are interested in having your child become bilingual, you may speak two languages to him, and he will learn both. This is a wonderful time for children to learn more than one language, and they are soon able to differentiate between the languages. Becoming bilingual may or may not slow him down a little in speech acquisition, but the language will come. In families where each parent can speak a different language, each can mainly use his or her own language with the child to help the child sort out the languages. But one parent may also use more than one language with the child. Sometimes a child will learn a second language from a grandparent, nanny, or au pair. Children can acquire all the inflections and phonemes of a language when they hear it spoken as a native tongue.

Communication is a key motivator for learning language, and young children quickly learn what language is understood by those to whom they want to communicate. If children are in a school or with other children who speak a different language, they will readily learn that language to communicate. I know English-speaking families where one parent has frequently (or exclusively) spoken a second language to the children for bilingualism. After the children started attending preschool, where only English was spoken, the children were reluctant to speak the second language—even to the parent whom they knew could understand English. On the other hand, I know a two-year-old who spoke a second language to her Grandmother because it was the only language her Grandmother could understand. I also know children whose families have moved from one country to another. These children have readily learned the language needed to communicate with their peers. To learn to speak a language well, it must be needed for communication. However, this shouldn't discourage parents from introducing a second language to their children. The children can learn to understand the language and will be able to speak it more readily when needed.

Rules

It's amazing how young children pick up the rules of a language. Before they can talk, they learn that we take turns in conversation and that we use eye contact. Some of the mistakes children make in language are due to the fact that they know the rules and are generalizing them. For instance, they might say "She *goed* to the store," knowing that you add "ed" for past tense. Similarly a child might say, "My *foots* are cold," or "The dog *runned* away." As children learn the exceptions to the rules, that kind of mistake is corrected.

Language blossoms as you talk to a child face-to-face.

Encouraging Language

Use clear, not-too-fast speech when speaking to your child, but don't overly exaggerate. Be sure to use single words, naming objects your child is looking at, as well as whole sentences.

Talk to your child about what you are doing and about what he is doing. Talking to a child before he can speak isn't easy for some parents, but it's essential to bring forth the child's language.

It's important to be a good listener as your child learns to communicate. Some parents are excellent listeners. They stoop, squat, or sit to be at the child's level and look him in the eye. Then they listen carefully to what he says and try to verify the words. Talking to a child about his interests brings forth language. Whereas, if a parent's language to a child is mainly directive, the child can do what he's told but doesn't need to respond with language.

Here's an example of encouraging a toddler's language and good behavior that I observed in a beauty parlor. But I don't recommend taking a toddler to your hair appointment if there are other options. Mom's haircut was nearly finished, and Marty, her 22-month-old, was sitting on her lap.

Mom: "There's a carnival today."

Marty: "Ammuls."

Mom: "Oh, you think you'll see *animals* at the carnival."

Marty, imitating a nearby hair dryer: "Uuuuuh."

Mom: "Yes, that's a hair dryer. . . . Hey, you need to sit very still. Toni's cutting my hair. Remember, we're going to eat breakfast."

Marty: "Going go?"

Mom: "Yes, soon as we're done."

Marty opens a drawer and picks up a hair brush: "Buh."

Mom: "Yes, it's a *hair brush.*"

Marty: "More buh."

Mom: "More brushes, yes."

As Mom is paying at the cash register, Marty tips over a box of shampoo: "B(r)oken." [It wasn't.]

Mom: "Put it away."

Marty puts box back and starts to open a door on a TV.

Mom: "Close it."

Mom, turning to the door to exit: "I thought we were getting donuts."

Marty lingers.

Mom, heading for the door: "I'm getting donuts. Are you going to come with me?"

Marty runs to her.

Mom: "I thought so."

Correcting Mispronunciation

Correcting a child's mispronunciation can lead to disfluency in his speech. As mentioned before, it's best to respond to the meaning and then pronounce the words correctly in your conversation. If, after your child is speaking well in sentences, you notice certain phoneme substitutions such as "th" for "s" or "w" for "y," you might think of some stories or games to play that use the missing phonemes. For one child, I made up a story about Sammy Snake who couldn't hiss like his brothers and sisters but just went "th." The child enjoyed learning with Sammy how to say "ssss." See if you can get your child to use the needed sounds in other stories or games, being careful not to push him to use them in his speech. You don't want him to feel badly about not using certain sounds but to feel good about his attempts to clarify his speech.

Books for Children

Books are a wonderful source of language. Many fine children's books are on the market today. Be sure to have a good selection available and read them often to your child. Babies and young children like the rhythm of rhymes. They also like the certainty of hearing the same word every time they look at, or point to, a picture. Even if your child won't sit to read a book with you, you can read a little at a time or continue after he walks away. He may be listening from afar.

Board books are best to use at first so the pages can't be torn.

Cloth books are also sturdy, but they get floppy and don't remain as appealing. Vinyl books are good for infants, as mouthing doesn't damage them. Chunky books are small and appealing. The pages spring open as they are turned. Your baby may be interested in books as hinged objects at first and enjoy opening and closing them. She may put a book in her mouth. If so, you can gently take it out saying, "We *look* at books. We don't put them in our mouth." Don't struggle with your toddler over trying to read a book from front to back. Allow him to turn the pages when he wishes.

At some point, your child will become attentive to the pictures in the book. See what picture he is looking at and label it. You can also point to a picture, tap your finger on it, and name it. Later you can ask your child to find a certain picture, and he will point to it. He may point to a picture with his questioning word and ask you to name it. Eventually, he will point to pictures and name them himself. It's fun when your toddler starts relating pictures to real objects. He may see a picture of a ball and bring you a real ball. You can show him other real objects that are pictured in books.

Children love to hear animal sounds. Many children can make the sounds before naming the animals. Your child may relate to vehicle or machine sounds also.

Your toddler will start bringing books to you when he sees their value. If you're sitting, he may back into your lap wanting you to read to him. At first, the toddler will want to open the book and have you name whatever picture he's looking at. Later, he will become willing to let you start at the beginning of the book.

He may have favorite pages or pictures he looks for in a book. At some point, he will have a favorite book and want to hear it again and again. Do read that book for the 58th time, and find other similar ones. Books with repetitive phrases are appealing. Allow your child time to respond to the book as you read. See how he enjoys a dramatic reading of a book. When your child has a specific, keen interest, he will enjoy having books about that topic—vehicles, animals, people.

Toddlers will often "read" a book on their own. At first they'll babble, pretending to read. Later, when they have heard a book a number of times, they might "read" it word-for-word from memory.

Books become friends to children. It has been interesting to note that when children are asked to choose a book from our toy library, they usually find one they love and have at home. Whereas, they almost always want toys they haven't played with before.

If your child loses interest in books, it may indicate he's ready for a more complex type of book. After books with simple pictures, children become interested in books with many pictures to study on a page. Then, the child will become interested in picture books with simple story lines, and later, more complex stories. Children may talk about the stories and integrate ideas from them into their play.

Stories are a wonderful teaching tool. In addition to teaching language, they teach many concepts. You may find yourself learning along with your child. I learned about parts of trains and other vehicles, the names of sea shells, and many other bits of knowledge from reading to my children. Books are also excellent for teaching values. You can find books showing the value of courage, cooperation, sharing, caring, and other qualities. This is a better way to teach values than to preach. Be selective in the books you choose. If a book contains something you don't want your child to hear or see, remove it. Feel free to edit if you find yourself in the middle of reading a book that contains something objectionable. You should be as particular about the ideas you expose your child to as the food you give him to eat. You can be discerning about your child's readiness to gain certain knowledge for his protection.

Your child will especially enjoy a book you make for him. Gather pictures or photos of favorite subjects or family members and add your own text. To protect them, you can laminate the pages, cover them with clear contact paper, or put them into a photo album. You can also put them in clear freezer bags and sew the closed edges together for a book.

Homemade books can be valuable for introducing a child to a coming experience such as an expected baby, a new home, a vacation, a coming visit, or a change to a new bed. They can also focus on a child's day, relatives and friends, favorite topics, or introduce a child to the ABCs. These books will be treasured.

Whether homemade of store-bought, enjoying books with your child will help him to become a lifelong reader.

14

Supporting
Your Child's Learning

*All thy children shall be taught of the Lord; and great shall
be the peace of thy children.*

Isaiah 54:13

Parents as Educators

Parents are prime educators of their children. Your children will learn more from you than from anyone else—not only skills and concepts but, of most importance, *values*. They will observe what matters to you and then adopt those values for themselves.

Education is not stuffing sausages—putting knowledge into a child, writing on a blank slate, or waiting for a child to go through pre-programmed stages. It is finding pearls—discovering the intelligence, wisdom, acuity, memory, strength, discernment, balance, grace, and beauty that is already there. The best teaching method is to recognize and acknowledge the presence of these qualities in your child. Your awareness of these qualities leads the child to see them in himself. For instance, you talk to your child as though he already understands your language, and he responds by understanding. This kind of expectancy brings fruit in other areas of learning as well.

In realizing the importance of our job as educators, we need to guard against the temptation to glory personally in our children's suc-

Single-piece puzzles provide opportunities for learning language, skills, and concepts.

cesses or be overly disappointed by their failures. We don't want to put undue pressure on them, or ourselves, in this way. We can gain a healthy sense of balance as parents by regarding them as God's children and by giving Him the glory for their goodness. Our children are placed in our hands, but we have their Maker's care and guidance for supplying their needs.

How Children Learn

Children love to learn. They learn through play or action and through imitation. They practice diligently those skills that interest them. When language is of interest, that may take precedence over independent play with toys, as we have seen. When a child becomes interested in mastering a piece of equipment such as the toddler stairs, he will practice going up and down again and again. I've seen a toddler practice walking up and down a carpeted inclined ramp while holding a rail for over 30 minutes. Similarly, toddlers will practice climbing on and off of chairs, a spring horse, or riding toys. If you try to help a toddler struggling to climb onto a chair, he will probably soon climb down and then try to climb up again. His purpose is not to be on the chair but to practice climbing up and down.

Children also learn many concepts by practicing and playing with objects. Toddlers will work to learn about object permanence by putting balls or other objects in holes to see them disappear and reappear. They'll watch cars or balls go down inclined ramps repeatedly, trying to figure out the effects of gravity. They learn to recognize shapes by putting them into shape sorters.

A good educator of young children looks to see what's on the child's agenda. Children surge forward in skills they're interested in practicing, then catch up in other areas as interests evolve. When an adult wonders along with a child, expects the unfoldment of his limitless capabilities, and provides a setting for discovery and communication, an incredible amount of learning takes place.

Training and Discovery

It's useful, as a parent, to know when training is needed and when to allow learning by discovery. Training is necessary to teach a child a skill where we see what the outcome should be. Teaching appropriate behavior takes training. We train a child by showing him the correct way to do something and giving him positive feedback for his attempts. For a time, the word "training" came into disfavor by those who feared adult domination of children. However, training is an important aspect of learning. Through it, adults pass along to children knowledge that comes from experience. Through training, children learn behavior that helps them fit smoothly into our society.

Discovery makes learning interesting and keeps the learner engaged. Parents and caregivers can set the stage for discovery to occur. Children learn many concepts through discovery, such as how to make toy figures pop up with different gadgets, how to balance blocks when stacking, what shapes will fit into which holes, how to nest a series of cans. Allowing the child to learn by discovery takes restraint on the part of the adult who wants to teach and show the child how everything works. But watching children discover concepts on their own is truly fascinating. You simply provide the child with appropriate equipment, toys, or materials, and opportunities to examine, explore, and experiment; then step back and let the discovery take place. I've seen children quickly lose interest in a toy when an adult shows them just how it works, whereas led by their own curiosity, children will play at length to figure out a toy's inherent concepts and skills.

Supporting a Child's Learning Through Play

Parents must take a directive approach when they see the need to change or teach appropriate behavior. But when playing, a child will learn skills and concepts best if the parent is *not* directive. Play is an area where the child should have some control. For instance, if a child is working to put pegs into holes, or disks on spindles, the parent should not say, "Put the peg in the hole. Put the yellow disk on the spindle." Support and language can be provided occasionally by describing what the child is choosing to do. For instance: "You're putting the red peg in the hole. You're putting it next to the blue one." "You're filling a whole row." "What a tall tower you're making!" Children will work longer and harder at a task which they, themselves, have chosen. For instance, your child may choose to put all of the blue blocks in a truck. If you wish to comment, you can simply say, "I see you are putting *blue* blocks in the truck." He will likely continue with this activity. Whereas, if you tell him to put a block of a particular shape or color in the truck, his interest will probably soon wane.

If you want to make a suggestion to your child, you can show him a possibility. For instance, if a child has worked with a shape-sorting truck for some time and not discovered that the shapes will also fit on the wheels, you might put one on a wheel and see if the child picks up on the idea. If not, disregard it. If a child nests cans for some time and ignores the stacking aspect, you might stack a couple and see if he wishes to pursue that activity. You can also ask a question and give the child a choice: "Can you stack these?" Then leave the answer up to the child.

Watch the Praise

Praise is best reserved for encouraging good behavior. It should be used judiciously and sparingly with a child's play. You can rejoice with a child when she accomplishes a task she's been working hard to do, such as climb onto a spring horse or get a shape into a shape sorter, by saying, "You did it!" or even by clapping. But if you say overenthusiastically, "Good girl!" your daughter may get the idea she's doing it to please you. Or she may assume that she's good if she plays with a toy the way you want her to and bad if she plays with it another way. I have seen children lose interest in toys when parents put pressure on them in this way.

We sometimes tend to be goal oriented and feel a child should play with a toy in a certain way. For instance, if he plays with puzzle pieces instead of putting them in the puzzle or puts construction toy pieces together without making a product, we feel we must intervene to get the child to use the toy in the correct way. Children will tend to be more creative and play longer with toys when we let them experiment in their own way.

Children don't like to be tested. If you ask your daughter, "What color is this?" she might not answer. Either she doesn't know the color word or she sees no point in answering the question to prove she knows her colors. She may discern that you're trying to show off her knowledge to someone else and doesn't want to be put on the spot. If you really want to check your daughter's color recognition, you can find occasions to ask her to choose an item of a particular color.

Learning Materials— Self-Correcting and Open-Ended

Who started the myth that children have a short attention span? Have you ever watched them play with water, sand, mud, cornmeal, or play-dough? Often the adult ends the activity while the child is still deeply involved. Children love to learn, to discover, to explore, and to create. Some materials offer more opportunity for these activities than others. Materials, no matter what they are, are merely symbols of ideas. Through their use, concepts and skills are discovered or developed, and this is the way much of a young child's learning takes place. Self-correcting toys teach different concepts than open-ended toys or materials, and both are important for a child to experience.

Self-correcting materials are ones where there is a goal for completion. The child learns a skill or concept and knows that he is correct when the task is completed. Puzzles and shape sorters are examples of this type of toy. As a child works a puzzle, he learns and practices shape discrimination, a skill needed for reading. He learns a sense of order. He is also learning puzzle-working skills, so he will be able to complete the same puzzle more quickly another time and will know better how to tackle subsequent puzzles. He will learn such skills as putting outside pieces in first or starting with the largest pieces. When a child has worked a puzzle or other self-correcting game a few times and learned she can do it, she generally is finished with it and ready to go on to something else. This type of toy is ideal for a toy library or parent toy exchange because it is useful (and hence interesting to the child) for a relatively short period of time.

It's important for self-correcting materials to be the right level of difficulty to maintain interest without causing frustration and discouragement. This type of material should provide for progressive skills. A toddler will be able to put balls and cylinders in a shape sorter first. Then hexagons and pentagons will be mastered. Finally, squares, rectangles, and triangles, which take more turning to fit, will be conquered.

Children as young as fourteen or fifteen months of age can begin working with simple puzzles. At first the child will just take the pieces out and play with them. You can name and talk about the pieces. Don't be discouraged if the child isn't interested in putting the pieces back for awhile. You can start teaching children at this early age that puzzles and self-correcting toys should be put away after play so that pieces won't be scattered.

When children are given self-correcting toys of gradually more difficult levels, their skill and self-confidence in working with these materials increases. If a child doesn't want to work with self-correcting materials, try to find some dealing with a theme that especially interests him, such as cars and trucks, people, or animals. Make sure the material is of a level that has some challenge—but not too much—so he will have success in completing it.

Open-ended materials have no definite rules of completion but offer endless possibilities for discovery and creativity. Clay, playdough, water, sand, paint, and construction toys are examples. These materials hold tactile as well as cognitive appeal. The child can pour, shape, pat, measure, build, and observe the many forms these materials take. With open-ended materials, the child asks his own questions and creates his own problems, so play will usually last longer. At first the properties of the material will be explored: "Will it pour? stretch? break? hold its shape?" The next question may be, "What can I do to change it (scoop, roll, pound, prick, smash, or pull)?" A child may ask himself, "Is it really the same thing when it's rolled up into a ball and when it's stretched out long?" Later, the child will ask, "What can I make with it?"

Construction toys are open-ended and bring forth creativity.

If a child is intent on putting a material into his mouth, try to teach him that it is for play only. Take it away momentarily and say, "This is not for eating. It's for play." Demonstrate how it can be played with. Give it to the child again and talk about it as he plays with it. Watch carefully, and if it goes to the mouth again, repeat the process. If putting the material in the mouth is too appealing, postpone its use until the child is older. There are some edible open-ended materials that a young child may use. Some parents are concerned that these materials might teach their children bad habits about what to eat; others enjoy using edible play materials with their children and experience no undesirable consequences. If you feel free about it, you can let your child use pudding as finger paint on a tray or in a clean bathtub. Peanut Butter Playdough is another fun edible material.

PLAYDOUGH RECIPES

Peanut Butter Playdough

In large bowl, mix:
1–16 ounce jar creamy peanut butter
1 1/2 cups dry powdered milk
5 Tablespoons honey
If mixture is too sticky, gradually add more dry milk.

Cooked Playdough

1 cup flour
1/2 cup salt
1 cup hot water
1 Tablespoon cooking oil
2 teaspoons cream of tartar

Mix ingredients. Heat in pan on stove and stir until mixture forms a ball. Store covered in refrigerator. Food color may be added before or after cooking.

Silly Dough

This is an unusual substance to stretch, break, and bounce, a bit like Silly Putty.

    1 cup Elmer's white glue (not "school glue" that has a water base)
    About 1/2 cup liquid starch (Look for bottles with the thickest starch.)

Add starch to glue, starting with a little less than 1/2 cup and adding more gradually, as you mix it with your hands, until it comes together and will stretch.

    If it's too hard and rubbery, it needs more glue. If it's too soft and sticky, it needs more starch.

Silly dough stretches and breaks.

Parents can learn a lot about children's present concepts by observing their play with open-ended materials. What questions might they be asking as they play? For instance, "How long a line can I make with these blocks?" "How big a mountain can I build with this sand?" "Can I make my hand disappear in the sand?" "How many spoonfuls will fill this cup?" "Can I make little pieces from this big piece of playdough?" "Can I cover the paper with this paint?"—and so on.

After a child has plenty of time to explore a medium, the play can be made more complex by adding other objects:

- to water—cups of different sizes and objects that sink and float
- to sand—scoops and containers of different sizes and shapes, water to change the consistency, and molds
- to playdough or clay—dull knives for cutting, cylinders for rolling, cookie cutters or commercial play-dough presses and tools

Blocks are a good open-ended toy. Children may stack blocks or simply line them up. Whatever they choose to do is fine. They shouldn't be urged to do something else. At some point, they will want to see how high they can stack blocks. If they aren't interested in stacking, and interest in blocks wanes, you might stack some and allow the children to knock them down. Then they might try to stack some too.

A toddler will probably be content to explore the simple properties of open-ended materials. Usually a child will not be interested in making a product from these materials until he is at least three or four, and he shouldn't be pushed to do so. Young children are more interested in the process than the end result. If you make a model, such as a recognizable animal, out of an open-ended material, you turn it into a self-correcting material. If the child can't make a model as good as yours, he may lose interest in experimenting with the material and depend on you to make a product for him.

I have known some children who prefer the precision and order of self-correcting activities and toys to open-ended ones. A child like this might lack confidence in his own creativity or be concerned about getting messy. Your fearless participation in exploring the materials at his level may be a help. If a child doesn't want to put hands into finger paint, he may enjoy pushing your hand around in it until he gets the courage to touch it himself. Don't be concerned if your child avoids certain materials. Present them periodically until you find a readiness for them. Creativity might be shown in other play such as pretend play.

Children learn through play. The homemade clothespin can develops small motor skills and color concepts.

15

The Play Curriculum
Expanding Interests and Skills

*But continue thou in the things which thou hast learned
and hast been assured of, knowing of whom thou hast
learned them;*

II Timothy 3:14–17

Children gain skills and concepts through their play. In fact, their play and toys may be considered a curriculum as their skills, concepts, and interests emerge. Besides the large-motor skills of walking, running, climbing, riding, throwing, and catching, toddlers are learning many small-motor skills from the toys and objects they play with.

In their first years, children learn most from experiences with concrete objects. These experiences form the foundation for later learning from representational materials, such as books, television, and the computer, and abstract concepts subsequently encountered in math, reading, and writing. A number of studies have shown that time spent in front of television or at a computer, at the expense of interaction with concrete objects, can be detrimental to a child's learning.

At around 12 months of age, the baby becomes interested in how one object relates to another, so toys with parts are most interesting. They learn to strike or pound one object with another; to place an object or peg into a hole; to put a disk or ball on a spindle; to rotate and fit an object, such as a shape or puzzle piece, into a matching hole; to carry, push, and pull objects; to slide, rotate, or wind knobs; to stack and nest.

At the same time, they are learning about basic concepts such as object permanence, size, shape, color, number, cause-effect, and effects of gravity. They discover these concepts as they play, and they learn language as adults supply words for the concepts. For example, it helps the child to grasp the concept of color if you repeatedly name the color of objects that are the same in size and shape and differ only in color. A child will show that he understands the concept of color first by matching objects of like color. It may be a while before he can find the color you name, but soon after that, he will be able to name the colors himself. Two-year-olds, whose parents have named colors for them during the previous year, usually can name many colors.

Despite all the interests and skills children are learning through play with toys in the second year, Velcro Time (see p. 191) may decrease interest in toys for a while. You, the primary caregiver and model for language, may be the main interest. You'll be the model for other learning as well. Your toddler is learning from watching you. He will hold a toy telephone up to his ear as he has seen you do. You'll find him imitating your motions, facial expressions, and tone of voice. He may pretend to clean or cook as he sees you do it. You can talk to your toddler about what you're doing, talk about the items he brings to you, and take moments, when you can, to look at board books with him. Your child will also learn from observing other children. You'll see him staring steadily at other children, and then you may see him trying some of the activities he's observed.

Interests and Skills
Unfolding in Toy Play

We can learn much from observing what is on a young child's agenda. The toy library is an excellent place to see the unfolding of children's interests and skills as we watch them play with appropriate toys. The skills and interests described in this chapter are ones I observed for many years working with children in the toy library. Your toddler or two-year-old will likely show similar interests, and you can watch his skills and concepts develop as you provide similar materials.

Look for your toddler's interest in the following skills:

Rolling Balls and Disappearing People

From 11 or 12 months to about 16 months, babies are fascinated by discovering object permanence. They love putting balls into holes and watching them reappear in another location. There are a number of toy houses on the market with chunky or rounded people that can be dropped through chimneys or doors to reappear in another location. These toys usually have other places to put the people as well, which extends the toy's interest range.

Carrying

Toddlers love to carry items from one place to another. Balls, small toy figures, plush toys, radios with handles, and toy purses or picnic baskets can be favorites. Sometimes the bigger the item to carry, the better. Wastebaskets or small chairs may be moved. A big beach ball may have appeal for its size and portability.

A toddler will carry a small ball or toy in each hand and sometimes try to pick up a third one, possibly using the chin to help. When you see a child carrying two items, you can help put language to his number concept by saying, "You have two!"

Pounding

Babies often love to hit a pan with a spoon or pound any object against another. Xylophones and toy drums provide opportunities to use this skill. When a baby's pounding skill improves, he will delight in one of the toys where he can hit a ball through a hole with a hammer and watch it reappear and roll down a ramp. A pounding bench, where he can hit a peg or shape through the bench is also popular. The child can start to learn color words as you name the color of the peg or ball he's pounding.

Disks on Spindles

Your toddler can learn to put a disk, ball, or bead on a spindle. A common variety of this toy has a graduated spindle that requires the disks to be put on in order according to size. It's better to look for the versions of this toy that have a straight spindle, since the skill of sorting by size is more advanced than the interest level of putting the disks on the spindle. As your child plays with this toy, you can name the color of the disk she is putting on.

Pegs in Holes

Another popular skill for the toddler is putting pegs into holes. Pegboards with large pegs work well, and these are ideal for learning about color. Many of the toys with small peg people use the same skill, and the child will enjoy putting the people into a car or bus. Children can learn about thickness by working with pegs and holes of different sizes. They learn about number as they work to fill varying numbers of holes.

Some of the most popular toys for children between 12 and 16 months of age are homemade clothespin and lid cans. Cover two shortening or coffee cans with contact paper, and cut holes in the plastic lids—a round hole in one for clothespins and a slot in the other for baby-food jar lids or frozen juice-can lids. Baby will enjoy putting the pins and lids in and out of the cans, first without the plastic lids and then through the holes in the lids. The toys are more appealing if you spray paint the pins and lids a few different colors. Then you can name the colors as baby plays. Counting, as the pegs are dropped into the hole, also makes a good game.

Two- and three-year-olds (who don't put toys in their mouths) can enjoy a pegboard with smaller pegs and a hundred holes. They will invent tasks such as filling all the holes by putting pegs of one color in a row or making fences for small, toy animals. This kind of pegboard can be made with golf tees and a pegboard found in hardware stores for inserting hooks and hanging tools. Cut the pegboard into a rectangle or square approximately 15" by 15", and glue $1/2$-inch wooden blocks on the corners for legs. You can spray-paint the board for a nice-looking finish.

Shape-Sorting

After becoming proficient at putting balls and large pegs into holes, a child can learn to turn a shape to fit into a shape sorter. This is an excellent way to learn about different shapes. The name of each shape can be given as the child puts it in. The ball is the easiest shape to fit into a hole. Next comes the cylinder. The octagon and hexagon are next in order of difficulty, followed by the oval, square, rectangle, and then the triangle. The equilateral triangle is easier than other triangles.

At first, the child will always try to put a piece, regardless of it's shape, into the hole he was successful at getting the last piece in. You can say, "Try another hole" as you point to the correct hole. Until the child learns to turn the shape to fit, you can help by tipping the container for the child so he finds success. You can also tell him, "Turn the shape," and show him what you mean. Your child will first show he recognizes the difference in the shapes by choosing all the round ones to put in. He has discovered that these are the easiest ones to fit in. Eventually, he will recognize the different shapes and be able to get them into the correct holes by himself.

Stacking and Nesting

It's fun to see a child discover the joy of stacking. Blocks will become interesting as he sees how high he can stack them without having them tumble down. This interest may start by allowing the child to knock down towers you build. Blocks of different sizes will be enjoyed, from the cardboard brick blocks to the small wooden table blocks. Cans from your pantry or empty cardboard boxes can also be stacked. Often a child prefers placing blocks in a line to stacking. Much is being learned

Stacking can provide joy in accomplishment.

about size and number by this activity, and it's best to let the child pursue this interest as long as it lasts. When this interest is at its height, cars, animals, and all sorts of objects will be placed in a line.

The concept of size can be experienced with stacking and nesting toys. The level of difficulty of these nesting toys advances from those round in shape, to the hexagonal, and finally to the square ones. Empty tin cans of varying sizes can be used for stacking and nesting. Be sure to smooth the edges so they're not sharp. The child will learn to dump the cans to separate them. Then, as he sees what will stack and what will nest, his concept of size will develop. He will learn to make corrections to get all the cans to nest or stack and eventually will be able to choose the correct size to fit by sight rather than by trial and error.

Cause-Effect

Cause-effect continues to be a prevailing interest for the toddler. This interest keeps the child working with a toy to bring a surprise effect. Some of these effects are: a tumble of pieces, as with a stacking Humpty Dumpty toy; the release of a spring that sets a toy in motion; the rotation of a top; the popping up of a figure by turning a gadget; or the playing of music by turning a crank or dial or by pushing a gadget.

Pushing and Pulling

Push toys may be interesting to a baby who is crawling and can get an effect by pushing and pulling the toy from a sitting or hand/knee position. Push toys are popular for their intended purpose after the toddler is walking well enough so that he doesn't need to raise his arms for balance. The child can walk and watch the effect as balls pop, chimes sound, or objects turn around when he pushes. A toy vacuum cleaner is a favorite when the child can push it hard enough to make the "rmmm" sound. He may be fascinated with (or fearful of) the real vacuum cleaner and love to push his vacuum to "help" with the cleaning.

Pull toys later become interesting when the child can walk backward, or become aware of the sound of a pull toy following him. Pull toys that also include other skills and concepts, such as pegs in holes or disks on spindles, may remain interesting for a longer period of time.

Stringing

As they near two, children can learn to string beads on large laces. There are a number of stringing toys available. Some have buttons of different sizes and colors with one to four holes in them. Thus they are good for learning concepts of size, color, and number. When learning to string, children usually get the lace through the hole without difficulty. The hard part is learning to grab with one hand the end that comes through, while pushing the bead down with the other. As you help them grab and push, the concept will suddenly click, and they will do it on their own. They may fill the lace and want you to tie it into a necklace. Stringing circular cereal pieces such as Cheerios or Fruit Loops can be fun, but you'll need rules about where to wear the necklace, so it doesn't make a mess all around the house when the cereal is nibbled.

Puzzles

Puzzles are excellent for learning language. The first ones can be used from the time a child is 14 or 15 months old, especially if he's interested in language. Wooden puzzles that have small pieces with knobs are the best for starters. Each colorful piece is the picture of a different object, and the child will simply take out the pieces at first and enjoy having them named. When his interest in playing with the pieces starts to lag, you can put them back for him. When he's ready to help you, put them partly in so that a simple push of his hand will slide them the rest

After experience with single-piece puzzles, children can learn to work composite puzzles.

of the way. You might maintain his interest at first by saying, as the piece is turned, "Turn, turn, turn, turn . . . plunky!" (as it fits). Then, as you show him how to turn them to fit and he succeeds at pushing them in, he will eventually become interested in putting them in on his own.

As your child nears two and has some experience with a number of single-piece puzzles, she may be ready for simple composite puzzles that take more than one piece to make a picture. A child's interest can depend on the success she has, so it's important to find puzzles on her level. A child may want to build confidence in working a familiar puzzle a number of times, but eventually she'll be ready for a new and more-difficult puzzle. Difficulty of composite puzzles increases with the number of pieces. After plenty of experience with composite puzzles, simple jigsaw puzzles may be enjoyed. Puzzles are good toys for a toy library, or for trading with friends as skill levels increase.

Pretend Play

Pretending is a type of open-ended play which can be beneficial as a child creates his own scenarios and solves his own problems. He is observing and synthesizing his observations as he acts out scenarios he has seen. A child will imitate parents or other children. He will use toy versions of real objects, such as the telephone, toy cooking and serving utensils, and tools. Interest in this kind of activity will usually start during the child's second year and continue to get more complex during the preschool years. The child will pretend on his own and with other children and will also love having an adult participate on occasion.

Play kitchens encourage lots of pretending.

As a child nears two or later, another kind of pretend play evolves. The child uses small people, animals, vehicles, and buildings to create scenarios. The child makes the toy people talk to each other and ride in vehicles or act out scenes. He is the director of the play rather than one of the actors. The most popular toys then will be the small houses, farms, garages, airports, playgrounds, or zoos that include the small toys. Both types of pretend will continue into grade school.

Individual, Specific Interests

After toddlers gain some language, they may develop keen, specific interests. Cars and trucks, trains, or airplanes may be intriguing. If so, the child will love to play with models of these vehicles. Books, songs, and videos on the subject will be adored. Dolls, dress-up, and kitchen play, or interest in animals can engage other children in a similar way. Some children will become engrossed in how things work or in building with construction toys. Though all children show some interest in these various subjects, the intense interest is often gender-related to the surprise of parents who are determined to provide liberal sex-role models. Usually boys are the vehicle-lovers and girls more often take to the dolls, though this is not a rule for all boys and girls. Children of both sexes often have a keen interest in animals. We have also seen special interest in music and in insects. Sometimes these early interests are so keen, they carry through the school years and into adult professions.

It's good for parents to encourage these individual interests—whatever form they take—and provide the information, books, and toys for the child to explore his interest thoroughly. This kind of exploration can be an introduction to research for the child. The parent shouldn't try to wean the child away from a keen interest with concern that it is too narrow or intense. The parent can broaden the child's interest by using it to introduce other concepts. Shape, size, and color can be learned through vehicle shape sorters or through play with vehicles of different sizes and colors. Dolls and clothing of varying size and colors can teach in the same way. Spatial concepts and the use of prepositions can be learned as toys go in, out, over, around, and through things—with the child directing the play, but the adult periodically adding the language.

Toys to Encourage Different Ways of Thinking

After a child is two and is interested in pretending, we usually send home from the toy library a toy for each of three major areas of play and thinking. 1) A self-correcting toy such as a shape sorter or puzzle, for *convergent* thinking. 2) An open-ended toy such as a construction toy for *divergent* thinking. 3) A pretend toy for the child to *synthesize* his observations.

How Many Toys Are Too Many, and What Kind of Toys Are Best?

You have probably heard the argument that children get spoiled from having too many toys and that too many toys can destroy a child's imagination or creativity. I agree that being surrounded by a jumble of all kinds of toys can be confusing to a child, and a child should not be given any toy he asks for. Also, toys should not be given to replace time spent with a child. Toys should be chosen carefully to be sure that they are safe, well-made, and of the correct interest and skill level for the child. The child should not have too many toys out at one time. Good toy management can help with this.

For awhile it was popular to sell very simple, unpainted wooden toys with the theory that these simple toys would cause the child to pretend more and be more creative. There were unpainted cars without wheels and dolls with mirrors for faces. Most young children played little with such toys. Young children usually prefer toys that are small replicas of real vehicles or babies. Playing imaginatively with unrealistic props generally comes later.

Many toys are advertised that have little value for children. After the age of three, children will see these toys on television and beg to have them. The toys end up being a disappointment because they often don't act the way they did in the commercial. Children learn little from mechanical toys that are just for watching. Most of the play should be in the child, not in the toy.

I have seen that access to the right toys at the right time can be beneficial to a child's learning. A toy library is ideal for providing children with appropriate toys to learn from, a few at a time. You might check and see if there is a public toy library in your area. Some public libraries are now sponsoring toy libraries. Otherwise, you can set up a toy exchange with friends and relatives to get more value from your toy dollars and give your child access to more good toys.

Toy Management

Toys get lost in the jumble of a toy chest, and the heavy lids of some toy chests can fall, making them hazardous. It's better to have low shelves for toys where children can see the toys, get them out easily, and put them away. Toys with parts become valueless when they are separated and scattered around the house. Regular pick-up times will maintain the usefulness of these toys. Toys that are outgrown should be put away or given away. Children can learn the joy of giving outgrown toys to younger children.

Good containers for toys are valuable for keeping pieces together. For toys with many pieces, such as construction toys or play sets, you can get large, plastic containers of varying shapes and sizes at discount stores. (Rubbermaid has good ones.) The containers should be large enough so the child can spread out the toy pieces in the box to see and choose the desired ones. Eventually the child can learn to take the box off the shelf, play with the toy, put back pieces, and then return it to the shelf. Puzzles and table toys should be put away after each use. For younger children, it's best to have these toys out of reach to be brought down for a particular play period and then put away. We found that parents who treated toy-library toys with parts in this way retained all the pieces more easily.

For other toys, you can establish a regular pick-up time, such as before lunch, dinner, or bedtime. Exceptions can be made if the child has a special set-up he wants to go back to. The rule of putting away one toy before getting out another works well for table toys with interrelated pieces, but it's difficult to enforce with other toys and prevents a child from relating toys to one another. You'll get more cooperation putting away toys if you do it with your young child. You can make a game out of it by counting the toys or talking about them as they're put away. One game might be to express gratitude for each toy and what it does as it's put away.

As your child gets older, he will be able to do more of the picking up, but a whole, messy room may seem to be an impossible job. Let your child know how nice it is to have toys put away neatly so he knows where to find them. Promote pick-up time as a rewarding activity and an opportunity to express order rather than as drudgery that must be done.

The Play Curriculum

Rotate Toys

Children lose interest in toys they see out all the time. To get more mileage out of your child's toys, rotate them. Gather up the ones he hasn't played with for a while and put them into two boxes, leaving out about a third of his toys. Place the two boxes up in a closet out of view and reach. After several days, perhaps when you have a phone call to make and want your child to be entertained for a while, bring down one of the stored boxes of toys for him to use, and gather up neglected ones to put away in the box. Then, after several more days, you can bring out the second box to keep the toys rotating. Of course, you will not want to rotate toys that have continuing play value or are cherished items.

Table Toys

Certain toys are best played with at a table to keep pieces together. A small table and chair is a good investment for a young child. Another alternative is to use a high chair pushed up to a counter or high table. Toys with pieces, such as puzzles or pegs and peg boards, can be kept for table play. These should then be put away when the child is through playing with them. Tables help to contain the messiness of materials such as crayons, paints, and playdough.

Favorite Toys

In the toy library, we found the following toys to be perennial favorites. This is just a guideline for finding suitable toys. You can find similar ones that serve the same purpose.

Thirteen to Sixteen Months

Balls and hinged objects are favorite items, so toys using these interests are popular.
Bumpin' Busy Balls (Playskool), Roll-a-Round Farm (Fisher-Price)
Baby Basketball (Fisher-Price)
Musical chime and corn popper push toys
Nesting and stacking cups
Popular toys at this time are homemade clothespin cans and lid cans for emptying and filling. (See p. 214.)

Wooden toddler gym with slide (Childcraft) or Step Up Slide (Step 2). There should be raised hand-holds at the top of the slide for the child to hold while repositioning feet.

Here are other toddler toys—some with ages at which they have been favorites:

Kitchen (Fisher-Price), Doors and Drawers Activity Kitchen (Little Tikes) 15–19 months

Busy Balls (Playskool) 16–34 months (24 mos. peak interest)

Puzzle Roller (Playwell) Musical Puzzle Roller (Constructive Playthings Catalog) Pieces squeak as they go into shape sorter. 15–20 months

Vacuum Cleaner (Playskool) 16–30 months

Weebles House (Playskool) 16–30 months (22–26 mos. peak) A real favorite!

Bumpin' Busy Box (Playskool) 17–19 months

Strike-a-Ball (now Hammer Away, Discovery Toys) 16–24 months

Tumbling Racers (Fisher-Price) 18–29 months

Key Plays (Kawada, Constructive Playthings Catalog)

Lock-a-Block (Ambi)

Wooden puzzles with knobs

Four-wheel riding cars—Little Tikes has some good ones

Book Worm (Discovery Toys) nesting plastic "books" with lids that snapped closed 23–41 months (No longer available. Look for at garage sales)

Car Alarm Key Ring (Fisher-Price) Buttons make sounds and the child has his own metal keys.

Lego Primo Duplo

Here are good toys for two-year-olds:

Little Tikes Party Kitchen, House, and other housekeeping toys

Cash Register (Fisher-Price)

Shape-Color Sorting House by Berchet. Very popular from 23–41 months (Constructive Playthings catalog)

School Bus (Fisher-Price)

Bead mazes (Beads go over bent wires)

Gazoobo (Chicco)

Noah's Ark (Little Tikes)

Jumbo Stringing Beads (Constructive Playthings)

The Play Curriculum

Three-Car Garage with keys (Constructive Playthings)
Little Tikes Family Van
Little people farms, houses, main street, garages, airports, zoos by
    Fisher-Price, Little Tikes, Playmobile, or Li'l Playmates
Mr. and Mrs. Potato Head (Playskool)
Toddle Tots Petting Zoo (Little Tikes)
Toddle Tots Community Playground (Little Tikes)
Bristle Blocks (Playskool)
Duplo (large Lego)
Wooden composite puzzles
Tricycles
Rhythm instruments

Music

Most children who hear music from the beginning are fascinated with it. Children's taste in music is developed by what they hear. So be sure to let your child hear lasting forms of music, such as classical and folk music. In their teen years, your children will enjoy the current, popular music with their friends, so you can establish broader tastes by early providing exposure to other types of music. Sing, play tapes and CDs, and have good music on the radio. But remember, as your child is learning the language, to allow some moments of quiet for him to hear the fine sounds of consonants when you talk to him.

In addition to singing songs you know or learn from tapes, you can make up songs that will be special to your child. Sing about what you or the child are doing: "This is the way we make our bed so early in the morning" or "We're riding in the car to pick up Blake." Sing a direction to the child, such as "Follow me, follow me as we go to brush our teeth." A song can change a mood and promote cooperation.

Children usually like to feel rhythm. You can sing and rock with them. Be sure to dance with your children. Sing or put on some rhythmic music, hold them, and dance around with abandon. Also encourage them to dance next to you in imitation. Adding claps to music is another good way to help them feel the beat.

Rhythm instruments, toy music boxes, and xylophones can be enjoyable for the young child. Your children will like to play rhythm instruments to hear the different sounds and rhythms they can make and to accompany singing and other music. Your participation will add to the enjoyment as they learn about playing ensemble.

Young children can learn about orchestral and band instruments from hearing them played by others and by seeing video concerts. We liked to take our young children to concerts in the park. As children get older, they are able to sit quietly enough for performances in concert halls. It's important to not subject serious audiences to a wiggly or noisy child. Music classes for young children are offered in many cities, and a fine Suzuki instructor can be a good way to start a child on an instrument at an early age. Be sure to check the quality of such programs through references and visits. It's best not to start study of regular-sized instruments until the child has the size, maturity, and discipline to continue the practice needed. You want continuing success. Most orchestral instruments, other than Suzuki violin, are not started until the child is in fourth grade. Piano is usually most successful when the child is seven before starting, though some highly motivated children with proper teaching start a little earlier.

Enjoying music and art with your children is the best way to start their enjoyment of these aesthetics.

Art Activities

Exposure to lovely art can also begin early to enrich children's lives. I know a parent who hung prints of masterpiece pictures where the baby could see them from the high chair or crib. These pictures drew the attention of the baby and were changed periodically.

When the child is able to keep crayons, markers, and paints out of his mouth, they are fine open-ended materials for learning about color. Washable markers make more dramatic marks than crayons but are messier. You can show the toddler how to use these materials, teaching that the color goes on the paper (not in the mouth). Large sheets or rolls of paper are good for making marks. You can enjoy experimenting with color along with your child, but if you make only recognizable pictures, your child may prefer to watch you and tell you what to draw rather than use the materials himself.

Child-sized tables are good for art work and can later be used for stickers, cutting and pasting, and playdough as well as drawing. Don't allow your child to take the crayons, paint, or playdough away from the

The Play Curriculum

table. You can say, "These stay at the table." If a child continues to take them away from the table, after a few reminders, you can simply remove them and tell him that next time he will remember to keep them at the table.

Chalkboards encourage drawing and writing, and easels are fine for painting. A young child can finger paint directly on a smooth table or tray. Then a print can be made by smoothing paper over the paint and lifting it. This way the child can work with the paint for a longer time than when using it on paper.

Take your child on some trips to the local art museum. You can look for themes. Our children enjoyed looking for paintings of animals, modes of transportation, pictures with the brightest colors, and paintings of people who followed us with their eyes. Looking for specific colors is also a good activity. Children can enjoy trips to museums as well as to the zoo.

Math is Everywhere

There are many ways to bring math naturally into your child's experience. You can count buttons, steps, fingers, toes, bites of food. You can use words describing size, shape, and distance. You can make your child aware of time by saying, "*After* your nap, we'll go to the store." "We wash hands *before* we eat." "*Tomorrow* we're going to the zoo." "*Yesterday*, we went to the park." "We can do this *quickly*. That will take a *long time*."

You can use words such as next to, behind, under, over, around, far, and near. These are all concepts needed for an understanding of math.

A few games that teach math concepts are given below, and you can think of others to play spontaneously with your child. Many math concepts will be acquired as you talk and play with your children. These concepts are the foundation for more formal math instruction later.

Math Games

- Most nursery rhymes can be changed to include numbers, shapes, sizes. For example, "The *first* little piggy went to market The *second* little piggy stayed home. The *third* little piggy had roast beef. The *fourth* little piggy stayed home. The *fifth* little piggy went 'wee wee wee' all the way home." Fingers or toes are used for this rhyme.

- When offering food such as grapes or crackers, ask, "Do you want one or two?" Then later ask, "How many do you want?" When the child responds, count out the pieces of food accordingly. If the child holds up fingers, count them and then count out the same number of pieces of food.

- Count to the music "one, two, three" or "one, two, three, four" depending upon the rhythm. Then see if your child will count with you.

- There are some commercial board games for young children that involve moving pieces around with simple counting. Don't use these games until your child is counting naturally high enough to play the game with success. Emphasize that playing the game is important, but winning is not.

Toddler Games and Activities

Enjoyable games and activities evolve as you and your toddler spend time together. Your creativity and your child's can spark an idea and develop it. Special rough-housing games, peek-a-boo, and hide and seek games evolve in this way. The parent should be alert to end these active games before the child gets too wound up or over-stimulated. Always let your child's interest lead the activity. All games should end as soon as interest begins to lag.

Much learning can take place through games. Here are a few ideas for games and activities. Timing is important. Use only ideas that appeal to you, and use them at times when both you and your child are receptive to them.

Active Games

- Let your child climb on you.
- Talk about an action while your child does it or looks at an action picture in a book (walking, running, jumping, cooking, eating, sleeping).

The Play Curriculum

Painting with water is a popular outdoor activity.

- Give your child a ride on a beach towel.
- Dance to music holding your child. For variations, let your child stand on your feet or let him dance alongside you or holding your hands.
- Play games in the mirror with your child. For instance, see if he imitates the faces you make. Hold something behind your toddler, while he looks in the mirror and see if he turns to find it.
- Play chase games: "Let's play chase. I'll run and you catch me. Oh, you caught me! Now I'll catch you." At other times, when needed, you can say, "We're not playing chase now."
- For throwing and catching, find soft objects such as soft balls, bean bags, or stuffed animals. Use newspaper balls covered with masking tape to throw into a laundry basket or other target.
- Give your child an empty carton to fill and push.

- Let your child hold your hands and jump. Sometimes count the jumps.
- Pretend to be different kinds of animals.

Games to Play in the Home

- Name pieces of clothing and their color when dressing your child. Watch for his readiness in dressing himself.
- Place a piece of cardboard vertically in front of your child. Move a small toy slowly behind the cardboard, and keep it moving until it shows up again at the other side of the cardboard. When you repeat this, see if he watches the second side of the cardboard ahead of time, anticipating your actions.
- Look at animal books with your child and make animal sounds. Later, play the "guess who I am" game—make the sounds and let him guess or point to the animal.
- Cut pictures from magazines and newspaper ads. Mount on cardboard, and cover with clear contact paper or laminate. Let your toddler match pictures to real objects.
- Hide a toy that plays a tune and let your child find it.
- Compare items that are alike except for size (shoes, other clothing, measuring cups, pans, spoons, balls, etc.). Use words comparative: big, little, small, short, tall, high, low, wide, long, etc.
- Look for the different textures of fabrics, carpets, walls, floors, and other objects—smooth, soft, rough. Feel and describe them with your child.
- Listen to the sounds in the home and outside, such as clocks, appliances, birds, airplanes.
- Talk about one and two objects. For instance, when your child picks up two balls, say, "You have two!" Talk about two eyes, ears, hands, feet, (etc.) and one mouth, nose, chin, belly button.
- Look for shapes inside and outside such as square and rectangular windows, round tables, or cookies, and the moon.

The Play Curriculum

Outside Activities

- Take exploratory walks around your yard or block, following your child's lead. Talk about the many things you see—the flowers, insects, animals, people, cracks in the sidewalk, and so forth. Our children learned about birds, seasons, deciduous trees, blossoms, fruits and nuts, and much more on these walks. Take walks in various kinds of weather.

- When walking outside and watching birds, you can start to count them (if there are only a few) and also talk about their size and color.

- Sit on the grass and talk about the sun, the air, and the wind.

- Look for your shadows.

- Let your toddler feel the difference between walking on grass and pavement and going uphill and down.

- See how the yard looks in the darkness, at daybreak, and at sunset. Look at the stars and moon.

- Give your toddler a cup of water and a paintbrush (about one-inch wide). Let him paint outside walls, doors, and cement with the water.

- In warm weather, let your toddler play with a hose that has a small amount of water running out.

- Let your child run on the lawn through a sprinkler.

- A shallow splash pool is great fun outdoors in the summertime. Add plastic containers, funnels, etc. for creative play.

Summary

In play, children choose toys and activities that allow them to practice the skills and concepts that are emerging. Young children learn best by having a rich environment to explore and by having a caring adult nearby to teach needed rules and to provide language for the developing skills and concepts. Children learn from each other, but in the early years one-on-one time with an adult is valuable in bringing out their full potential. Observing and participating in a child's education can be intriguing and fulfilling for the parent, particularly when we remember that intelligence comes from a divine Source.

16

Living With Others

Thou shalt love thy neighbour as thyself.

Leviticus 19:18

And as ye would that men should do to you, do ye also to them likewise.

Luke 6:31

Beloved, if God so loved us, we ought also to love one another.

I John 4:11

At some point, we all learn that we are not alone in this world. We can cherish and be cherished by others. What we think and do affects others. Helping our children fit well into their social surroundings and make a contribution to others is one of the most valuable lessons we can give them.

First Social Scene

Infants' first form of communication is the cry. They learn that they are part of a caring world as their cries are understandingly responded to. In turn, they respond to the loving care that is given them and early give their caregivers smiles and responsive "conversation." Thus the first social interactions are with the parents or caregivers. The dependability of loving care shapes the way for positive expectations from others.

Parents give their children needed love, caring, and hugs. Babies

Children can do their part to help make others happy.

are then strengthened by being allowed to learn their responsibilities and capabilities such as how to comfort themselves to sleep, how to entertain themselves, and how to practice appropriate progression of physical skills. As needed and appropriate rules are lovingly established, taught, and enforced, children gain the foundation of principle and love that sets the stage for a rewarding social experience with others.

Babies love to look at faces. It's natural for them to respond to others. You can provide them with opportunities to see and interact with people within and without the home. Grandparents can form a special bond with children, and it's a big advantage to provide regular contact between children and their grandparents.

First Play with Other Babies

Babies usually get excited when they see children and other babies. Parents can provide regular opportunities for their infants to watch other children. When the baby becomes mobile and starts exploring with hands and mouth, it's necessary to be watchful and physically separate babies who are climbing on each other, pulling hair, poking eyes, or biting. They don't seem to understand in the first couple of years that others have feelings and are more than objects to explore. You want your baby to have positive experiences with others, so their protection is necessary.

You can let babies interact as long as they are not bothering each other. In the second half of the first year, they will watch each other and may give toys back and forth. But they'll need to be shown repeatedly how to pat each other gently. Likewise, a toddler or older child will need to be taught ways to interact that are safe and comfortable for the baby. Keen watchfulness is always necessary for baby's protection. In the second year, toddlers can be taught further how to play with each other. You can help them roll balls to each other and work with them to take turns.

Need for Teaching

If young children are allowed to play together without supervision or teaching of social skills, "the survival of the fittest" can hold sway. I've heard caregivers say, "Let the children work out their problems by themselves," but children need to be taught tools to use in working out their social problems. As with other teaching, early input is invaluable. It takes time and alertness on the part of the caregiver, but the time taken in early teaching social skills will benefit children and lead to peace and harmonious interaction with others in the future.

When you place your child in group situations where you will not be present, such as day care or preschool, it's important to familiarize yourself with the caregivers and the setting well enough to be sure there will be careful supervision and the kind of teaching that will strengthen social skills.

May I Have a Turn?

Most squabbles with young children revolve around possession of a toy. A toy becomes fascinating when another is playing with it, and the toddler heads right over to get it. It's not socially beneficial for the child playing with the toy—or the one taking it—to have this type of interaction. We can teach children to respect the property and rights of others. A valuable rule to set up and teach when young children are together is as follows: **Children may not take a toy from another. They must** ask, **"May I have a turn when you're through?"** When the adults working with children consistently monitor the play and teach this rule, children learn that their rights will not be invaded and are more happy to share toys with each other. Even toddlers unable to say the words can be taught this rule. The caregiver stops the child who is starting to take a toy away from another and speaks to the other child for him. "Jamie would like a turn when you're through with that truck." Perhaps you can help Jamie say, "Turn please?" or just "Turn." Try to interest him in another toy. When the other child loses interest in the coveted toy, help him take it to Jamie.

We have learned in our program that when parents and teachers all work together to teach and enforce this rule, the children play together peacefully. We hear the two- and three-year-olds asking for turns, and we see willing sharing take place. This doesn't prevent the need for continued supervision and reinforcement of the skill. The teaching works best when the adult sees the interaction begin and guides it as above. If that moment is missed, and the children are in a fray with no obvious perpetrator, it may be necessary to remove the toy and put it in "time out" for a few minutes until the children have calmed down and are willing to work out a plan for taking turns or sharing. It's always best if the intervention is done without anger.

If there is one coveted toy that many children want to play with, it's necessary to teach turn-taking. Tell the children that everyone wants a turn with this toy, and set up a method of determining when a turn is over. You may use a timer, or count (as with number of swings or rides around the playground). As with ball playing, sometimes children can be helped to use a toy together. When they near three and start pretending with little people, children can be helped to interact using different figures in a play home, garage, zoo, or park. At times, adults can join the interaction to model dialogue for such scenarios. For instance, they can take a figure and say, "Knock, knock. May I come in?" "Would you like to come to play at my house?" "May I please have something to eat?"

Some rules that can help children play well together are: 1) We never hurt another. 2) We use only nice words with each other. 3) If we make someone unhappy, it's our responsibility to help them feel better. 4) Whoever builds a block tower gets to knock it down. When the above skills and rules are introduced and taught to young children, they become part of the child's repertoire to use in later social experiences.

Respect Baby's Property

It's best to prevent a toddler from getting into the practice of taking toys away from a baby even though a young baby will not object. If the toddler repeatedly grabs baby's toys, it teaches the younger sibling to become overpossessive or to grab toys from others when he gets older. Yes, it takes alertness to prevent a toddler from grabbing baby's toys. You can make the toddler give back the baby's toy and say, "You may not take baby's toy away. I will not let someone take toys away from you, and I won't let you take baby's toys away. You may play with toys baby is *not* playing with." Sometimes toddlers cleverly bring another toy to baby while taking away the toy the baby is playing with. This is all right if the baby puts down the toy and starts playing with the toy the toddler has brought, but the toddler must learn to wait until that moment and not remove the toy from the baby's hands. If the toddler continues to grab baby's toys, he may need to be separated from the baby for a brief time (just a few minutes) as a teaching method "until he can remember the rules about being with baby." Then the older child should show you that the rules are being remembered and followed.

Sibling Friendship

An advantage to having more than one child is that the children can play together, entertain each other, and learn from one another. They can learn social skills for dealing with others near their age, and the parents don't have to be the child's sole entertainers within the home. These children can have best friends among siblings for the rest of their lives.

When observing children's first three years in the home, Burton White[13] observed so much squabbling between siblings close in age, and abuse of the younger by the older child, that he recommended spacing children at least three years apart. The reason for this inharmony may be that parents don't know how, or aren't able or willing, to

---

[13] Burton L. White, *The First Three Years of Life, Revised Edition*

take the time and effort during those early years to teach the children appropriate social skills. I have seen parents of twins and children close in age commit themselves to teaching these social skills with notable results. In the following years, the children have not only become great playmates, but teachers have commented that these children are teaching other children how to solve social problems.

Parents with more than one child must begin with a goal and commitment to peace in the home. A "come what will" approach simply doesn't provide the fabric to establish lasting sibling friendship. Parents can decide on maintaining peace between themselves and with their children. As they practice the communication and qualities of fairness, trust, and love that make for peace, they model and experience that harmony in the home. This determination means the need to talk over and solve problems as they come up. Turning together to a higher power as head of the household is the best approach. This can bring about the needed humility and reduce willfulness. Young children respond to the parents' values.

If one is looking for rivalry and jealousy in siblings, one is likely to find it. But the joyous expectation of harmony brings harmonious results. Contention between people is usually based on the belief that there isn't enough love or goodness to go around. A faith in the infinite presence of Love can replace those fears and lead to peace.

It's easy for parents of children close in age to feel torn and at times to accept the belief that there isn't enough time or love to go around. At those times, if parents learn to turn for reassurance to the thought that infinite Love is caring for these children, and that they are being directed to do the right thing at the right moment, the ideas and opportunities that meet the immediate needs will come. The children will learn, when they see the needs of a sibling being met, that their needs, too, will be met. Patience is a good quality children can learn when they have to wait their turn.

I was once fearful of jealousy and felt I should be careful not to show too much love for the baby in front of the older child. I later learned how much better it was to demonstrate to the older child the love I felt for the younger child. Then the older child saw the younger one as an object of love and learned how to express love himself.

It's important to see each child as an individual and to look or plan for one-on-one time with each one. If you see a trait that's not good in your child, it's helpful to know that it isn't a real or permanent part of his individuality and can be changed. You don't want a child to get the idea that he's the "bad guy," or he'll act the part.

If a brother, for instance, is seeing himself as the aggressor, separate that behavior from him rather than merely scolding or punishing him. Let him know how much his sister loves him and appreciates kind things he does for her. Tell him she likes his *gentle* hands. When needed, comfort her and seek his help in comforting. Encircle them both in love. Tell him, "I can't let you hurt her, and I wouldn't let anyone hurt you." Get him to look at her face to see if she looks happy. Rather than forced apologies, which can be mere lip service, try to gain true repentance and caring. Controlling or eliminating your anger will help with this. Then, when you see genuine concern and the desire to make amends, you can suggest, or demonstrate, an apology as a way to help.

Look for qualities you like to see expressed by your children, and "catch them being good." This approach is far more effective than catching a culprit and then punishing.

Learning to Get Along

When your children are young, you can establish some rules and help the children gain social problem-solving skills that will stand them in good stead later. If a parent takes the side of the younger child, the older one may feel he has to give up whatever interests him when the younger one is around.

Most siblings spend far more time playing together happily than in conflict. The strife often seems worse to us because it attracts our attention. If you are concerned about sibling conflict, take time to observe your children playing together. Make notes about what they are doing and jot down conversations. See what is causing arguments, and see if the children are finding solutions. If one child is always getting his way, you will need to intervene, talk about fairness, and teach problem-solving skills.

To help solve problems, you can use this method or a variation of it: 1) Help the children define the problem—"You would both like to play with this toy." 2) Help the children think of many solutions—"You could set the timer and take turns. You could play with it together. We could put it up, and you could each play with something else. Can you think of other solutions?" 3) Help children evaluate solutions and add, "What could you each do while the other has a turn?" 4) Let them choose a solution both can agree to. At first, you will supply most of the questions and answers, but as the children grow and see how to do it, they will participate more in the process until they can do it on their own.

As parents value the individuality of each child, the children can learn to respect each other. Children don't have to be treated quantitatively alike. Parents can explain to their children that parents show love to children in different ways according to the need. Love is shown to babies by carrying and caring for them. Love is shown to older children by talking and listening to them, reading to them, and taking them places. Stories about when they were babies can appeal to older children, and comments about how much fun it is to have them older and able to do more can emphasize their progress. Of course, affectionate terms and hugs are always welcome.

Space

Children all need their own space, even if it's only a bed and dresser. Whether or not it's best for children to share a room will depend on their age and the parent's ability to provide separate rooms. Sometimes young children like to sleep together for company. This can be done if they don't disturb each other or keep each other awake. It may be necessary for a time to put young children to sleep at separate times, or in separate rooms, and move them together once they're asleep. Some young children can get to sleep in the same room at night but need separate rooms for daytime naps.

When children sleep in the same room, as they get older (pre- and elementary-school age), they can be taught to quiet down for sleep. I remember my parents allowing "talky time" after bedtime until we heard a knock on the door. That meant time to be still and go to sleep.

Children should have a place to go when they want to be alone. You can look around the house and see where that place might be. One child loved a soft spot of her own in a closet where she had a light and some of her own books and toys. Parents can determine if having separate bedrooms will be best as the children grow and need more privacy or independence.

Sharing Toys and Play Space

When children are close in age, it works best for most of the toys in the home to be common property. The possessiveness of keeping "my toys" and "yours" separate leads to many needless hassles. Special favorite toys or lovey items may be respected as private property, but the rest should be considered "our toys" and kept accessible with the rule that the possessor may have the turn. Teach the children to say, "My turn," rather than "My toy."

New toys given to a child may be kept for a time in a special place and used by that child (or by the other with permission). When the newness wears off, the toys can then be moved into the common pool.

Of course, an older child's toys with small pieces must be kept away from a baby. The older child must learn where to play with these toys out of reach of the baby until the younger one is old enough to not harm or be harmed by them. An older child must be given a place to keep certain toys out of reach of a toddler as well. A kitchen counter and stool can be a good place for an older child to play or work out of reach of a young toddler, or a separate room with closed door or gate may be needed. The children's interests and ability to play with the same toys will determine when and how to set up the common-toys pool.

Remember to rotate young children's toys as described in **Toy Management** (p. 221).

Contributing to Peace on Earth

Peace established in every home would surely lead to peace in the world. As a popular song goes, we can help our children "let it begin with me." Of course this means letting it begin with us—with striving to use discipline that is consistent and loving, ruling out abusive behavior or communication, and showing love in different ways within the family. We can express appreciation for each other. We can talk to our children about how others think and feel and about what they might do to help. We can help children communicate with others by letter or telephone. Children can participate with us in giving in the church, school, neighborhood, and community.

Our children learn attitudes from us, and we can give them the heritage of appreciating and looking at others without discrimination. Look for opportunities to get together with those of other races and religions. Your children will see you reaching out with love, and it will be natural for them to follow suit.

Everyone can find his own way of contributing to the world, and we can help our children find theirs.

17

Tuning in to Your Child's Spirituality

*And thou shalt love the Lord thy God with all thine heart,
and with all thy soul, and with all thy might. And these
words, which I command thee this day, shall be in thine
heart: And thou shalt teach them diligently unto thy children,
and shalt talk of them when thou sittest in thine house, and
when thou walkest by the way, and when thou liest down,
and when thou risest up.*

Deuteronomy 6:5–7

Spirituality is a quality that is innate in our children. It is there for us
to behold and help our children recognize. We see it as our children
give and respond to love, as they struggle to use their physical capabilities freely, as they honestly "tell it like it is." Spirituality is evidenced in
innocence, in the intelligence that continues to amaze us, and in the
unique identity that unfolds before us.

We teach the things of spirit more by our lives than by our words.
We want to avoid the preaching that gets tuned out and be prayerfully
led to say only what is truly inspired. Parents who are turning to God for
answers grow spiritually along with their children.

The form of discipline we choose teaches children about our concept of God and what we value. If we think of God as Principle and
Love, we won't be punitive or wishy-washy. We'll be firm in holding our
child to what is right but do it in a loving way that makes them see the

joy of dropping their misdeeds. The on-going challenge is eliminating our anger or laxity. But we can progress in doing this, with God's help, as we see the value this growth has for our children.

Trust

Our understanding of trust expands as our children look to us with complete trust, knowing that they will be fed and cared for. They rely on us for assurance in new situations. They reach for our hand and turn to us for comfort whenever the need arises.

In the same way, we can reach out to the Creator and show our children the way to a deeper trust. Our children can become aware of our trust as we say: "I'll have to listen to God for an answer to that question." "Let's see if God shows us what to do about that." "Let's think about what's the right thing to do here."

Then, we can let gratitude flow from our lips: "Thank you, God, for this happy day." "Thank you, Mind, for that good idea." "Thank you, Love, for supplying that need."

Our children see where we place our trust. Their reliance on us strengthens our faith as we see that of ourselves we cannot supply all their needs. The responsibility of parenthood has led many parents to reactivate church attendance or Bible study. It has also encouraged some to drop other trusts such as smoking or alcohol. I have seen children bring much good to families and believe we can attribute that to their spirituality.

I liked to sing hymns to my babies as I worked beside them or held them. I would tell them from time-to-time that they were God's children. When one of our sons was about 19 months old, he awoke one night crying loudly. I took him from his crib, held him, and tried to comfort him, but he only cried louder. I carried him and sang hymns, but nothing would stop the screaming. Finally, I headed back to his crib and mentally put him in his Maker's arms. "Father-Mother God, he's Yours. Please tell me what to do." The next thing I knew, I heard myself asking as I put our son in his crib, "Who are you?!" He immediately stopped crying and replied, "God's child." He then put his head down and went to sleep. I returned to bed in awe that the question and answer had both appeared to come from the same source.

Such experiences strengthen our trust that we and our children will be cared for. When children see us trusting in a higher power, it's natural for them to trust as well.

Expecting Good

As one definition of God is "Good," we can look for goodness in our experience with our children. That means dropping cynicism and approaching our days with joy. Occasionally we may find ourselves looking at the hole instead of the donut. When we can catch ourselves at such times and, with God's help, change our attitude, we see the change reflected in our children.

As problems arise, it's easy for a child to get labeled: "the aggressive one," "the hyperactive one," "the defiant one," "the slow one," "the shy one," or "the naughty one." If we accept such labels and voice them, the children take on those labels for themselves. It's not always easy, but we can do much to eliminate labels. Children act out their concept of themselves, and we can help them change that concept. This is done mainly by catching them being good rather than dwelling on, or punishing them for, the difficulty. For instance, if a child is aggressive, we clearly define the rules for treating others gently. We show the child how to play gently and appreciate gentleness when it occurs. We then need to watch carefully to prevent moments of aggression. As we hold his hands, we can say, "Remember you're Love's *gentle* child." Other labels are overcome in the same way. The change starts with our acknowledgment that change is possible. We then work with the child to achieve the change rather than accepting the label and looking for its verification.

Truth and Honesty

Children can embarrass us when they tell the whole truth before learning the art of tact. Children naturally value truth and their trust in us is strengthened as we're consistent in being truthful with them.

We can set an example of honesty for our children from their infancy. As mentioned before, we should always tell children, from babyhood, where we are going and when we will be back, using terms that they can understand. Sometimes parents try to avoid a scene when putting their children in the care of others by slipping out without saying goodbye to them. If you have ever seen a child's face when he discovers his parent is gone, you will not do this. The child gets over his tears, but trust in the parent has been weakened. The child isn't sure when the parent is going to disappear and may cling more in the future. Children can learn by example the useful rule that family members keep each other informed about their whereabouts. Then it's natural for them to tell or ask us when they're wanting to play outside or with a friend.

A child's honesty is tested when parents see the result of a mishap such as a spill or a mess, and ask, "Who did this?" or "Did you do this?" A child between the ages of two and four will almost always deny responsibility. The reason is that, at this age, children's desire to please the important people in their lives is far more important to them than telling the truth about an incident. They say what they think the parent will want to hear and thus disassociate themselves from the problem. The parent's question in that case promotes the fib. If you know your child is responsible for a mess (or whatever), the best thing to do is to focus on what needs to be done rather then trying to assess blame. For example: "I see you spilled the water on the floor. We need to wipe it up. Here's a cloth." As you are wiping it up together, you can discuss what brought about the mishap and how it can be avoided in the future. As children get older, and responsibility needs to be determined, you can talk to them about "what really happened" and let them know how pleased you are that they can tell you the truth.

Being able to pretend is a skill most children gain as they near age three. They may be able to fabricate elaborate stories. Learning the word "pretend" is then useful in helping them differentiate between truth and fiction. You can talk to them about what is pretend and what is the truth.

If your child catches you exceeding the speed limit or merely pausing at stop signs, you know he is valuing the truth and will put you on guard. Many parents improve their habits under the watchful eyes of their children. Also, our children remember times we have returned excess change given by a cashier or when we have gone out of our way to return a lost item to its owner.

Loving God and Our Neighbor

When children see our desire to make spirituality a top priority in our lives, they come to accept similar values. When we are acting in accord with our highest sense of right, we are showing our love for God. Our children take note when we admit our mistakes and strive to do better. They accept the regularity of church attendance and see us turning to prayer for answers.

Our children's love of others starts with the love they give and receive from us. A warm, nurturing relationship spawns an attitude of caring. We don't want to nurture the self-centeredness that comes from putting children on a pedestal and doting on them. We can help them correct mistakes and do their part to make others happy. We don't want them to think that the world revolves around them but that they have an important part in the expression of God's love.

We are teaching our children to love their neighbor as we make peace a priority in our homes and as we help them learn social skills. They soon pick up any prejudice we have or emulate our ability to love and accept others who are different. We can talk to our children about how others feel and about what we can do to make them feel better. We can show our care for the environment by not wasting our resources, not littering, and by picking up litter dropped by others.

It may sound as though more is expected of us than we imagined when we first thought of having a baby. And so it is. We grow along with our children, but that's half the fun. And that's how we truly LOVE THAT BABY.

Conclusion

*Continue thou in the things which thou hast learned and
hast been assured of, knowing of whom thou hast learned
them;*

II Timothy 3:14

You have given your child a strong start and have witnessed your own growth as well. You and your child will continue to progress as you see each problem that comes up as a learning opportunity. Don't be upset over mistakes you may make as a parent. We all make mistakes. Just see mistakes as information and an impetus to try another way. The love you feel for your child, tempered with wisdom, will continue to lead you to make decisions in his best interest. Be assured that the Love which is God will always be with you and your child to guard and guide.

Appendix 1

A Day in the Life of a Child: Sample Schedules

What is a typical day in the life of a toddler or young child? That depends on the size of the family and the schedule of the parents, as well as the needs of the family. The following sample schedules shared by parents in our program reveal commonalities as well as differences. Some parents have given more detail than others. A schedule can be fairly predictable but should allow for flexibility. There will be variation from day to day, and weekends will probably look different from weekdays. No one else's schedule will perfectly meet your needs. But seeing what others do may give you ideas for how to structure your child's day.

Alan[14], 13 months, has an older sister and two school-age siblings.

Time	Activity
7:00 a.m.	Out of bed and dressed for the day.
7:30	6 ounces of milk, half banana, $1/3$ cup cereal or waffles or pancakes cut up into squares. Once a week may have strip of crisp bacon.
8:00	Independent play in family room.
8:30	Quiet play in parents' room with older brother and sister while Mom gets ready for the day.
9:00	Leave for errands or school parent-toddler program.
11:00–11:30	Home and clean up for lunch.
11:30	Lunch: Sandwich with thin bread (peanut butter and jelly or cream cheese and jelly), frozen peas, vegetable baby food, yogurt, custard or fruit. Sometimes turkey or ham (from deli).
12:30 p.m.	Book time, then nap.
3:00	Play with toys.
3:45	Leave for school to pick up siblings. Home or in car to take siblings to sports. Plays with brother and sister.
5:00	Plays in kitchen with pots and pans while Mom makes dinner.
5:30	Dinner: casserole, combo dinner, $1/2$ jar fruit or fresh fruit, milk. Followed by playtime.
6:30	Family dinner. Sits in high chair.
7:00–7:30	Bath every other day. Hymns, rocking, bed.

[14]Names have been changed

Greg, 14 months, is the only child in this family.

Time	Activity
6:30–7:00 a.m.	Awakens, snuggles, and plays with mama and papa (brings first book of the day).
7:00	Breakfast: Cream of Wheat, banana, egg, yogurt, apple, milk.
7:15–7:45	Dresses, teeth brushed, bath if Cream of Wheat was a disaster. Comb hair.
8:00	Plays. Mama tries to encourage independent play, but he generally insists on being in the same room with her. In kitchen—plays with pots, pans, spoons, and spatulas; in bedroom—sits in laundry basket and reads books. Mama will stop periodically to build with blocks or read a book with him.
10:00 or 10:30	Snack: fruit, Cheerios, juice, cookie—whatever is on hand.
10:30	We run errands if necessary or just go outside for awhile. Coming back indoors can be a challenge.
12:00 or so	Lunch: usually leftovers. He likes tuna, omelets, kidney beans, noodles. Milk.
12:30 p.m.	Nap.
2:30	Awakens. Game with Mama—"Do you know who you are?!!"
2:40	Snack: cheese, Cheerios, crackers, fruit. Then books, books, books!
3:00	More play: exploration with Mama cutting in or out to entertain or distract.
6:00	Papa's home! Runs around silly with excitement.
6:30	Dinner with family.
7:30	Family playtime: toy-library toys, building, books, wrestling, chase.
9:00	PJs, bath if necessary, teeth, story, rocking, bedtime.

Abby and Blaire, 15-month-old twins, have just dropped their morning nap. They have an older brother who attends preschool.

Time	Activity
6:30–7:00 a.m.	Wake up, diaper change, have a drink of milk from a sippy cup. In high chairs they nibble Multigrain Cheerios, Kix, or Rice Chex while brother is readied for school.
8:00	Instant oatmeal with milk or water for breakfast.
8:30–10:30	Supervised play and book reading.
10:30–11:00	Diaper change and dressed for day. Play in room while Mom straightens it.
11:30	Lunch—Gerber Graduates dinner with vegetable, an other vegetable, fruit, banana, Ritz crackers, milk.
12:00–2:45 p.m.	Nap. Mom does spiritual study and listens to inspirational tapes.
2:45	Up from nap. Change diaper and dressed. Drive to school to pick up brother, or stay home.
4:00– 5:00	Play with brother.
5:00	Dinner in high chairs. A Graduates baby food dinner with meat, if meat wasn't included in lunch food. A vegetable such as green beans, milk. While Mom prepares family dinner, brother plays nearby.
6:30	Family eats. Twins play.
7:00	Bath some nights. They love bath time.
7:30	Bedtime after some lotion and cream.

Perry, 19 months, has an older brother who attends preschool.

Time	Activity
7:00 a.m.	Awakens, has breakfast of cereal, toast, eggs, French toast, waffles, milk.
7:30	Helps dress himself.
7:50	Into car to take brother to school. Juice in car.
8:30	Errands with Mom, or play at home. Sometimes has a snack mid-morning.
11:30	Lunch—milk, sandwich, fruit, yogurt, crackers.
12:00–2:45 p.m.	Nap.
2:45	Up from nap. Change diaper. Drive to school. Juice in car.
4:00	Home from school. Play outside, read books, play games and with toys. Sometimes go to library.
5:30	Dinner. Sometimes Dad is home—often he isn't home yet.
6:30	Bath time.
7:00	Dress for bed and start reading books.
7:30	Lights off, rocking, prayers, cuddling.

Danny is 21 ½ months. His Mom says he thrives on a regular schedule. Days that stay close to the schedule go best.

Time	Activity
7:30 a.m.	Awakens, plays until about 8:30.
8:30	Breakfast: likes oatmeal, pancakes, cereal with bananas, bacon, Nutrigrain bars, toast with peanut butter, fruit (grapes, cut-up apples), milk.
9:00–11:00	Plays nearby while Mom works around home (doing laundry, paying bills). Mom stops to read books with him periodically; or he goes on errands with Mom in car.
11:00–11:30	Lunch: cut up hot dogs, string cheese, fish sticks dipped in catsup, grilled cheese, applesauce, peaches, vegetables (corn, green beans, lima beans), rice with cream of chicken soup, and milk. Will eat one bite of a new food.
12:00–2:00 p.m.	Quiet playtime: play dough, coloring, puzzles, together time, or watch video.
2:00–4:00	Nap preceded by routine: chooses crib toys and three books for Mom to read. Plays about 20 minutes alone, then falls asleep.
4:00	Wakes up, cuddles, snack of crackers and cheese with milk or juice. Wakes up with Barney or Sesame St.
5:30	May help Mom cook dinner or play with his play kitchen or train table nearby.
6:00	Family dinner. Tells Dad what he did during the day. Likes spaghetti, noodles, rice, chicken—wide variety of foods. Milk.
6:30–8:00	Time with Daddy (hide and seek or rough-housing) while Mom does work for pay on computer.
8:00	Bath with Dad. (Brushes teeth in bathtub just before getting out.) Mom joins for story time (4 books). Prayer, kisses, lights out.

LOVE THAT BABY

Dale, 24 months, has an older brother who rides the bus to preschool.

Time	Activity
6:30 a.m.	Awakens, has juice, then plays.
7:00	Breakfast: milk and cereal.
7:30	Diaper change, reads books, playtime with toys.
Morning	Watches Sesame Street or video, sometimes with snack of crackers. Errands if needed. If weather permits, plays outdoors or goes for walk in backpack or stroller.
12:00	Lunch: peanut butter and jelly, grilled cheese, cottage cheese with fruit, milk.
12:30–3:00 p.m.	Nap.
3:00–5:30	Juice, plays computer game, books, play dough, puzzles. Snack of crackers if wanted. Pick up brother at bus stop. Plays with brother— dinosaurs or coloring. Daddy comes home.
5:30	Dinner: likes chicken nuggets, rice dinners, fish sticks, fruit, milk. Plays with Daddy and brother—chase and wrestle.
6:30	Bath with brother.
7:15	Two to four books.
7:30–7:45	Hymns, songs with cuddling, to bed.

JoAnn, 27 months, has a baby brother. Her Dad is the primary caregiver during the day when her Mom teaches college.

Time	Activity
7:00 –8:00 a.m.	Awakens. Breakfast of variety of cereals, eggs mixed with cheese, milk or juice.
Morning	Dresses, free play, music, and dance, mixed with book reading. Diapers changed as needed. Errands in morning as needed.
11:30–12:30	Lunch—foods eaten by parents: turkey, chicken, soup, macaroni and cheese, salad, juice or milk.
1:00–2:00 p.m.	Nap, between $1\frac{1}{4}$ and $2\frac{1}{2}$ hours, depending on rising time and previous night's sleep.
Afternoon	Plays, reads, sings as in morning.
5:30–6:30	Family has dinner together. Some playtime after dinner.
7:30–8:30	Bath starts.
8:00–9:30	To bed after bath.

Edie, 28 months, has no brothers or sisters. Her mother cares for her during the day and works in a library for a few hours in the evening.

Time	Activity
7:00 a.m.	Awakens and plays.
7:30–8:00	Breakfast: waffles (frozen) with butter and syrup or she helps Mom make pancakes, bananas, toast with butter and sugar, cold cereal, milk Dresses herself, which takes awhile.
8:20	Plays independently while Mom works around the house.
9:00	Errands or outside play if it's nice, or parent-infant program.
10:00	Snack, if home: water and crackers (Ritz Bits) or animal crackers, or fresh baby carrots.
12:30–1:00 p.m.	Lunch: rice made with cream-of-chicken soup, peas, homemade pizza with pepperoni and olives, fruit cocktail, grilled cheese, Bagel Bites, chicken chunks, scrambled eggs with cheese, sliced ham and turkey and cheese "shapes," fresh or steamed carrots, salad with a little ranch dressing and croutons, milk.
1:30 or 1:45–2:30	Plays with Mom (puzzles, quiet toys, books, listen to music on the stereo and dance, play house with baby dolls) Independent play if Mom needs to finish cleaning kitchen, etc.
2:30–4:30 or 5:00	Quiet time or nap time in crib. Listens to tape player and knows to play quietly even if she doesn't take a nap. Reads books, plays with babies. Usually falls asleep.
5:00	Awakens, snack and cuddle. Plays with Mommy, and helps Mom prepare dinner until Daddy gets home.

5:30 or 6:00	Dinner together: Each talks about what they did during the day.
6:30–7:30	Helps Mommy and Daddy do dishes and clean up. Independent play.
7:30	Bath time.
8:00 or 8:30	Bedtime, story with Dad or Mom. Listens to music until she falls asleep.

Helen, 34 months, has two older sisters in school.

Time	Activity
7:00 a.m.	Awakens, has breakfast of cereal or toast and juice, milk.
8:00	Goes with Mom to take sister to bus stop.
8:15–9:00	Plays independently with toys while Mom cleans breakfast dishes and does laundry.
About 9:30	Midmorning snack of juice or milk, fruit, and dry cereal. After snack watches a little TV, follows Mom around while she works, pretends, or colors at the table, plays outside, or goes on errands with Mom.
11:00–12:00	Lunch: may be fast food—meeting Dad for lunch—or leftovers from night before, or sandwich; sometimes soup, with juice or milk.
Afternoon	Goes on errands, walks around neighborhood, outside play, or plays as Mom works around house. Nap time is optional. Usually falls asleep in car following errands. Plays with or alongside sisters when they come home from school.
5:00 p.m.	Supper. Lots of vegetables, chicken and pasta meals. Stir-fry with vegetables, chicken and rice is a favorite. Conversation about each one's day.
Evening	Playtime, reading books with Mom while big sisters do homework. Bath time is a favorite.
8:00–9:00	Hugs each family member, bedtime.

Appendix 1

Angela's mother is expecting a baby. Angela is 38 months.

Time	Activity
7:15–7:30 a.m.	Awakens, potty. Breakfast: chooses a cereal to have with raisins and banana, milk.
8:30–9:30	Dresses, watches half hour of Sesame St. or Barney.
9:30	Plays, gets ready (potty) to go out for errands or school program.
10:00–10:30	Snack (usually while out): grapes, graham crackers, pretzels.
11:30–12:00	Potty. Lunch: grilled cheese, hot dog with mac'n'cheese, fruit and milk or juice. Once a week meets Daddy or a friend at McDonald's for chicken nuggets, French fries and juice.
1:00–1:30 p.m.	Potty. Nap time. Picks three books to be read. Nap time is a question these days. When she takes one, sleeps 1 or 1 1/2 hours.
3:00–3:30	Wakes up, potty, more books. Quiet play (Duplo blocks, puzzles, pretends with teddy bears and stuffed animals).
5:30–6:00	Potty. Dinner with family: likes meatloaf, baked chicken, pot pie, roast beef, mashed potatoes, rice, cooked carrots, fruit, milk.
After dinner	Play with Daddy: usually rough-housing, play with toys, or reading comics.
7:00–7:15	Bath, if taking one.
8:00	Cleaned up and "jammies" on. Read books with Daddy, potty, usual stall tactics.
8:30 or so	Lights out.

June, 39 months, has an older sister and brother in school and a baby brother. She is toilet trained and goes throughout the day whenever she needs to.

Time	Activity
7:00–7:30 a.m.	Awakens, dresses for day.
7:30 or 8:00	Breakfast—one or more of: cereal (hot or cold), scrambled eggs, waffles, pancakes, bananas or raisins, orange juice, milk.
9:00 or 9:30	May go out for morning for errands or a parent-toddler program. If home, quiet independent play while Mom does chores or helps baby.
9:30 or 10:00	Plays with special toys from toy library. Plays with baby brother.
10:00 or 10:30	Book time with or without Mom. Likes to "read" by herself. (Mom may read her own book.) Or art work, play dough, drawing, painting.
10:30	Snack if hungry: fresh fruit, fig bar, fish crackers, Teddy Grahams, juice.
11:00 or 11:30	Play outside if nice weather: ride tricycle, sandbox play, play house, take walk, play with baby brother.
11:30 or 12:00	Lunch: sandwich or bagel, fresh fruit; may have yogurt, vegetable sticks, milk.
12:00–12:30 p.m.	May enjoy 30 minutes of sing-along video.
12:30 or 1:00	Book time, quiet on bed. May go to sleep, or reads several books with Mom.
1:30 or 2:00	Plays with Mom—cooks and bakes with Mom while baby naps.

Appendix 1

3:00 or 3:30	Gets ready to pick up older siblings from school.
3:45–4:30	In car taking older siblings to after-school activities.
4:30–6:30	Plays with older siblings inside or outside.
6:30 or 7:00	Dinner with family.
7:30 or 7:30	Bath, story, prayers, hymns, bedtime.

Appendix 2

Cameos of Individual Toddlers

Cameos are included in the first part of this book as examples of what individual babies might be doing throughout their first year. The second part gives topical information about one- and two-year-olds. Now, cameos from toy-library sessions are again presented so that you can become acquainted with some individual children between the ages of 14 and 36 months. Ages are given merely as a handy guideline to the continuing progress of these children. You will see similarities, but as age increases, so does the diversity of these wonderful children. When we compare the cameos at the end of this book to the ones at the beginning, the progress is unbelievable!

Fourteen to Eighteen Months

∞ Brett[15] ∞

14 mos. 20 days. Brings stool to kitchen counter and table to get what he wants. Has good focus and attention span when playing. Cheers for himself when successful. Nests four cans repeatedly. Puts row of pegs in holes.

15 mos. 4 days. Says "Hi," "Mama," "Dada." Questioning word—"Eh?" Keen interest in Musical Activity Center attached to stair rails. Frequently went to it and pulled gadget to activate music box. Mastered four-piece shape sorter.

15 mos. 18 days. Velcro Time (see p. 191). Wants to be with Mom at home. Said "off" while sliding off Mom's lap and "up" while pointing up at airplane.

16 mos. Loves books. Still asking "Eh, eh?" about everything. Experimenting with making sounds he hears—truck and siren.

---

[15] Names have seen changed.

Starting to "give it back" to older brother and gaining more respect. Loved steering Playtime Driver toy and working key.

16 mos. 15 days. When asked if he wanted a cracker, ran to pantry and pointed to shelf where the crackers are stored. Shape sorter favorite toy.

16 mos. 29 days. Has learned which kitchen cupboards he can open, and which he can't. Put all clothespins through hole in can—a favorite toy. Put pegs in board, then started throwing them when Mom didn't pay attention.

∾ **Phil** ∾

14 mos. Eating well. Likes vegetables. Says "mo(re)." Said a version of "Daddy" and "tick tock." Started walking, and walks all around now. Works all but one lever on Busy Surprise Box. Likes to put pins in clothespin can, pull off lid, and dump pins.

14 mos. 13 days. Talking in jargon and with some words. Favorite book: *Donald Duck's Trucks*. Likes to find tractor. New words: "bo(ttle)," "ho(le)," "off." Liked pegboard. Pointed to hole and said "ho(le)." Asked for toy by saying "ho."

15 mos. 5 days. Makes questioning sound. Made riding horse whinny, then made same high sound vocally. Likes putting spools on and off a pull toy. Got round and square pieces in shape sorter.

15 mos. 26 days. Says "Mama" and "Nani" (great grandma). Says "out" and "jacket." For first time sat on Mom's lap while Mom read book. Liked making kitty sound by pulling string on Activity Cube Center. Liked putting shapes in Sound-Puzzle Box.

16 mos. 9 days. Loved book, *Early Words*. Points to pictures and relates to objects in house. New words, his version of: "milk," "circle," "mama," "broccoli," "snow," "in," "out," "star," Said, "up" and "down" as he climbed in box. Very busy. Takes items out of his drawer in kitchen and puts back. Makes animal noises while looking at animal book. Pulled dinging clown pull toy around house and asked for it by name, "c(l)own."

17 mos. 14 days. Velcro Time. Mom is primary interest. Using questioning word to get Mom to say words. After hearing word "snowsuit" twice, said it. Brings things to Mom. Loves having Mom read books. Favorite: *Goodnight Moon*. Says, "Moon" when it's bed-

time. Liked Toddler Kitchen toys, especially dropping cups and shapes down chute.

∽ **Marilee** ∽

14 mos. 10 days. (Velcro Time) Walking since her birthday. Recently climbing on furniture and up and down steps. Goes up stairs and down slide of activity center again and again. Not interested in food. Picky eater. Pays attention to sounds—dogs, fire engines. Says "Mama," "Daddy," "llllight," "ball." Peg board favorite toy. Would bring to Mom to work with it, listening to color names.

15 mos. 1 day. (Velcro Time) Took trip with family and learned from cousin about feeding bottle to doll. Loves books and people. Focuses on Daddy when he's home. Likes tickling and rough housing. Makes up her own songs. New words: "wff wff" for dog, "Uh oh," "eyes." Enjoyed Hammer Balls, Toddler Kitchen, and Pet Shop with doors and four toy animals.

15 mos. 22 days. Loves books. Constantly playing with Baby Beans doll. Makes animal sounds—dog, cat, cow. Carries around balls and small toys. Carried toy picnic basket like a purse. Liked putting colored clothespins through hole in can. Pretended pins were crayons.

16 mos. 5 days. Loves crayoning in high chair—only activity she'll sit to do. Carries around baby doll. Sits it in corner and laughs. Puts it in her high chair. Takes place mats out of drawer and puts baby to bed—"night night." Calls all men "Daddy." Figured out how to push over gate at stairs. Grabs parents' finger and pulls to show what she wants. Weebles House with dog and boy were favorite toys. Pretended with them in house and carried it around with her. Pushed toy vacuum all around.

17 mos. 3 days. Pretends to stir and eat with Mom. Only interested in toys with animals or people. Tries to put her shoes on doll. Toy flexible people favorite. Worked to get shapes in holes of sound shape sorter.

18 mos. 7 days. Getting into everything. Starting to put two words together—"Read book," and "Me eat." Climbs out of playpen. Takes off her clothes and diaper after nap. Babbles while she reads book. Distinguishes between hot and cold. "Col(d) baby." "Aw done."

❧ Denny ❧

14 mos. 24 days Throws diaper away in trash. Came back into bedroom announcing "Dah Dah Dah" when Dad came home early. Likes to bother brother by turning off TV while he's watching. Curious about doors. Loves to climb. Gives kisses! Musical Pusher favorite library toy.

15 mos. 8 days. Imitates movements of others. Climbs out of crib and gets on rocking horse alone. With Hammer Balls, pounded all balls down. A big hit.

15 mos. 22 days. Cutting teeth so likes to have something in his mouth. Likes to hear Mom play nursery rhyme on piano. Learned shapes of Shapes and Slides Playground. Enjoyed clothespin can.

16 mos. 9 days. Imitates brother, Mom, and Dad. Laughs when others laugh. Communicates with brother. Takes purse and says "bye." Goes upstairs "shopping."

16 mos. 20 days. Having fun with brother, wanting to do what brother does. Learned to open all doors of Pop-up Pets. Said "c(l)o" when he closed doors.

17 mos. 3 days. Loves electronics—Dad's computer and tape deck. Has old phone of his own. Says, "Hi dah," "Mama," "ta tah" (thank you). Grabs a finger to take adult to show what he wants. Climbs everywhere—stools, countertops, dining room table—"Quite a challenge!" Shape sorter favorite toy. Triangle shape was hardest, but mastered it.

17 mos. 17 days. Says, "Hi Mom." Very affectionate with kisses and hugs. Catches on quickly to toys requiring attachment like locks and train couplings. Fascinated by key in Lock-a-Block. Mastered shapes too.

Eighteen to Twenty-One Months

❧ Stan ❧

17 mos. 22 days. Hugs and kisses with open mouth. Played with cousin, running and giggling. Working at eating with spoon. Had oatmeal all over head and elbows. Says "poopy" when needs a change. Pulls everything off a shelf and piles it somewhere else. Shakes head "no," but can mean "yes." Has words for brother and sister. "Guck" = stuck. Says "uh oh."

18 mos. 12 days. Recognizes many new words and loves books. Saying words for: apple, juice, bath, shoes, coat, jacket, hi, thank you, light, pretty. Making connections between pictures in book and real objects. Likes game of climbing on chairs and counter to have someone take him off. Loves music. First puzzle: took pieces out listening to words, but then threw on floor.

19 mos. 10 days. Losing interest in books except to turn pages. Climbing on everything. Lots of words and repetition of words using "b," "d," and "m" sounds. Longer attention span and more deliberate and orderly in play. Liked Pet Shop toy, opening and closing doors and putting animals in and out. Put one at a time on chair, then back. Says "turtle" and "bunny."

19 mos. 25 days. Velcro Time is over. Saying many words but not always clear to people other than Mom. Keen interest in vehicles. Longer attention span. Now likes books with short story line. Bumpin' Busy Box favorite toy. Put balls in repeatedly and manipulated gadgets.

20 mos. 8 days. Exploring possessive concept, "Mommy('s) shoes," "Daddy('s) shoes." Joked: "Mommy('s) pacy" (pacifier), "Daddy('s) pacy," "Nana('s) (dog) pacy." Having movements on potty. Runs on toes everywhere. Liked Lock-up Garage, putting cars in and out and pushing them around. Didn't work key.

20 mos. 22 days. Parents trying to discourage him from being the clown—food in hair—making brother and sister laugh. Has developed special fondness for dog. Riding tricycle is the big thing.

✎ **Mickey** ✎

18 mos. 7 days. Imitates crazy sounds brother and sister make but not saying other words yet. Loves to read books with Mom. Communicates with "uhhh" and body language. Liked Unimax Work Bench using all tools.

18 mos. 21 days. Came and sat right down at table to work with toys at toy-library appointment. Loves to draw. Mom noted: will sometimes say a word, then won't say it again. Sings something that sounds like "Rocking Rocking" song at bedtime. Filled every hole in Graduated Pegboard with satisfaction.

19 mos. 7 days. Says, "Uh oh." Says "I do" or "how do" a lot. Mostly referential language for social communication. Doesn't label objects.

Says "Mama" and Dada" to get attention. Likes containers and is starting to like vehicles. Short attention span for toys today. Likes balls.

20 mos. 3 days. Says "Ah do," in response to "Who wants to eat?" Repeating some words after Mom but still not very vocal. Likes books. Attention span short with toys now. Didn't want to leave toy library but finally left with smile and a finger wave.

20 mos. 18 days. Saying more words. Making attempt to say words he hears. Favorite is "Mm?" Says "dink," "p(l)ease," "meow," "woof woof," "uh oh." Brother taught him "pooh pooh." Loves to kick ball and go with brother to soccer.

21 mos. Loves balls. Enjoys going outside. More talking.

✎ Linda ✎

18 mos. 13 days. Has keen sense of order. Wants to put things away where she found them. Likes to play hide-and-seek with Mom and Dad. Using words to get what she wants. Uses word "color" and knows some of the color words. Has definite ideas about clothes and hairstyle. Says, "No way!" if she doesn't want what's suggested. Picks up mannerisms from parents. Wants to do things by herself. Pretended to bake with Toddler Kitchen.

18 mos. 27 days. Parents took her to her first movie, *Pinocchio*. She didn't like the donkey part and said, "Home," so they left.

19 mos. 5 days. Lots of words. Language biggest thing on her agenda. Says, "appoh" (apple), "te'y bear," "red," "g'een," "yeh'woh." When she heard the word "bath" at the dinner table, hopped down and headed for it. Urgently wants to dress herself completely. Helps put on shirt and pull up pants. Does well with slip-on shoes.

19 mos. 18 days. Brought doggie puppet over and said, "woof woof." Says "Mine," "Go way." Told Mom she had pizza and milk for lunch at school. Loves books. Says, "Re(ad) t' me." Enjoyed shape pounder, pounding all down with determined expression. Pretends to feed her dollies and stuffed animals.

20 mos. 3 days. Surprised Mom by counting to five this morning. Copies everything. Lots of new words: "platypus," "acorn," "catch," "up," "down," "out," "in," "big," "small." Expanded with hands—"big, big, big." Makes meals for parents with play kitchen.

20 mos. 16 days. Loves books and the library. Requests favorites. Active in play kitchen, taking dishes out and putting away. Follows directions. Trying to dress herself—shoes off and on. Said, "Too hot for my coat." Good cooperation with other children—more willing to share.

20 mos. 30 days. Wakes up in the morning and says, "Read, read." Using verbs. Said, "Mommy sew bow on it." (A dress without one.) Lots of pretending with dolls. Sings "Twinkle," "Baa Baa Black Sheep," and part of "Old MacDonald." Eats everything parents do, now. Watches in kitchen and wants to help. Enjoyed pretending with flexible toy people.

Twenty-One to Twenty-Four Months

✺ Stan ✺

21 mos. 5 days. More interested in active, than quiet, play. Falls asleep quickly and easily now. Got towel and Windex to polish his trike when Mom was cleaning table. Loves indoor and outdoor riding. Mimicking language and practicing words he hears. Keen interest in Weebles House. Found all the places to put boy and dog.

22 mos. 3 days. Parents' alertness needed. When he finds a cup, goes to get water from the toilet. Dipped sister's Barbie in toilet. Favorite word: "OK" = time to go, time to get out of the car. Likes pouring water from plastic bottles when in tub.

22 mos. 17 days. Good focus. Sat at table in toy library and played a long time with each toy. Talking well in two-word sentences, enjoying communicating. Said expressively as he pulled out book, "Oh, book!" Said "Peek-a-boo." Learning not to throw things when he's through with them. Water big fascination. Liked stacking and tumbling Humpty Dumpty toy. Play with toy phone started him talking on real phone to Daddy.

23 mos. Sings "Head, Shoulder, Knees and Toes" so Mom recognizes it. Lots of language. Loved pushing lawn mower.

23 mos. 14 days. Repeats what you say: "Dare's 'orse." "Here guck." If he needs help or wants something makes "unh, unh" sound. Pulls over a chair to get something that's high.

∽ Brad ∽

21 mos. 13 days. Loves to be with older sisters. Plays well by himself for extended periods of time. Acquiring new words. Loves cars and trucks! Joyful disposition—ready for fun. Small, painted, wooden cars and trucks favorite toys.

21 mos. 27 days. Seems happy with very little interaction from others. Long attention span. Likes to be outside. "Gah gun" is " thank you." Enjoyed Tumbling Racers and vehicle puzzle.

22 mos. 11 days. Talking a lot, quite clearly: Says "please," "thank you," "airplane," "car." Is a great buddy to sisters, but sometimes mischievous with cat. Preferences emerging. Loves black jacket.

22 mos. 25 days. Helping dress himself. Brings Mom's shoes and checks to see if she has coat when they're getting ready to leave. Has definite ideas about eating: "Doan like it." Turned down some toys with that statement today.

23 mos. 28 days. Becoming considerate of sisters. Comforts them: "What happened?" Helps Mom in kitchen. Makes roads out of toys. Learns routines quickly. Difficult to take shopping. Expects milk at night in Mickey Mouse cup, but won't take it from Dad. Carries red Porsche everywhere.

24 mos. 26 days. Loves *Freight Train* book. Rides four-wheel riding toy around house. High sense of order—puts things away carefully. Likes to make things happen. With rhythm instruments, whole family got into a marching band.

∽ Linda ∽

21 mos. 13 days. Sings *Frosty the Snowman* for friends. Says "poo poo" for pillow. Had success on potty three days in succession. Now "checks" doll's pants. Loves books. With play food and utensils served food to dolls and stuffed animals.

22 mos. 11 days. Took three days to open Christmas gifts—played with each after opening. Pretends to cook and feed a lot. Lots of pretending with pink Lego set. Liked nesting books. Would say, "I'm building." When she got them out of order as she tried to nest them said, "Not working." Enjoyed Little Tikes Family Van. Talked as she played with it: "Eh, eh, eh" (baby crying). "Bye, see next time day." "It's too hard." "Di-boh (driver's) seat."

22 mos. 24 days. Loves pretending with little toy people and has them

talk to each other. Dresses herself completely. Says "Myself." Likes books with a story line. Now likes to sit next to parents rather than on laps. Enjoyed toy farm. Put animals in and out of fence. "Go in here amal." Works composite puzzles. Said, "I'm going to do a puzzle. Do you want to watch?" Named parts as she put them in.

23 mos. 8 days. Likes to share play food with Mom and Dad. After hearing *How Do I Put It On?* put hat on leg and said, "I'm funny." Runs and says, "I'm running." Said: "I'm working, Mommy. Be ready in a minute. Almost done." Liked playing with people in Playmobil Playground Set.

23 mos. 22 days. Has memorized *Peter Rabbit* book. Won't let parents skip text in books. Likes to dress and undress and make choices about what she wears. Likes independence. Goes to swimming lessons and library.

24 mos. 6 days. Listens to books over and over. Likes having toys organized on shelves now. Liked giving baths to pliable family toy.

ᴄᴏ **Seth** ᴄᴏ

21 mos. Sat perfectly still for a haircut. Brings books to Mom to read. Practicing with basket ball—puts in overhead shot. Starting to imitate sounds and say words: "bye-bye," "dere (there)." Steps down front steps all by himself.

21 mos. 14 days. Interest in toys short now. Likes putting Duplo together. Seems to go in and out of Velcro Time. Wants to help Mom in kitchen. More interest in toys when Mom sits with him, but doesn't want Mom to direct. Loves books. Orderly about putting things away.

21 mos. 28 days. Velcro Time. Now full of hugs and kisses for Mom (unlike before). Prefers Mom to Dad. Wants books all the time. *Freight Train* favorite book. "Eh?" means "what's that?" or "Look at this." Says "more more" when he wants something. Says "Mommy," "Daddy," "no," "down," "dog." "Psss" means "please."

22 mos. 12 days. Follows Mom around, but now crazy about Dad. Up with Dad in the morning, watching him eat breakfast. Trying to copy sounds. Said "br-sh" for brush. Likes to read and shoot baskets. Enjoys dancing and listening to Raffi tapes. Carried around Hickory Dickory Dock Clock (music box).

22 mos. 26 days. Would read books and shoot baskets all day long if he could. More interest in people than toys. Doing well on potty. Needs constant supervision—testing limits. Marching Band was favorite toy. Argued with brother about it for two weeks. Then yesterday, figured out a way to share—each taking one drumstick.

23 mos. 23 days. New words every day. High energy. Likes to be with Mom or brother all day. Little independent play. Lots of singing. Recognizes color "blue." ("Boo.")

24 mos. 7 days. Cars and trucks are current favorite interest. No longer interested in reading books. Just likes to talk to family members. Favorite birthday gift was a ball from his brother. Also enjoying new colored pencils and a puzzle. Favorite toy from library was Tumbling Racers. Named colors "ye(ll)ow, b(l)ue, re(d)."

Twenty-Four to Twenty-Eight Months

✍ James ✍

23 mos. 25 days. More interaction with other children in co-op class. When another child wanted the doll he had, found another doll to give him. Took a toy over to baby brother. Interested in how things work.

24 mos. 9 days. Uses questioning "Uh?" and lots of body language for communication. Likes toys with keys like Key Plays and Locking Garage. Liked using hammer with Strike-a-Ball, but Mom put up when he started throwing balls.

24 mos. 22 days. Learned how to work the drinking fountain. Going up and down stairs on feet. Gets into refrigerator but learning to wait for Mom to help. Loved Tumbling Racers. Worked for a long time at stringing shapes.

25 mos. 6 days. Chose a book he had before, and shook his head when Mom asked if he wanted others too. Liked putting Creative Train together.

25 mos. 20 days. Likes vehicles. Can put jacket on himself. Playing longer independently. Lots of jargon but few words. Says "dog." Pointed to seat asking me to sit down and play with him. Throws things when frustrated. Played long time with Weebles House—liked dog best.

26 mos. 17 days. Good understanding of what is said, but talking jargon. Held baby brother and gave him book, blanket, and toy.

27 mos. 1 day. Made muffins with Mom. Saying more words. Used potty independently.

27 mos. 29 days. Said, "I go car." Chose toys he wanted to take and loaded into bag.

✎ Jim ✎

24 mos. 1 day. Sings "ABC" and "Twinkle" songs all the way through. Fills in words for fun like "Twinkle twinkle little mommy." Imitates Mom's sentences. When he wants help, says, "Let me help you." Coughed and said "Excuse me" without coaching. Pointing to book said, "Dat's a moon—a yellow one." Pointed to rocking chair, "Dis is a red rocker." Favorite toy was homemade magnetic letter can. He matched letters and color with traced letters on metal shortening can covered with white contact paper.

24 mos. 29 days. Likes computer game with letters and pictures Dad bought. "E" and elephant is favorite. In bathtub saw water drip and said, "Dere's a piece of water." Visited zoo and liked alligator and elephant best. Made up nonsense words for "Pony Boy" song. Favorite toy was Chicken Dinner and Hot Dog Play Food Set.

25 mos. 13 days. Climbs on mulch pile. Picking up words like, "government" and "mankind." Teased Dad by saying "pine cone" for ice cream cone. Fit together nesting plastic "books."

25 mos. 29 days. Talking a lot. Asks what words mean. When Mom said "Just a minute," asked "What's a minute?" While playing "Piggies," asked "What does 'none' mean?" Learning names of all Dad's tools.

26 mos. 12 days. Loves wrestling and climbing with Dad. Has discovered numerals, recognizing many.

✎ Kendra ✎

24 mos. Talking more in sentences. Loves puzzles. Working composite puzzles every day. Prefers self-correcting toys to construction toys.

23 mos. 28 days. Has been doing a lot of jumping up and down. Works with Little Tykes Kitchen at home. Enjoyed taking play food and utensils from toy library.

25 mo. 26 days. Likes to cook with Mom—pancakes and muffins. Helps

set table. Pretends to cook. Talking more and more. Learning to pedal tricycle. Initiated play with "I know, Guys." Started potty training last week, and yesterday had no accidents. Learned to turn jack-in-the-box, and liked to pretend she was a jack-in-the-box.

26 mos. 23 days. Matched words on puzzle with pictures. Long attention span—especially with puzzles. Lines up pieces on table, then puts in. Chose puzzle with "I like dis one."

27 mos. 25 days. Very observant. Noticed same picture of rabbit fishing in *Goodnight Moon* and *Pat the Bunny*. Responds quickly to correction. When three people said "no" at the same time, dissolved in tears.

28 mos. 4 days. Still working on potty training. A new dimension of thinking is going on with puzzle work. It's as though she wants to make each piece go in a different way, so it's not going as easily. Lined up toy farm animals, naming them and making sounds. Put pig next to sheep and said, "He can be your friend."

∾ Alicia ∾

24 mos. 12 days. Clinging to Mom exclusively at home. "Helps" cook. Loves books—especially peek-a-boo Spot books. Picked up cordless phone, "Daddy here. Mommy here." Wants to do everything herself.

25 mos. 24 days. Mom noted language is increasing dramatically. Found crackers and asked, "Can I have these?" A little sing-song, "No more jumpin' on the bed." Saw bottle lying on side in refrigerator and said, "pleeping (sleeping)." Likes making tall block towers and working puzzles.

26 mos. Lots of independence—resisting help. Will accept some help from older brother. Mom's learning to take the five extra minutes, when she screeches, to help children find solutions to disagreements. Mastered Postal Box Shape Sorter.

26 mos. 28 days. Saying new things all the time. Dad picked up book, and Alicia said, "I read that already." Puts own shoes on and takes off all the time. Chose toys, "I wanna take dat one home." Sustained interest in Change-a-Tune Carousel with small people and records, and in Key Plays.

27 mos. 12 days. When asked to help, answered "I'm busy." Said "I'm

hungry." Says "My go. My do it." Mom noted comments, "Too hard for me" and later "I think so." Volunteered, "I had a good time at Dorie's." Liked hammering Hammer Balls.

27 mos. 26 days. Prefers knees to booster chair. Asks, "May I be 'cused?" Uses own fork and spoon. Undresses self before bath, and puts clothes down chute. Likes to choose own clothes. Found markers in trash and said, "Awesome! What are these?"

Twenty-Eight to Thirty-Two Months
∞ Phil ∞

28 mos. 8 days. Interested in trains. Told about a big train he saw by ice cream shop. Repeats prayers with Mom at bedtime. Liked pretending with a shopping toy—especially liked the wallet and calculator. Played with people and keys in Shape-Color Sorting House.

29 mos. 13 days. Takes himself to potty sometimes. Uses spoon and fork regularly. Enjoys painting and riding cars in co-op class. Enjoyed puzzles.

29 mos. 27 days. Takes self to potty often. Really talking and expressing himself. Said, "Mommy's wearing earrings." Mom said, "Mommy has the holes in her ears to wear them." He said, "When I get older, I can wear earrings, and that's soon." Worked every game and puzzle on table in co-op.

30 mos. 10 days. Told Mom at dinner he loved her. Repeats what he hears. More talkative at dinner. Now toilet trained day and night. Loved Power Workshop. Tried each tool.

30 Mos. 24 days. Favorite book is *Wheels Go Round*. Often "reads" it from memory. Doing some testing at home.

31 mos. 8 days. Good at choosing which toys he wants in toy library. Liked building with Bristle Blocks and putting faces on Mr. Potato Head. Mom working to keep her cool at trying times when he wants his way. In co-op, enjoyed pumping up balloon and letting it go. Created many things with Bristle Blocks.

32 mos. 6 days. Having to adjust to younger brother's mobility and interest in every thing that's on the floor. Doing nice job of sharing toys. Checked out children's lyre from toy library and spent long time making music with it. Made instrument with construction

toy. Used Connecting Shapes to make towers, airplanes, motorcycles, fish, bridges.

33 mos. 3 days. Interested in book, *Busy Wheels*. Remembered a crane from an earlier book, and when he saw picture of a cherry picker said, "Oh look, Mommy! There's a boom." Getting better at putting his clothes on. Still has trouble with shirts. Learning that if he doesn't cooperate at home, he doesn't get what he wants. Keen interest in Fisher-Price Power Workshop.

✎ Stan ✎

28 mos. 13 days. Excited about coming to toy library. Told Mom he wanted a car. Chose Lock-up Garage. Spent more time with imaginative play with this than using keys. Made many different instruments with Fisher-Price Crazy Combo. Learned to differentiate between kazoo and horn mouthpiece and played each.

28 mos. 27 days. Initiated shaking hands today. Counts to 10 by rote. Toilet training has had top billing this week. Saw fire engines in truck book and wanted one. Checked one out, but Fisher-Price Marching Band (rhythm instruments) was favorite toy.

29 mos. 11 days. Interested in trains, cars, and trucks, as well as music. Learned to put Little Tikes Waffletown Building Set roads together and ran cars around on it. Recognized Grandpa dressed as Santa.

31 mos. 13 days. Talks about school and teacher at home. Put Hey Diddle Diddle puzzle together repeatedly wanting to hear song again and again.

31 mos. 27 days. Now interested in puzzles and is seeing shapes better. In co-op class tried spitting a few times on various things. Went willingly to sink when told to spit there.

32 mos. 25 days. Enthusiastic about trying toys. Likes making believe with toy people and pretend toys. Plays a lot with older sister and her dolls, taking roles she assigns. Liked moving animals and people up and down ramp of Noah's Ark toy. Took Marching Band toy home again and kept trying to organize band with family members.

✎ Jan ✎

28 mos. 9 days. Mom has been talking Spanish as well as English to Jan, and she recognizes many words in both languages, including

names of colors. When ready to go said, "Juntos" (together) as she picked up one handle of the bag. Loved Fisher-Price Breakfast Play Set. Pretended to crack open eggs and cooked breakfast for Mom. With play waffles said, "My ha' waffohs today."

28 mos. 30 days. Takes good care of her toy babies. Loves to pretend and to help Mom—"He'p you Mom?" Dresses self and has very definite ideas about what she wants to wear. Likes to string buttons.

30 mos. 12 days. Likes elephants. Saw baby elephant at the zoo eating a carrot. Now will eat carrots if told that the baby elephant eats them. Enjoys wearing stick-on earrings. Takes good care of them and was unhappy when Dad got them wet in the shower. More imitation play with objects than pretend with play people.

30 mos. 26 days. Likes to answer phone and talk on it. Does well with sorting toys and puzzles.

31 mos. 9 days. Put pieces on Potato Heads and asked, "How you like it?" Wakes in morning and gets completely dressed by herself—including socks.

31 mos. 24 days. Doing lots of things "all by myself." Can zip own jacket, and took long time to button own overalls. Remembering things—"Member Dede and me outside last summer?" Asks, "Dis funny Mom?" Uses tongue when she concentrates.

32 mos. 15 days. Doing lots of talking and asking questions. Asks "What's did?" Mom repeats "What's this?" and she answers, "It's a . . . ." Frequently uses word, "also." When she finally gets a point across, says, "Dat's what I meaning." Likes playing with little farm pieces.

∽ **Dede** ∽

28 mos. 4 days. Loves puzzles. Interested in wearing big-girl pants and toilet training. Says "Mmmmm," for "thirsty." Likes playing with dolls. Feeds, undresses, and tries to dress them. After she made a painting for Mom, asked to make another for Daddy. Loved playing with Little Tikes Community Playground last two weeks. Played cooperatively with brother.

29 mos. 2 days. Starting to be interested in colors and numbers. Interest in potty training comes and goes. Learned to open doors with keys

in Shape-Color Sorting House. Loved harmonica in Marching Band. Had bands with brother.

29 most. 23 days. Saying words more clearly. Playing more with brother. Loves puzzles.

30 mos. 15 days. Keen interest in babies. Enjoys pretending kitchen and store activities. Likes to dress herself. As they were leaving, said, "Dank you for a toy 'ibrary."

30 mos. 29 days. Potty training going well. Starting to tell Mom and wait. Wants to do things by herself. Gets dressed in the morning. Knows her own dressing routine and wants to stick to it. Love 'n Care Baby big hit. Changed diaper and pretended to sit doll on potty.

Thirty-Three to Thirty-Six Months
✍ Pablo ✍

32 mos. 17 days. Loves cars and trucks. Asked for cars when he came in. Knows many letters. Excited about Motor Mat and Vehicles.

33 mos. 14 days. Is loving trains now. Working to use gentle hands and not vie for attention with younger brother. Received new book and "read" by himself after two readings. Has two computer-matching programs that he works very well, matching shapes and letters. Liked Shape-Color Sorting House. When he got the key turning correctly, played with this for long periods. Set up all people in house. Liked matching pictures in a lotto game.

34 mos. 26 days. Trains are main interest. Played with Fisher-Price Zoo at length—especially the train. When cars came apart, said "Shoot!"

35 mos. 9 days. Drawing small circles and straight lines. Drew circle and line and called it a "p." Pointed to word in book and asked, "What is this word?" Carried Duracell Flashlight from toy library everywhere and took it to bed with him. Made roads for cars, and put Lego trains on the Waffletown Building Set.

35 mos. 23 days. New words this week: "Actually, yes," and "probably." Plays well independently. When he wants something, wants it now. Interested in Cash Register. Works puzzles well.

❧ **Linda** ❧

32 mos. 21 days. Interest in categorizing items—plastic, wood, reptiles. Mom and Dad read a lot to her. Came up after final play-in singing time and said animatedly, "I brought back my toys! It's toy-library day!" Showed good patience in an elegant restaurant. Pretended at length with Fisher-Price Super Market. Enjoyed counting and money. Assigned roles to family members. Decided what she wanted to buy and its cost. Used with other toys. Put pieces in Fun Card Puzzle with great enthusiasm. At home gave each animal a different voice.

33 mos. 4 days. Loved book, *Angel Mae* by Shirley Hughes. At home said, "Mommy, I'm going to the potty. Go out now." With Airport Play Set, put man and girl in airplane and said, "Daddy and I am flying."

34 mos. 23 days. Reads to herself and her stuffed animals. Will say, "I want to read it to myself." Magna Doodle was favorite toy. Showed creativity with drawing, naming pictures, and trying to be representational. Interested in the power of erasing. Put a number of Connecting Shapes together, naming her creations, though parents didn't see relationship between the creation and its name. Lined up and played with animals from Noah's Ark.

35 mos. 6 day. Enjoying using new words such as "correct." Likes pretending with small people. Delighted with Community Playground. Took other toys and dolls to playground. Shared two people with Dad and Mom while playing.

35 mos. 22 days. Dancing and ballet is latest interest. Likes to wear Princess Jasmine attire so belly button is exposed. When Dad asked her, "What does expensive mean?" She answered, "My Mommy doesn't want me to have it."

36 mos. 4 days. Loves dressing up and play-acting. For birthday had a Wizard of Oz costume for each guest. She was the witch and enjoyed the role. In play-in, likes to wear tutu, crown, and wooden shoes. Used Tikes Peak Road and Rail Set for play rather than construction.

∽ Seth ∽

33 mos. 2 days. Started Sunday school. Good progress using words to work things out. Takes down pants by himself. Can take off all clothes and put on all but his shirt. Good obedience for a time—now testing again. Fisher-Price Power Workshop was favorite toy of all time. Used all the tools and polished the whole house with the buffer. Likes trains. Makes tracks on carpet with tinker toy or fork and drives toy trains on them.

33 mos. 16 days. *Ferdinand* is favorite book. Wants to hear it over and over and has memorized it. Working out disagreements with brother without screaming. Loves to pretend. Peter Pan is favorite video movie. Enjoyed Little Tikes Waffletown Building Set.

33 mos. 30 days. Uses potty independently. Using sophisticated words such as "actually." Made a car with a construction set and put in five people. Said, "Dese aw ba(d) guys."

34 mos. 11 days. Loves to pretend. Can readily name all primary colors except brown. Lines blocks up neatly. Creatively put together Tikes Peak Road and Rail Set.

35 mos. 24 days. Talks things over in grown-up way with brother. Saying phrases he hears, i.e. "I really think so." Plays alone well. Enjoys story books. Put together and used each part of Fisher-Price Little People Main Street. Fascination with small letters, mail truck, and mailbox.

∽ Stan ∽

33 mos. 8 days. Decided to throw his pacifiers away. Staying in bed at bedtime is becoming a challenge. Sings "Twinkle" and "Old MacDonald." New interest in where the teachers are after school. Fascinated by idea that the teachers have husbands. Interest in pretend now. Put Fisher-Price Crazy Combo together in different ways and played each combination. Showed keen interest in an airport play set relating all pieces to recent airplane trip he took.

34 mos. 6 days. Tells stories to himself in bed before going to sleep. Enjoyed play farm set. Named animals and stood them up.

34 mos. 20 days. Asking lots of questions. Asks "Why?" Talking in longer sentences. Loves physical activities now. Enjoying stories. Getting better at puzzles.

35 mos. 3 days. Can say "Grandma" now. Loves baths. Takes two or

three a day because he likes to play with the water toys. A lot of imaginary play. Says, "These are bad guys. This is a good guy." Mom has to limit TV watching.

35 mos. 17 days. Has a new trike. Played each piece of Fisher-Price Marching Band and marched with the instruments, wearing the hat.

∽ Alicia ∽

32 most. 29 days. Lots of language. Long attention span. "I have sunglasses." If not understood says, "Look at my lips." Uses "mines" and "I be." When neighbors moved away: "Where's Iowa? How'd he get dere." Chose all square beads to string. Said, "I like that much." Turning a rod said, "Dis tan move awound. Dese tan move." Liked Color-Sorting House.

33 mos. 12 days. Methodical a she sets toys up for play. Able to find picture on Tupper Blocks and put pictured figures inside. When Mom was working with twisty ties asked, "Do you need a key?"

33 mos. 26 days. Likes to swing in back yard and take walks with grandma. Counts two objects and working on "three." Corrected Mom when she said, "Two deer." "No, two *deers*." Says "anio" for "piano." Said to Mom, "I'm too heavy for me to carry you." Keen interest in Airport Play Set. Brother likes airplanes.

34 mos. 10 days. Enjoys pretending with older brother. He makes train and she adds people. When Mom bought set of four sponges, she said there were two for brother and two for her. Saves and shares cookies for Dad and brother. Lots of hugs and tenderness. Eating less. Pretended to bake cookies, cake, and cupcakes with Magic Glow Oven. With Deluxe Peg Set, made a "fence to keep the cat in." Put in all one color very methodically.

34 mos. 24 days. Lots of pretend play. Likes playing by herself. Some counting. Likes dolls but not one special doll. Lots more "whys." Enjoys puzzles.

35 mos. 7 days. When Mom called her a little girl, said, "No no, I'm a *big* little girl." Enjoyed puzzles. Teased Mom saying pieces didn't go where she knew they went. Loves puzzles. Asks for help when she needs it.

Appendix 3

❦

Velcro Time:
The Language Connection

Mildred E. Cawlfield

Parents, caregivers, and researchers of toddlers can attest that there is a period in which the toddler's interest in toys and independent play is largely replaced by interest in the primary caregiver. I have observed that this behavior occurs simultaneously with a notable spurt in language development and thus appears to have a significant developmental purpose.

Robin* came into our toy library one day last April and sat down at the table to work with the toys I introduced. With a good attention span, he put shapes into the shape-sorter trailer. If a shape didn't go in, he said, "No," and put it in the correct space. He put many large Duplo™ blocks together, then listened intently to the Tote-a-Tune Music Box Radio™, asking me to wind it when it stopped. His mother reported that Robin was now imitating many words—mostly one syllable, except for "Da-y" (daddy) and "bunny." For "turtle" Robin made a guttural sound, moving his tongue.

*Children's names have been changed.

Mildred E. Cawlfield, after more than 10 years of experience in early childhood education, developed and has directed, since 1974, a program for parents of children from birth to age three. This program has provided a unique vantage point to observe and record data on individual children.

At 18 months, 29 days, this was a different Robin than I had seen two months before. At 16 months Robin would explore toys briefly, moving quickly from one thing to another. At 17 months, 4 days, I noted on his record, "On the move. Briefly explores toys, then with a high 'Mmmm' reaches out for something else. Loves books. Went over to book box repeatedly. Looked at many toys today, with brief interest." At that time Robin's mother reported that at home, he was sticking to her closely, going off to explore, then coming back, often bringing something for her to comment on. He would watch her mouth as she talked (as he did mine), and he was beginning to say some words. Now, at almost 19 months, he was again playing independently for longer periods of time, and he was much more capable of communicating with words.

Following Robin's appointment that day, Justin came to the toy library with his mother. He had been an avid explorer, focusing intently on toys as he discovered how they would respond to a shake, twist, tap, or toss. Two weeks before, at 15 months, 27 days, I had noted, "Good receptive language, but not saying many words. Getting shapes in shape sorters." His mother had reported good interest at home in toys he returned, especially the Li'l Tykes Pet Shop™.

Now, at 16 months, 10 days, Justin's interest in toys was markedly shorter. His mother was distraught, reporting that he was not playing as long independently. He was sticking to her and constantly bringing toys to her, trying to involve her in his play. She was concerned that he might be getting spoiled.

I pointed out to her how he was watching our mouths as we talked. I said, "I call this 'Velcro™ Time.' Justin is keying in to language, and the only way he is going to learn is to hear it. Don't worry about giving him the attention he seeks, and talk to him a lot. He won't be spoiled if you consistently enforce the limits you have set for his behavior."

In the weeks that ensued, Justin followed mom around, wanting her to label items. At 17 months, 8 days, I wrote, "Language coming now: 'down,' 'hi,' 'Daddy,' 'Teddy.' He's copying what is said to him. Points to items wanting to hear words. Using words to get what he wants more often. Interest in toys returning."

A few weeks later, his mom reported, "I feel like my own person again. Justin is again happy to play independently." At this point Justin was communicating with one and two words in telegraphic speech.

A developmental marker

The behavior commonly noted in this toddler, Velcro™ Time, includes the following:

1. decreased interest in toys or independent play, often noted as *decreased attention span*

2. increased interest in the primary caregiver, frequently bringing objects to her for comment

3. increased interest in books; particularly enjoys having an adult label objects in pictures

4. watching the caregiver's mouth; obvious interest in language

5. attempts to say words

The end of Velcro Time is notable in the child's marked increase in attention span with toys. This attention span is often accompanied by a specific interest, such as cars and trucks, airplanes, the kitchen, dolls, or music. The child seeks toys and books related to this key interest and shows fascination with them. The ability to pretend frequently surfaces at this time. This may be an important culmination to Velcro Time because pretend play is dependent on the emergence of symbolic thinking (Piaget, 1962).

The observation and description of these toddler behaviors is not new, but my data implies a direct relationship between this behavior and language development, a connection I have not seen made by others. I have also noted that when parents understand this connection, they deal more understandingly with the behavior.

White (1985) describes the time when toddlers' interest in the primary caregiver and in practicing physical skills overtakes their interest in exploration of objects. This is a time when it is difficult for a caregiver to keep these two main interests in balance. My observations suggest that encouraging the caregiver to recognize the child's need for closeness—for linguistic purposes—makes this period more rewarding and profitable to both child and adult.

Mahler (1975) calls this period *rapprochement* and notes the emotional need of the toddler in attaining his separation and individuation from the primary caregiver. These conclusions are supported by the works of Bowlby (1969) and Ainsworth, Blehar, Waters, and Wall (1978). Brazelton (1989) also describes the play of toddlers in terms of Mahler's interpretation. Brazelton explains "This is not a time for long, involved play alone. [The child] is too aware of her

struggle about separating and too afraid of losing touch with her anchors." Not only does this period of heightened proximity serve a critical emotional and survival need during the second year of life, it appears to support the emergence of linguistic capacities as well.

Experts in language acquisition examine and describe the progression of language, but usually do not connect language development with other toddler behaviors. One reason the connection may not be obvious is that there appear to be several factors working simultaneously, or at least overlapping. A toddler is fascinated with practicing his physical skills. This gives him the ability to separate from and come back at will to the primary caregiver. At the same time, there is mental development as the child develops object permanence, an emerging sense of self, and a new capacity to appraise the unfamiliar (Schaffer, Greenwood, & Parry, 1971). The primary caregiver acts as a secure base from which the toddler may venture forth to explore and return to safety.

The emotional need for a caring adult protects the child in his important explorations and gives him a "haven of safety" when distress occurs, but the keen interest in language that occurs simultaneously with the change in play behavior in secure toddlers points to another developmental purpose for this behavior—a linguistic one.

Observing Velcro Time

The relationship between Velcro Time behavior and language acquistion became obvious in the unique laboratory of our parent/toddler program's toy library format.

For 15 years I have been observ-

ing and collecting anecdotal material on children from birth through age three as director of the parent/infant-toddler program *Acorn* at a private school in St. Louis County, Missouri. Parents enter the program with their infants shortly after birth and usually continue for three years. They come every two weeks to seminars with infants under one year, and every week to play-ins/seminars with one- and two-year-olds. In addition, parents and their children come every two weeks for an individual toy library appointment.

Before each toy library appointment I examine the child's records and select several toys (out of approximately 600) that, according to previous experience, will come close to matching the child's current interests and skills. In this way the toy library becomes a type of curriculum.

I show the child each toy one at a time, working and talking with the child as the parent observes. It is usually obvious which toys are most interesting to the child, and based on his response, we choose three for him to take home for the next two weeks.

During and after each appointment I note my observations, and the parent's, about the child and ask the parent what she notes about the child's current interests and abilities. "Anything new going on?" is one of the questions I frequently ask. There is free communication with the parent. I record comments of how the child plays with each toy at the appointment, including toys not checked out, and I log the parent's comments about how the child plays at home with toys being returned. For the past three years the information has been entered into a computer data base.

We have had an average of approximately 30 children in the program each year—10 new and 20 continuing. I don't have data on all of the over 100 toddlers I have worked with because some of my earlier documentation was incomplete, and some parents pulled out of the toy library sessions at the critical time. Parents may sign up for parts of the program, and some parents of toddlers have dropped the toy library sessions during Velcro Time because of the child's loss of interest in toys. I generally have to show more toys at appointments during this period in order to find ones that will catch the toddler's interest.

When much of the data was recorded, I was not looking for the Velcro-Time phenomena, but I searched the records later to find relevant data. Summer vacations have made unfortunate gaps in data, but in several cases a child would enter Velcro Time before vacation and definitely be through upon returning in the fall. Some data showed just the beginning or just the end of the period.

The table on this page graphs the number of children according to their age at the onset and at the end of Velcro Time. The modal beginning age is 15 months, and the modal ending age is 19 months. The median beginning age is 14.6 months, and the median ending age is 18.8 months.

From data on 61 toddlers (33 boys and 28 girls), 49 (80%) showed signs of Velcro Time. Of those 49, I omitted three from the graph data because I observed only the on-

set of Velcro Time (13, 14, and 15 months) and didn't have data on the ending time.

Some children were in Velcro Time for as little as two months and two children for as long as eight months. The mean duration was 4.19 months. In each case, the length of time appeared to be related to vocabulary acquisition. Some children learned to communicate verbally, increasing vocabulary more quickly than others. Also, because of individual differences, some children tend to have a much longer attention span than others, so Velcro Time would appear to be less intense or shorter.

The records of the 12 children (8 boys and 4 girls) who don't show this drop in attention span for toys are also significant. Ten of these children gained language earlier than usual, with many words in place and advanced communication skills by 14 months. They seemed to have

discovered early that verbal sounds have meaning and that they had the ability to imitate those sounds. The parents of these children had been attentive to tuning in to the children's early speech.

Late talkers showed an unusual pattern of Velcro Time: They seem to go in and out of Velcro Time rather than remaining in it for a shorter, intense period. Eric had good receptive language and spoke jargon at 12 months, 19 days, and could point to objects in books upon hearing the words. He was able to physically make himself understood. Interest in toys continued until 18 months, when it was supplanted by a keen interest in books until 21 months. Then toy interest returned until 24 months, when he was staying close to mom and obviously working on language. At 25 months he started parroting language, and by 26 months he was saying more words.

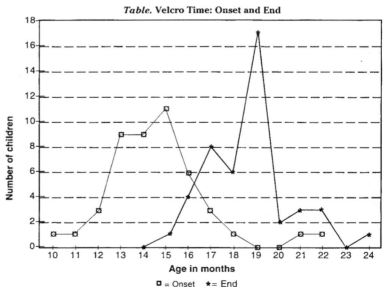

Table. Velcro Time: Onset and End

Number of children

Age in months

□ = Onset   ★ = End

Implications

The implications of Velcro Time for children in day care warrant further study. According to my observations, the need for bonding with and closeness to a caregiver serves a linguistic purpose as well as an emotional one. This substantiates the need for a caring, dependable, familiar caregiver who can tune in to the developing language of the toddler.

Parents and caregivers can make the most of the sometimes difficult Velcro Time and can better deal with the stress involved when they understand the behavior's developmental purpose. They can rest assured that they are not necessarily spoiling the child by giving him attention and language experience at this time. The caregiver should understand that the solution to Velcro Time is not to forcefully separate from the child, but to feed the desire to hear language. Soon, a more independent, verbal child will emerge with a longer attention span and with new ideas and interests.

References

Ainsworth, M.D.S., Blehar, M.C., Waters, E., & Wall, S. (1978). *Patterns of attachment.* Hillsdale, NJ: Erlbaum.

Bowlby, J. (1969). *Attachment and loss: Vol. 1. Attachment.* New York: Basic Books

Brazelton, T.B. (1989). *Toddlers and parents* (rev. ed.). New York: Dell Publishing.

Mahler, M.S., Pine, F., & Bergman, A. (1975). *The psychological birth of the human infant.* New York: Basic Books.

Piaget, J.(1962). *Play, dreams, & imitation in childhood.* New York: W.W. Norton Co.

Schaffer, H.R., Greenwood, A., & Parry, N.H. (1971). The onset of wariness. *Child Development, 42,* 165–176.

White, B.L. (1985). *The first three years of life* (rev. ed.). New York: Prentice Hall.

Appendix 3

Index

ॐ

Index

Index

LOVE THAT BABY

Mildred E. Cawlfield

The author has consulted with hundreds of parents and children throughout their first three-to-four years in a parent/infant-toddler program she developed and directed for 24 years. She met with each family from one to three times a week in group play sessions or individual, half-hour toy library appointments. She kept a computerized database of information as each child progressed from birth through age three. She has observed many of these children excel throughout school with continuing parental support and graduate with honors and awards. From this wealth of information and observation, she has prepared this book for all parents and caregivers.

Focusing on education, Millie Cawlfield received her B.A. degree from U.C.L.A. and Masters degree from Webster University in St. Louis. She taught kindergarten and first grade in the California public schools. She taught pre-instrumental music, piano, and recorder. She and her husband, Bill, raised four sons. For 24 years, she edited and wrote *Acorn Newsletter,* a quarterly publication subscribed to by parents around the world and gave workshops to parents in cities throughout the U.S. and in Canada. She has made presentations to local educational conferences and published an article in the NAEYC journal, *Young Children.*

To order additional copies of
Love That Baby
Clip out and mail to:

Peaceful Parenting Press
602 Rue Montand, Ballwin, MO 63011-2809

Please include check or money order
$16.95 plus $5.00 shipping & handling first book,
$2.00 each additional (If sent to Missouri, add $1.10 for tax)

Please print or type

- -

Send **Love That Baby** to:

Name _____

Street _____

City _____ State _____ Zip Code _____

Your name, if gift _____

Your phone number _____

❑ Gift card to read _____

- -

Send **Love That Baby** to:

Name _____

Street _____

City _____ State _____ Zip Code _____

Your name, if gift _____

Your phone number _____

❑ Gift card to read _____

Notes

Notes

Notes